I0866385

IT

AY

IEU,
WAY

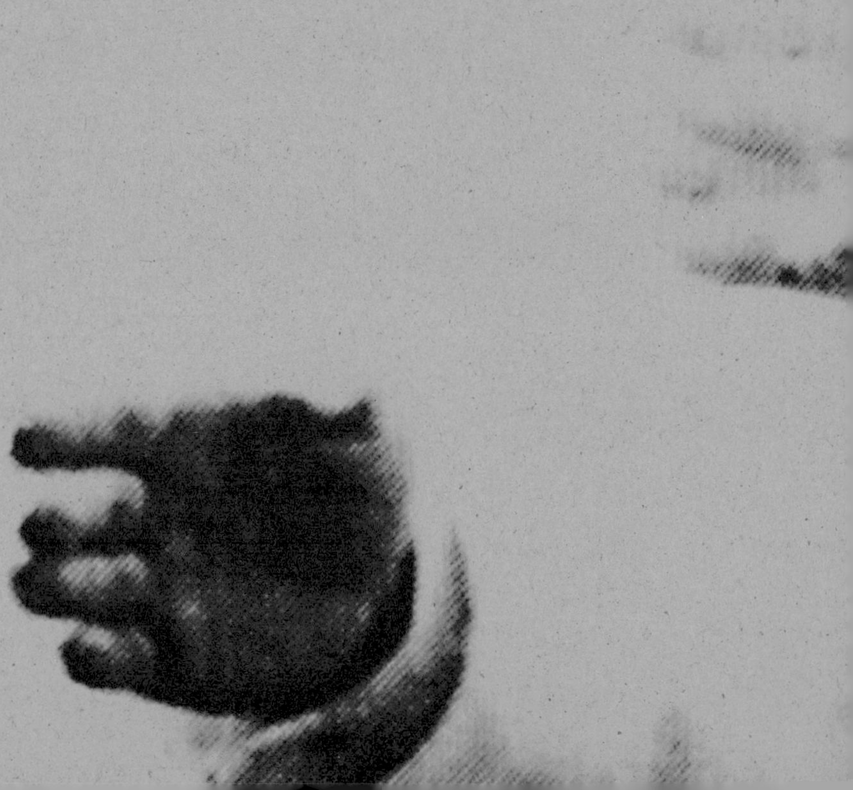

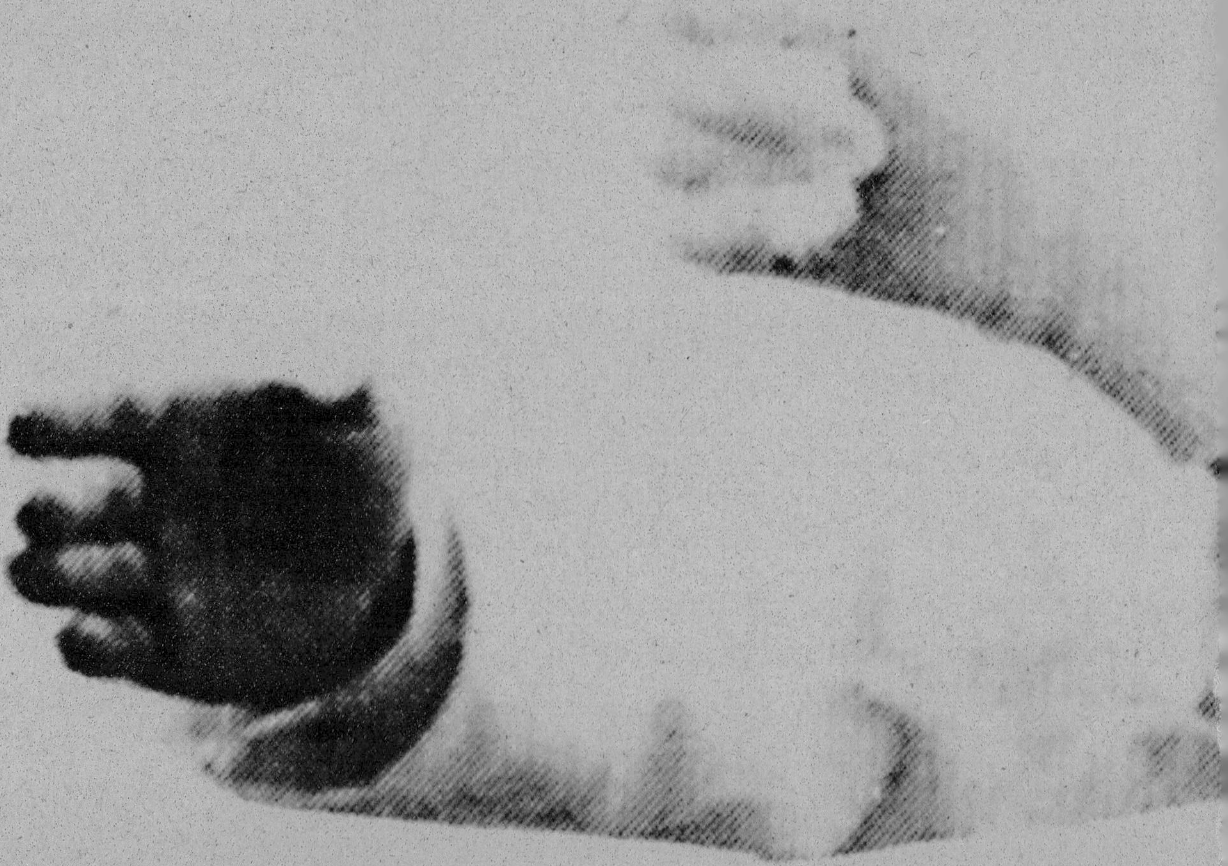

condominium became

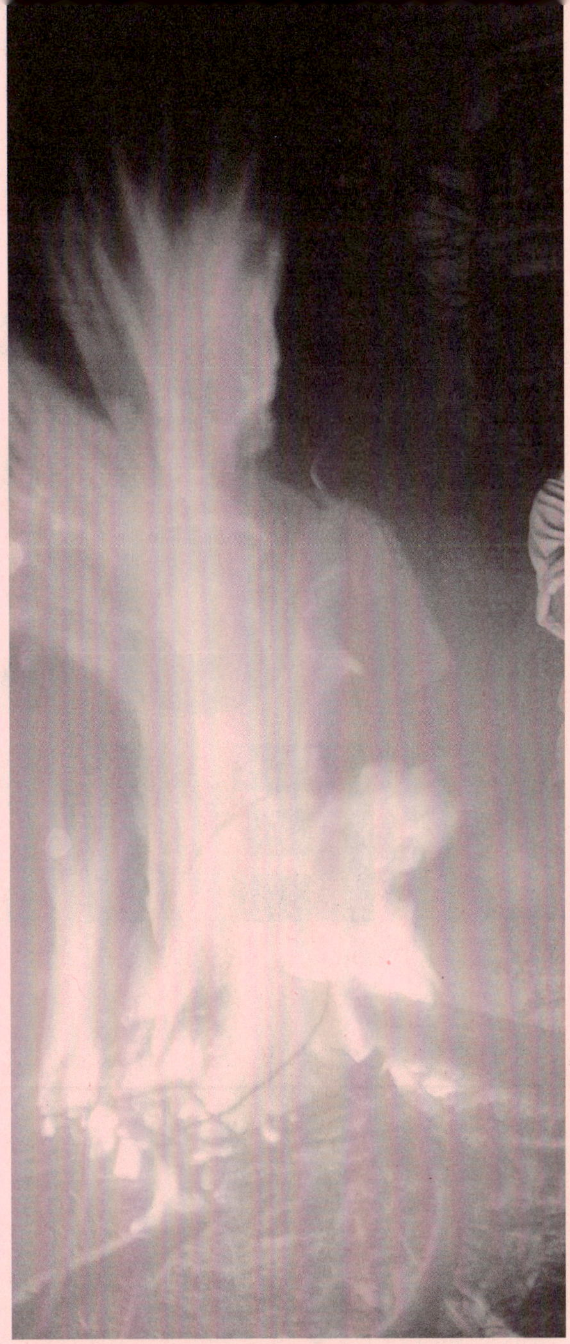

THE MEN WHO WOULD BE KING

Dewi Lewis Publishing

THE MEN WHO WOULD BE KING

Photographs Jon Tonks   Text Christopher Lord

John came in 1930. He stayed for about ten years.

It began when the ladies of the village went down to the beach to play. There is a game we play called 'kalabus', where we chase each other - if I touch you, you have to stay still. The ladies were playing this game when suddenly John came and joined in. But they were scared of him, so John went off and hid.

The ladies told the men of the village what they had seen: a white man down at the beach. The next day the ladies went back there and tried to catch him by again playing kalabus. When John reappeared, an old fella named Jack Kahou was waiting in the bush, and he grabbed John and brought him back to the village.

Asked where he came from, John said "I am from the US". The villagers said, what's your name, and he said, "My name is John Broom".

John Kaurua, Green Point, Tanna

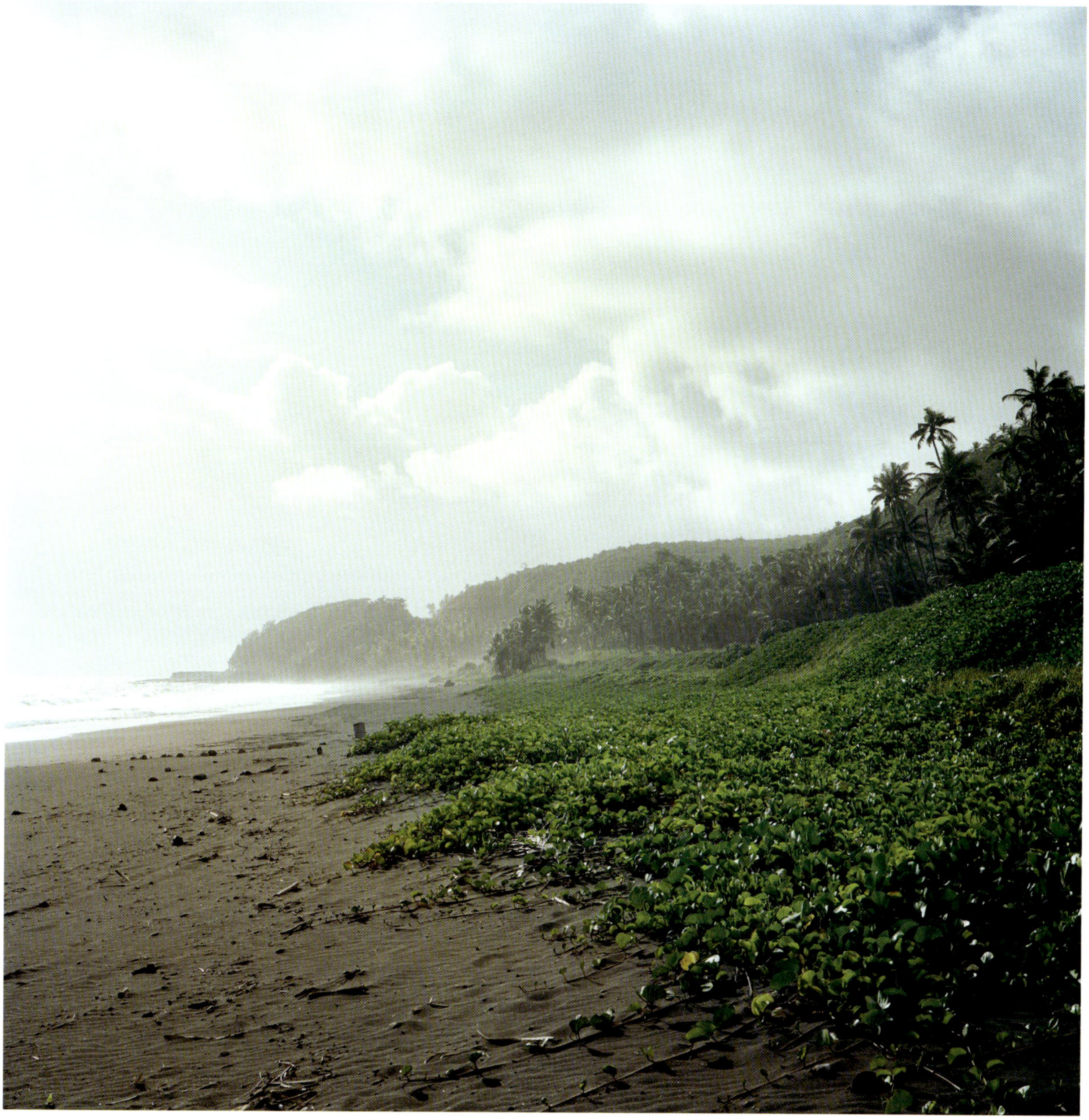

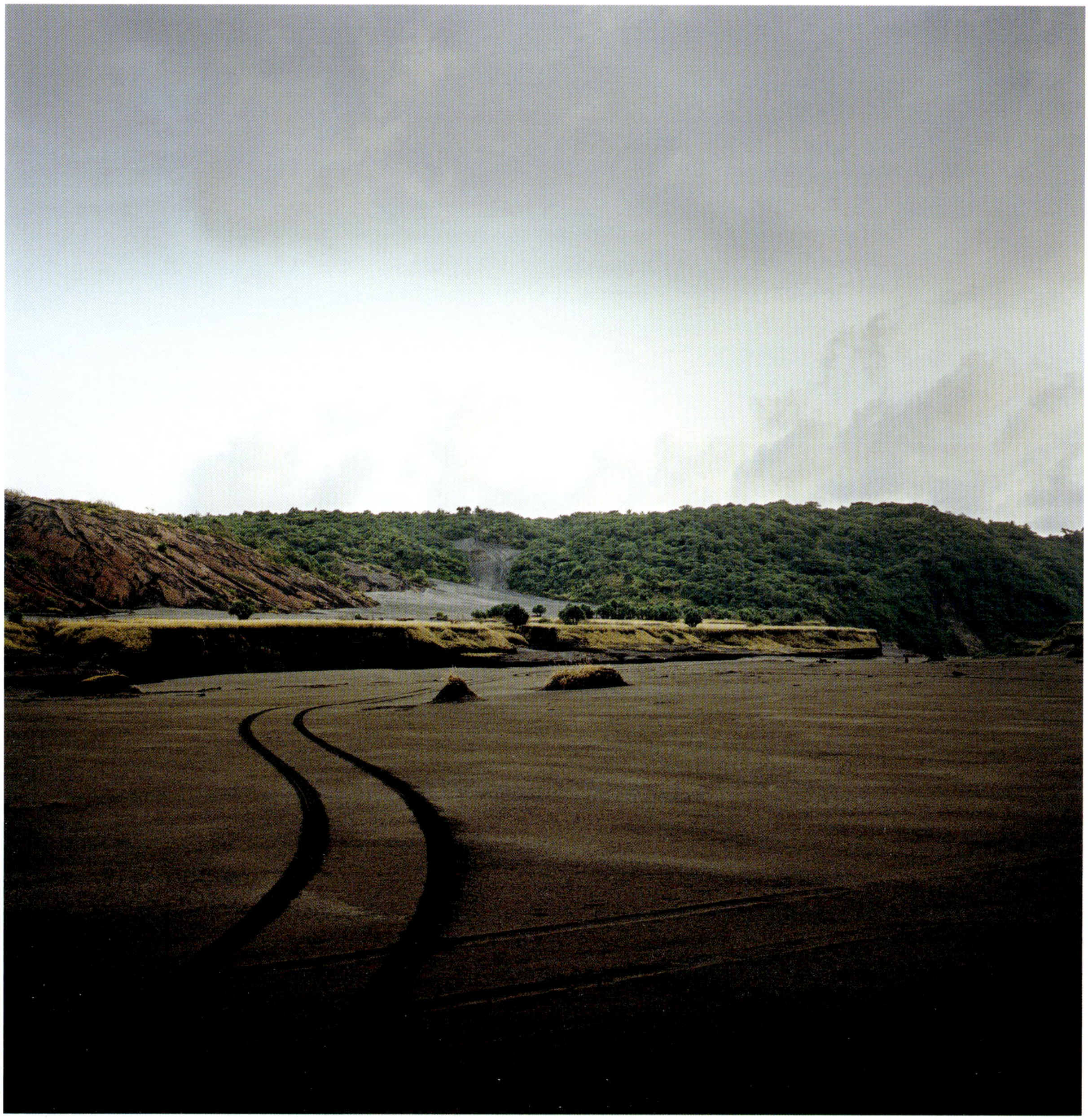

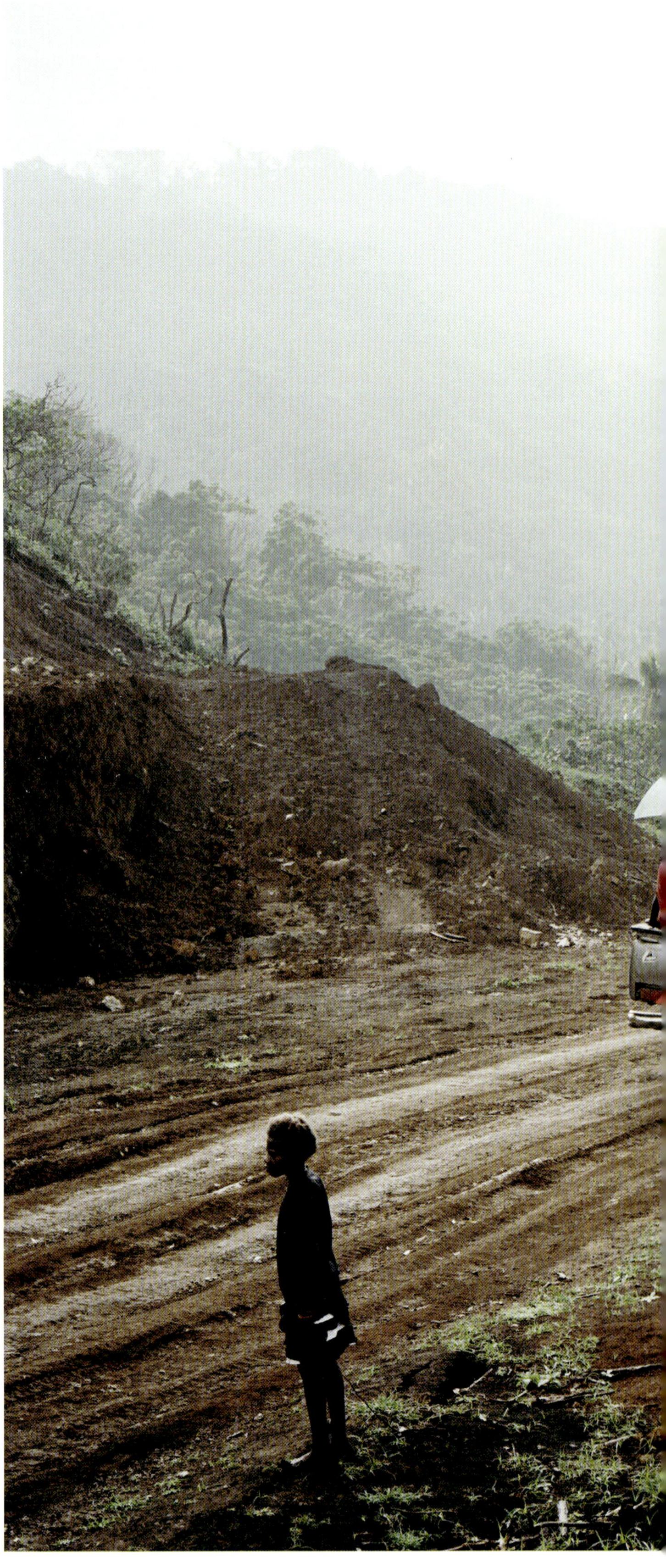

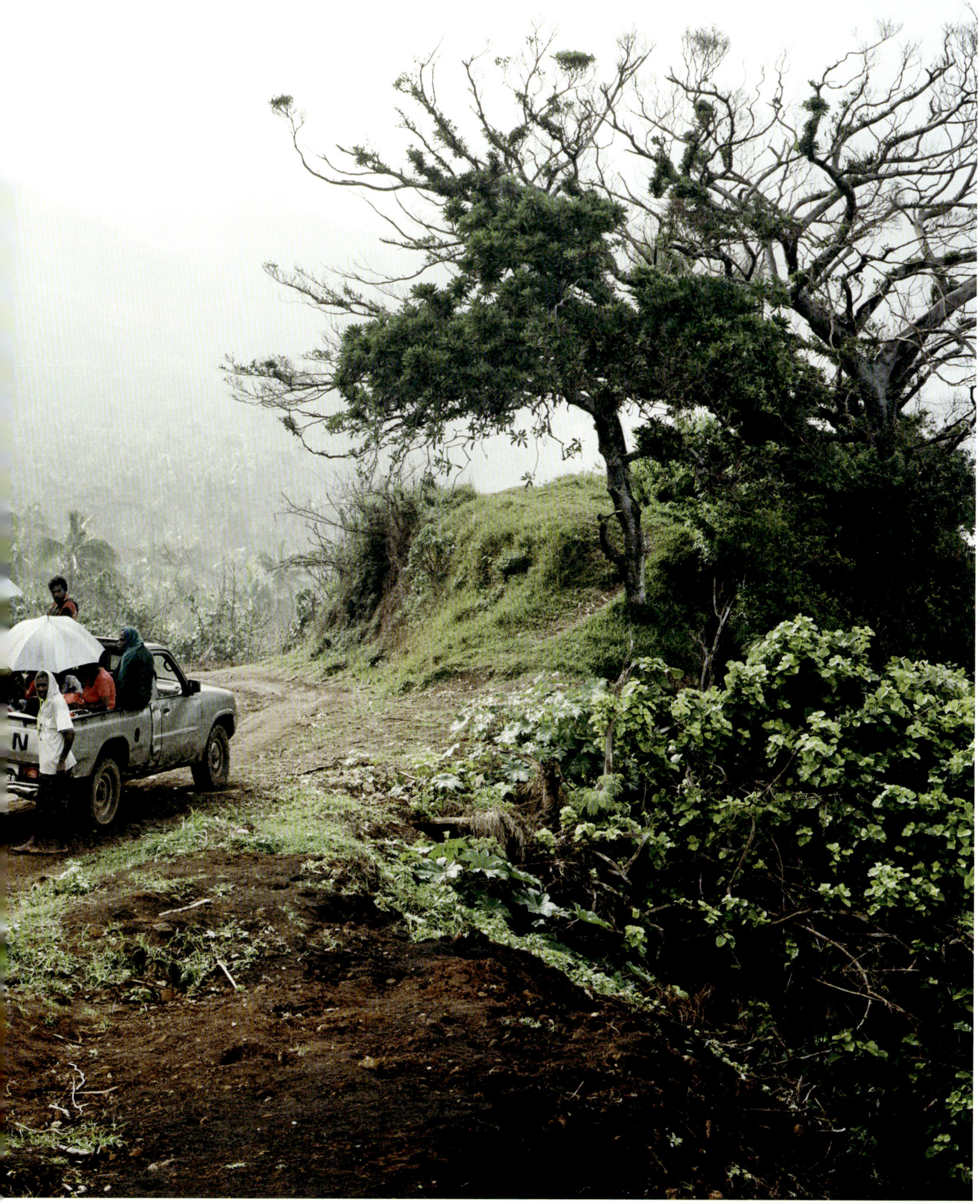

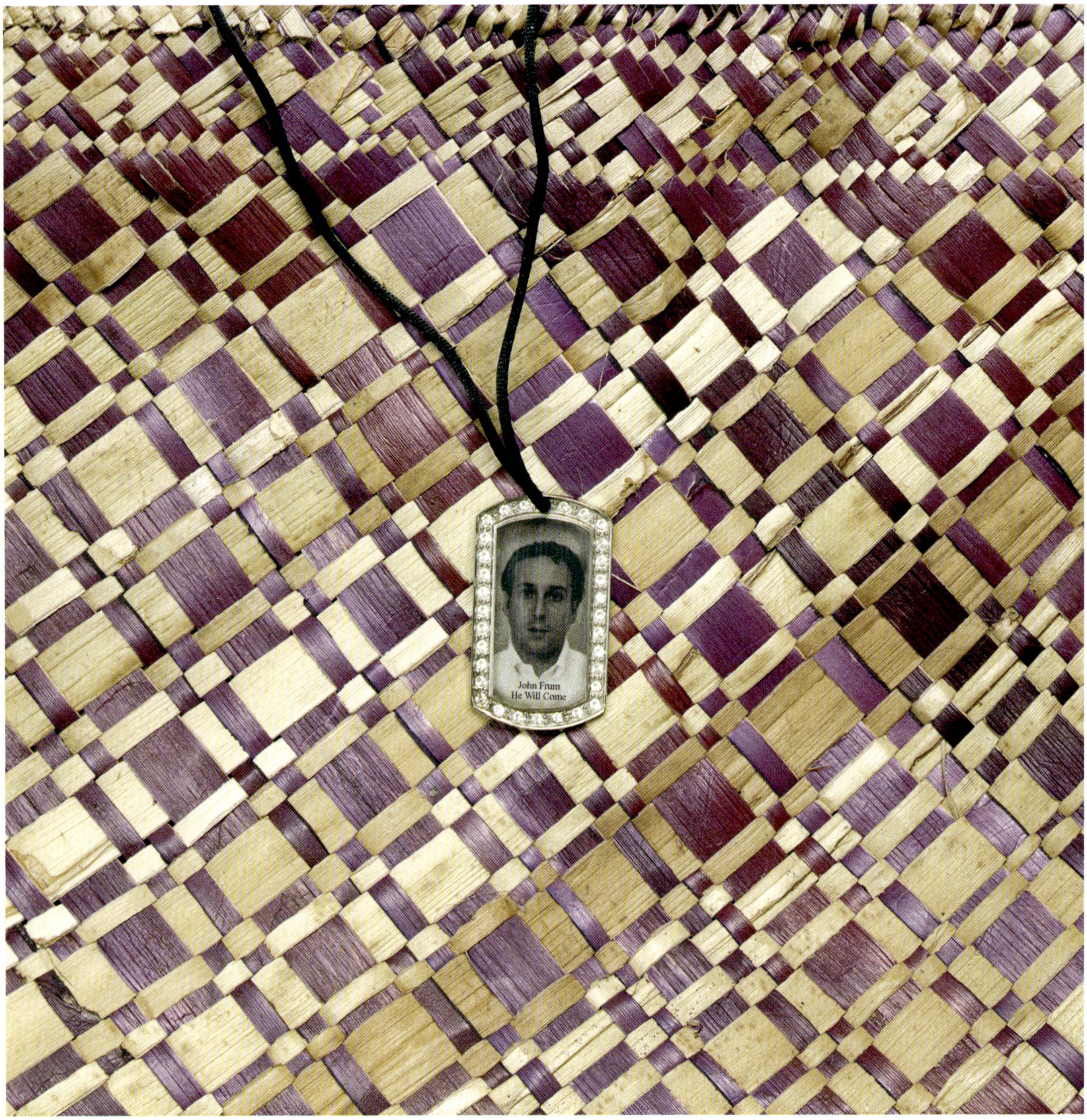
John Frum
He Will Come

Of all the places we went to in the course of researching this book, we can vividly recall the atmosphere of a beach called Big Bay, on a day when the air was luminous with spray from the Pacific Ocean.

We were there on one of many wild goose chases, looking for a crashed wartime plane that we'd heard was rotting somewhere in the bush. We never did find it. But we did leave Big Bay with a feeling: a strange sense of foreboding that rolls onto that beach with the breakers. Perhaps because it was here that the first Europeans landed on the islands we now call Vanuatu.

They came in two boats of 300 sailors, believing they were bringing Christian light to the dark corners of the Earth. Their Portuguese captain thought he'd found the outlying islands of a new continent, what he called *Australia del Espiritu Santo* – the Southern Land of the Holy Spirit – and founded a city called New Jerusalem. They went to great lengths and ceremony deciding who among the crew would be the nobles and knights of their new world. That was May 1, 1606.

A month later, the crew were paddling back to their boats. In 35 days, they had unleashed every atrocity on the inhabitants of this island; fearing revenge and sick with a bad batch of fish, they fled. Mercifully, it would be another 162 years before more Europeans came to these islands but that first contact sowed the seeds for a powerful idea.

Vanuatu was not part of a lost continent. It's a volcanic archipelago of 83 Pacific islands, due east of Sydney, and the people who live there are called Ni-Vanuatus. Today, it is a deeply Christian nation. But there are also communities on the islands who believe that a different kind of divine figure will soon arrive to initiate the end of days.

According to this prophecy, a messiah will come to reinstate a pre-colonial way of life in Vanuatu, return things to how they were before the centuries of interference by missionaries and imperial powers. They say he will come from a distant land, bringing health and prosperity, splitting the land open.

These beliefs have endured with their own myths and rituals. Today, incredibly, they also attract some unexpected pilgrims: Europeans and

Americans who travel thousands of miles to Vanuatu claiming – or believing – they are the fulfilment of the prophecy.

Their motivations differ. But while plenty of books have been written on the prophecy itself, the practice of Western men ingratiating themselves in these complex beliefs has been going on largely unseen for half a century.

Ours is not a study of the complex firmament of mythos and oral traditions that criss-cross Vanuatu. It is a series of encounters, between 2014 and 2018, with the labyrinthine tales that underpin those beliefs and the myriad foreigners who get lost in them. If there is any anthropology here it is of an idea, an old dream, that has persisted since a time when the responsibility of the world was thought to rest on European and American shoulders. What was once called 'The White Man's Burden'.

Over the course of four years, we made several trips to the South Pacific, as well as to America, France, and Germany. This is a story about storytelling – the ones we tell ourselves about who we are and our place in the world. The stories, one might say, that we live by.

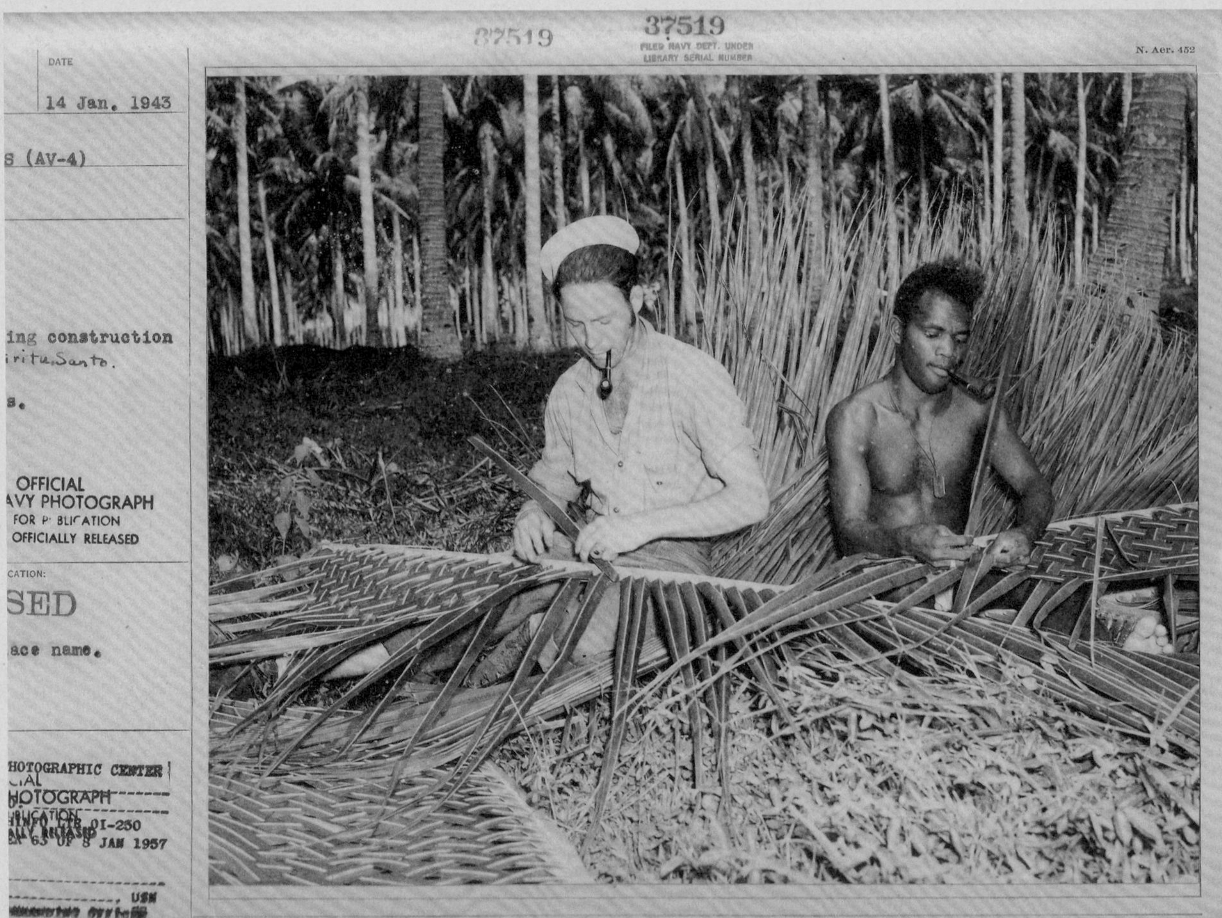

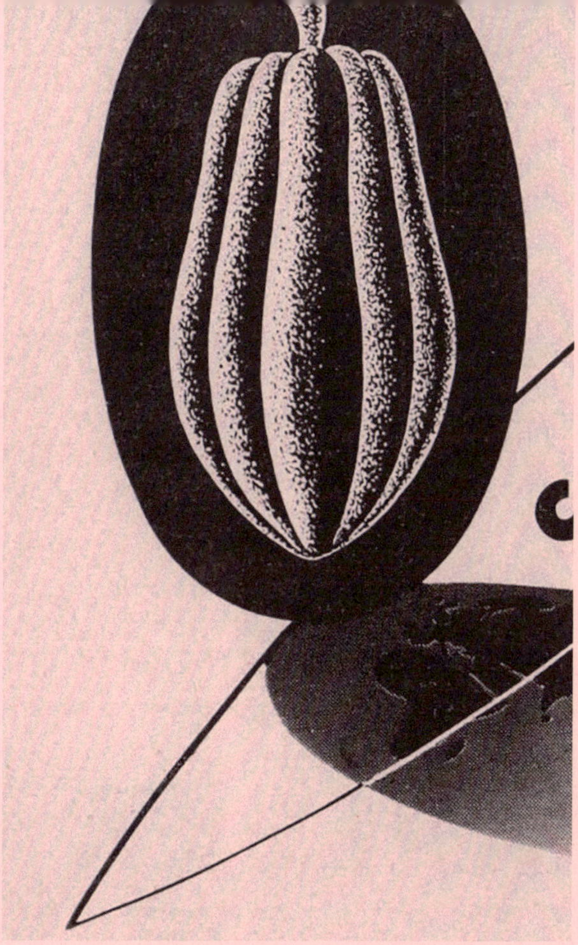

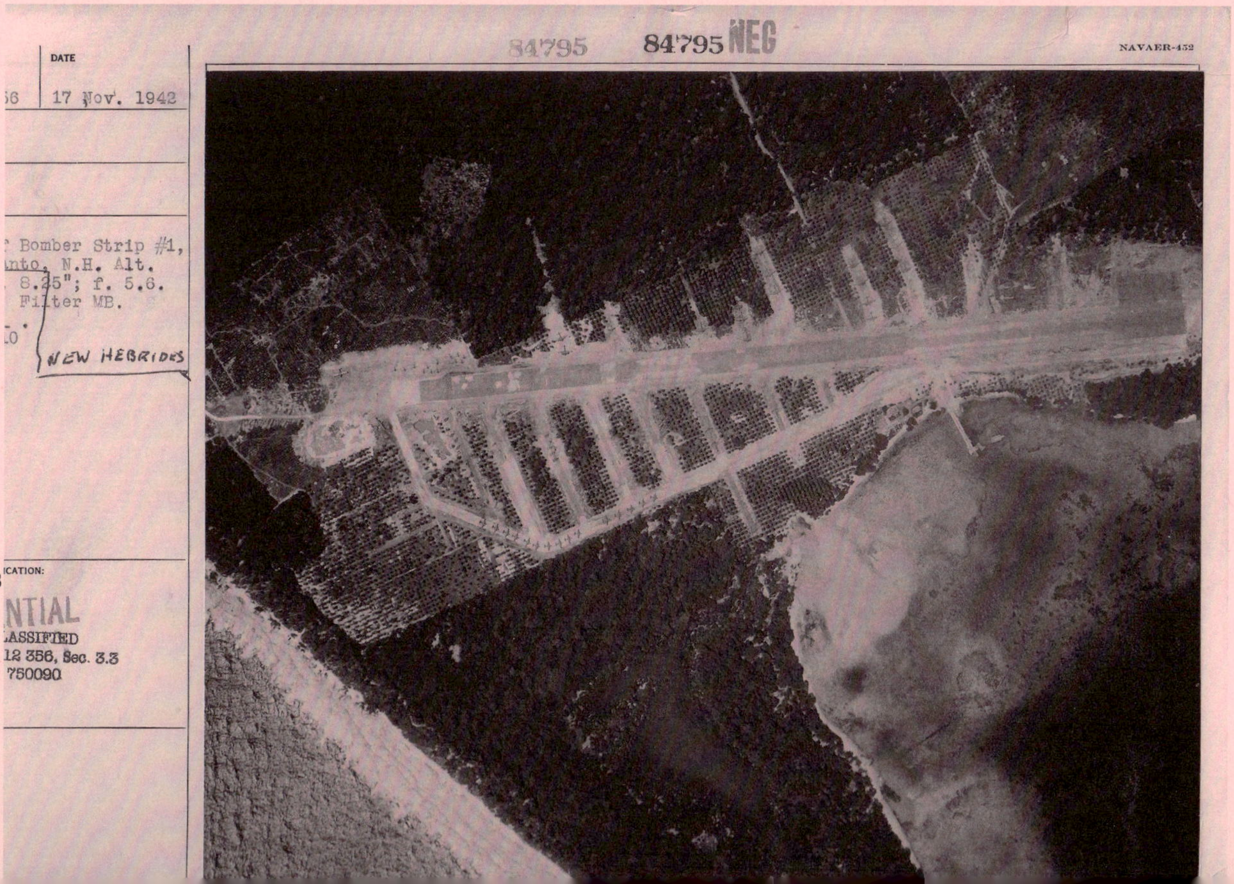
84795
84795 NEG
NAVAER-452
DATE
56
17 Nov. 1942
Bomber Strip #1,
anto, N.H. Alt.
8.25"; f. 5.6.
Filter MB.
NEW HEBRIDES
CATION:
NTIAL
LASSIFIED
12 356, Sec. 3.3
750090

13

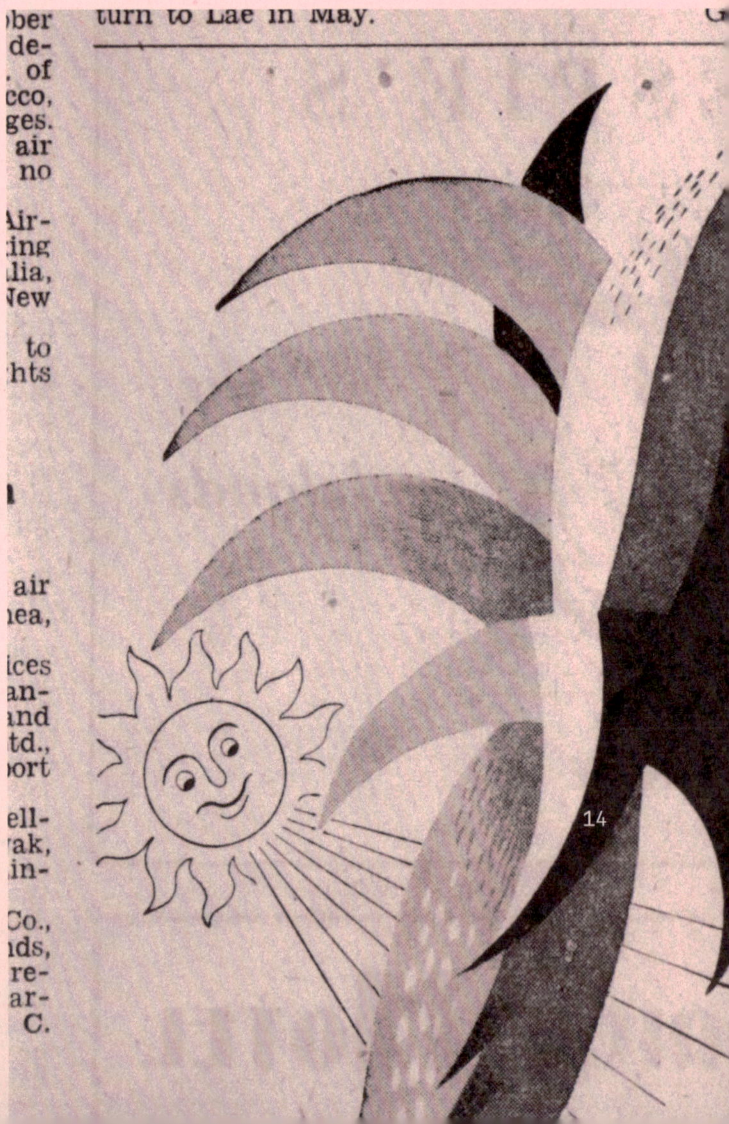
turn to Lae in May.

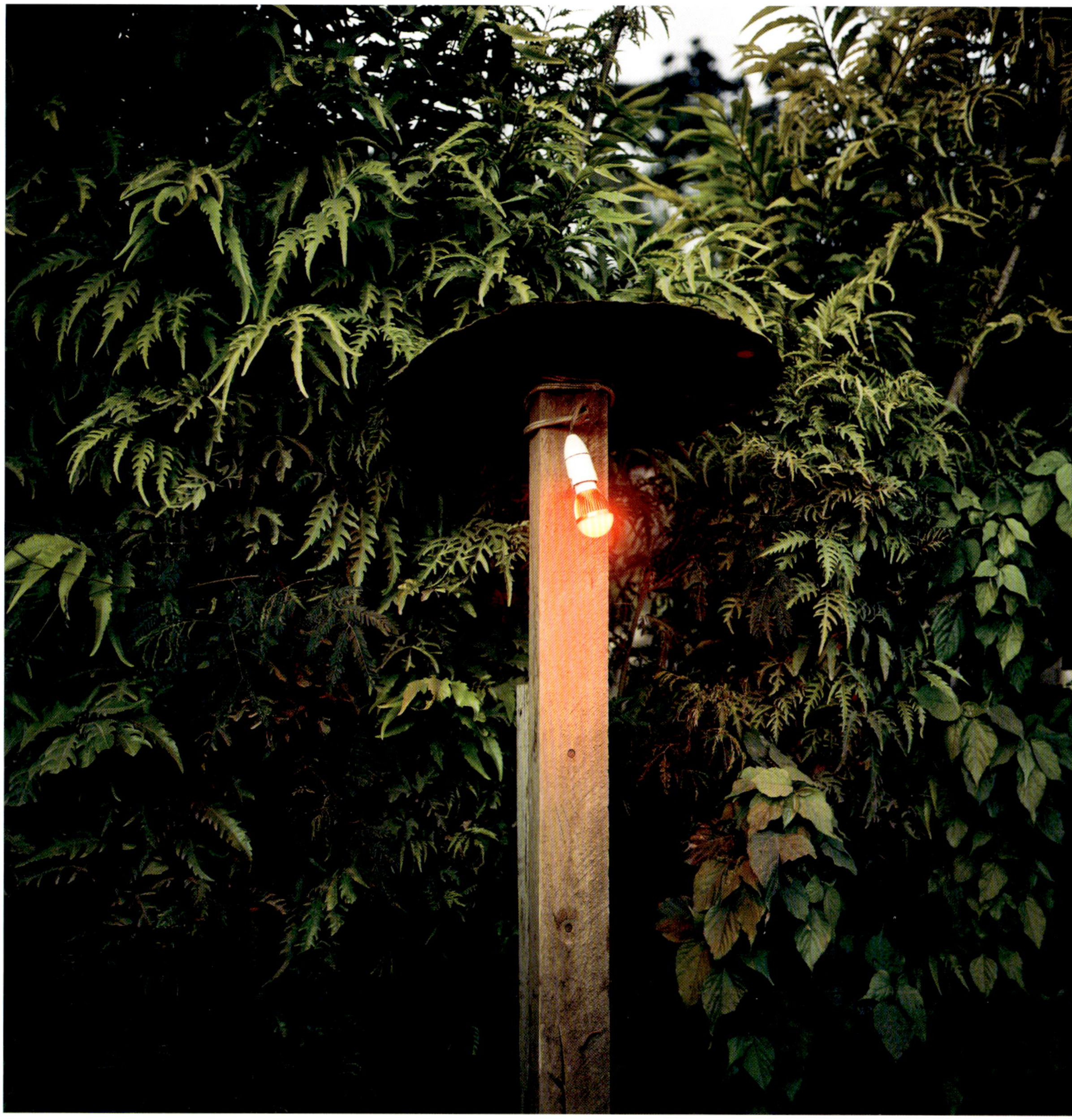

Mount Yasur, Tanna

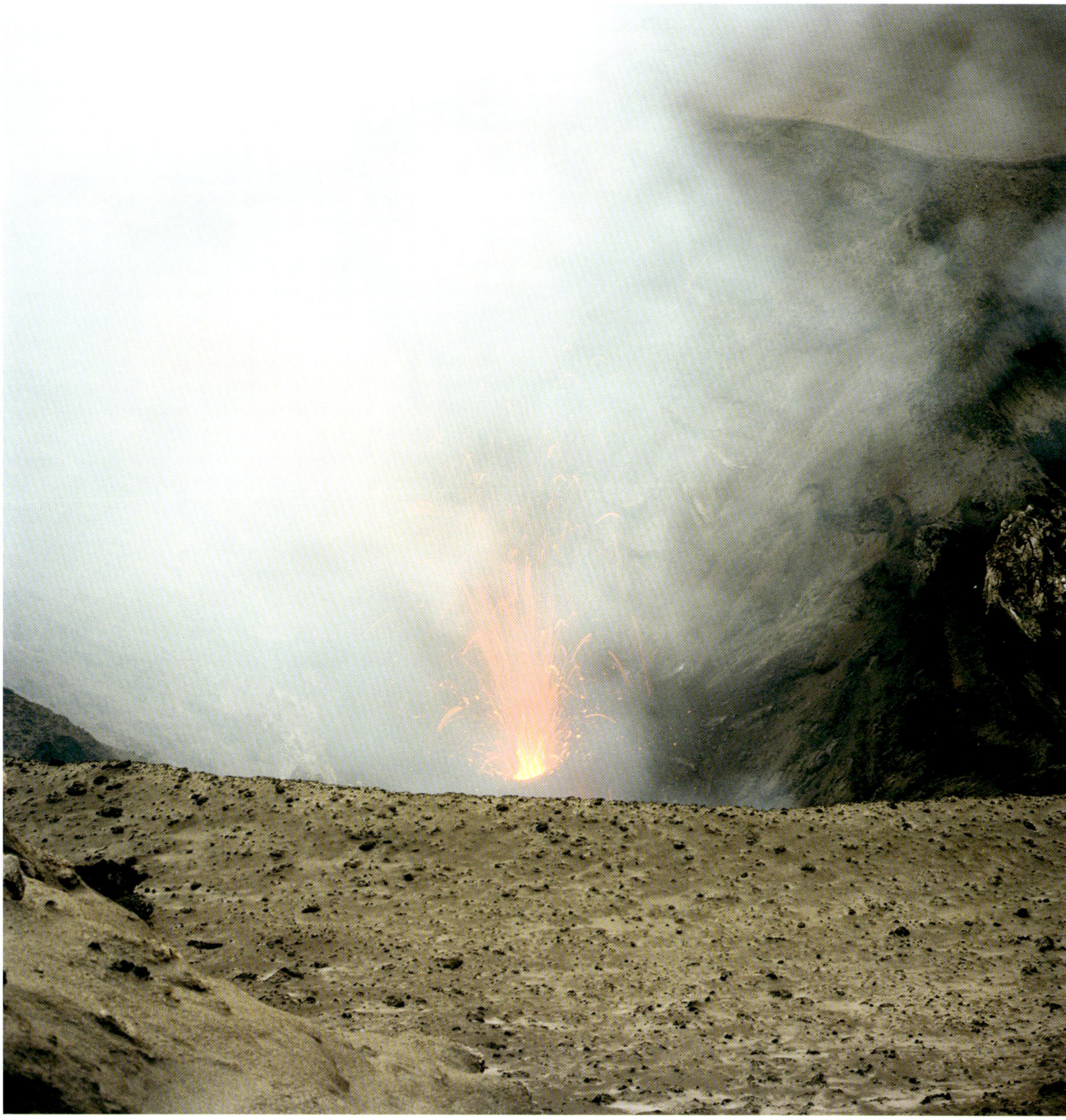

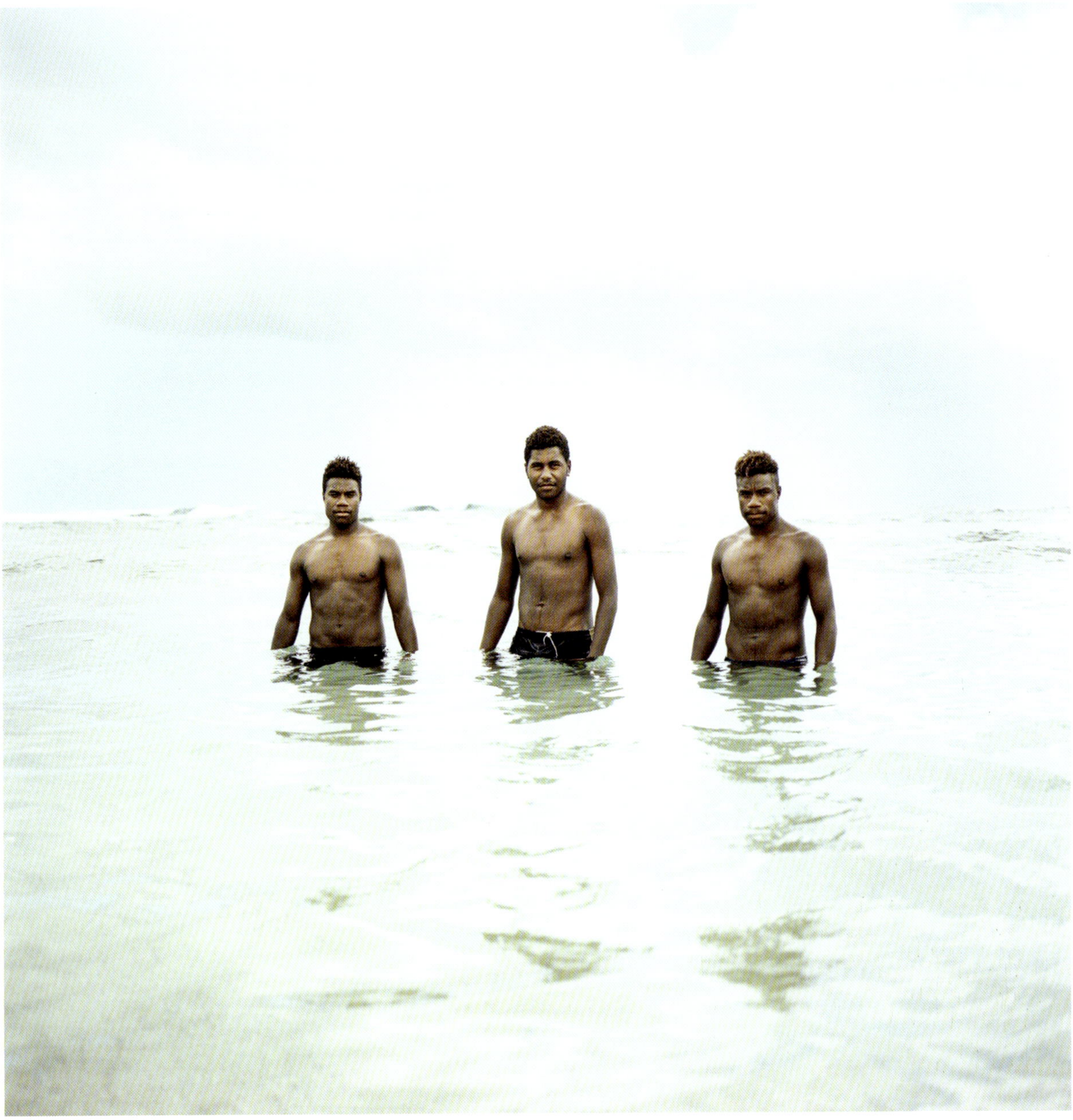

Barve, Patten and James, Lowanatom, Tanna

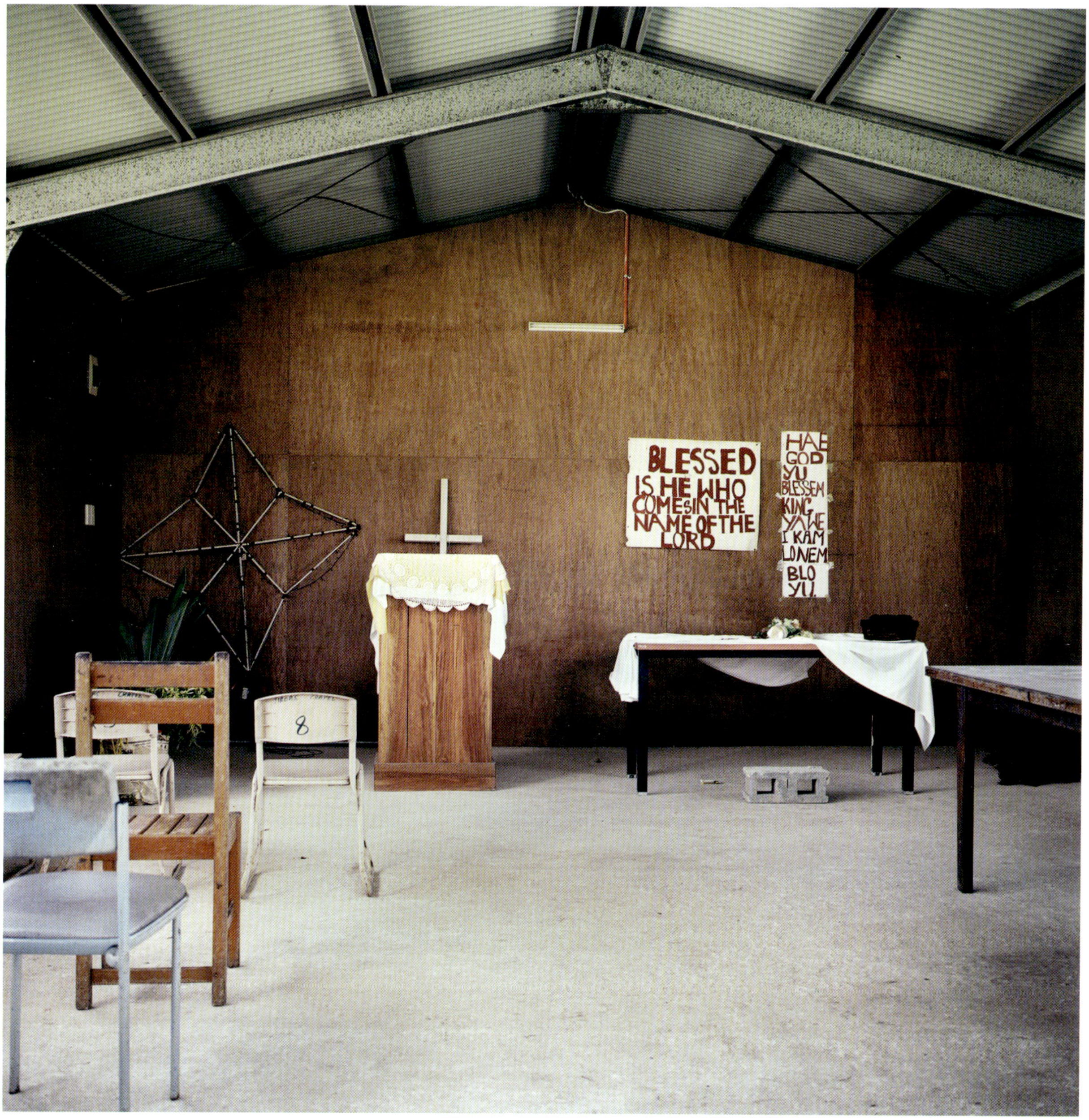
BLESSED
IS HE WHO
COMES IN THE
NAME OF THE
LORD
HAE
GOD
YU
BLESSEM
KING
YAWE
I KAM
LONEM
BLO
YU.

Toilet facilities, Mount Yasur, Tanna

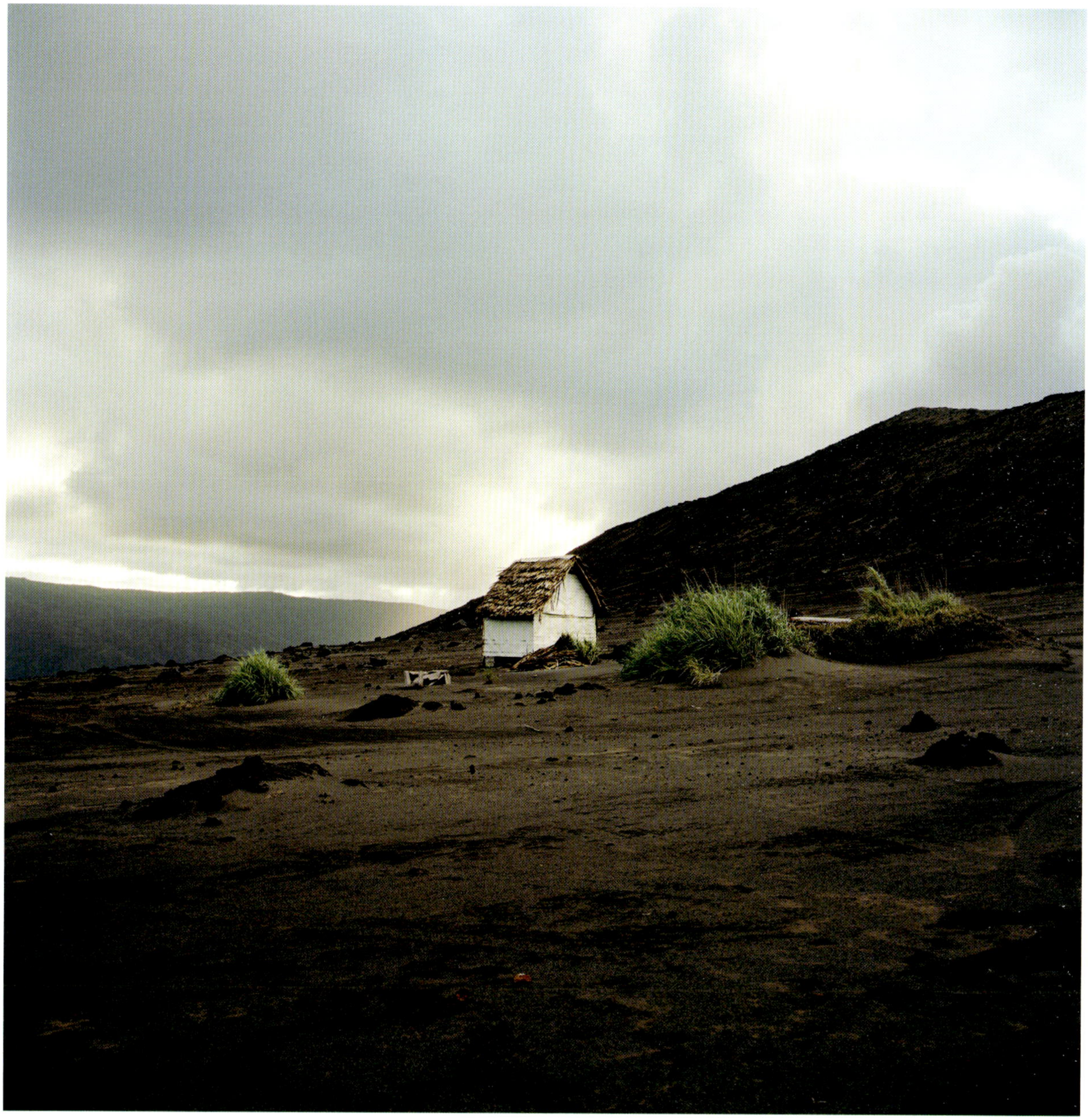

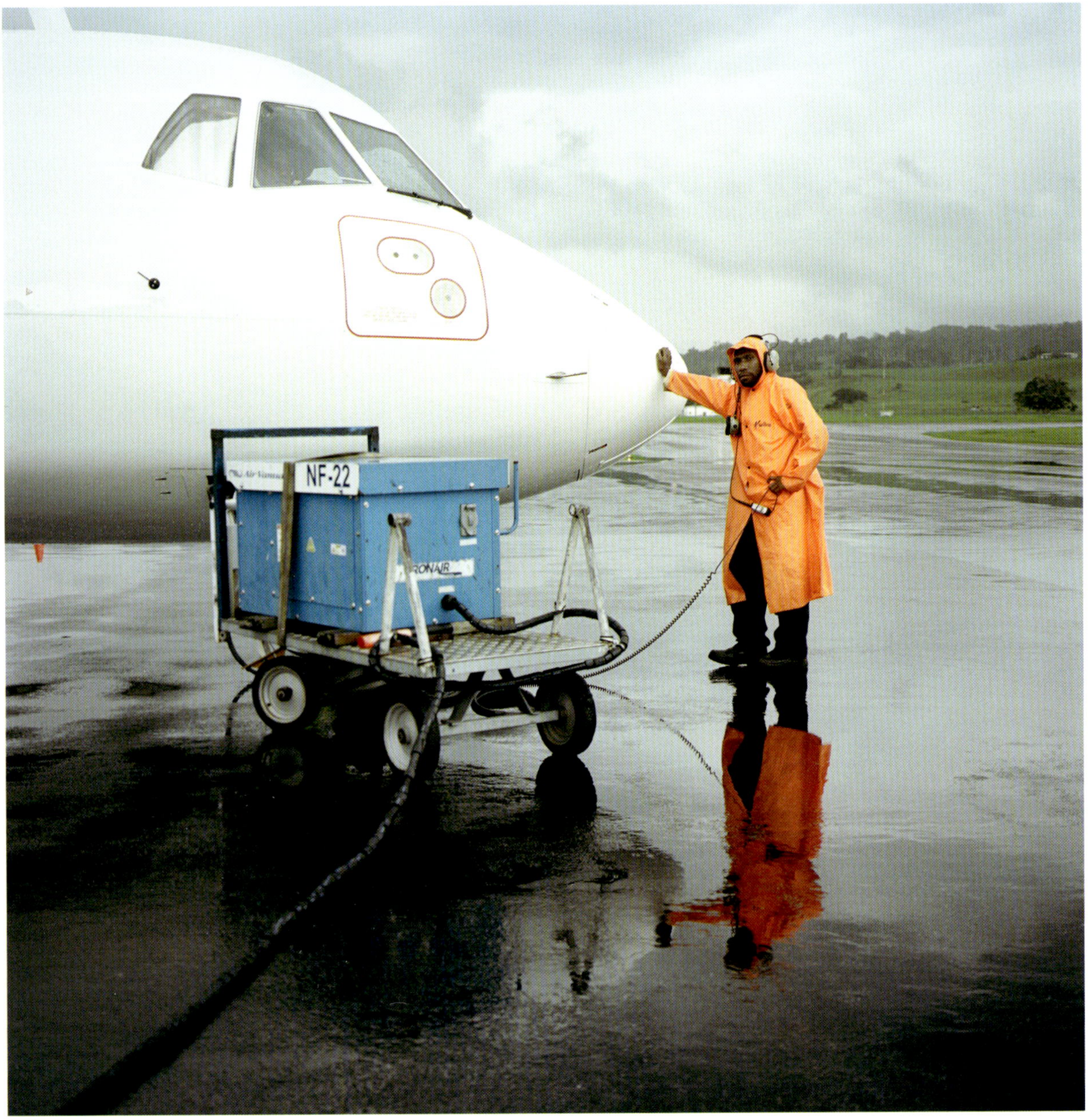

Godfrey Felix, Bauerfield International Airport, Efate

COME FLY WITH ME

At a business hotel in West Berlin, in a drab conference room where the windows didn't open, we met Claude-Philippe Berger – the man who would be king.

He was late for his own party. A line of ageing counts, countesses, dukes, and hangers-on had gathered. The corridor was full of their excited chatter in Flemish, German, and French.

"You may address the king only as *Majesty*," whispered a doughy-faced German count. He was solemnly tying on a black cloak sewn with Knights Templar-looking symbols while a few doors down, in another world, a trade symposium on dental hygiene was about to get underway.

Claude-Philippe claimed to be the exiled king of an island in Vanuatu called Tanna. Jon and I had come to the 'royal gala' to find out if Claude was a real king, even if we thought we already knew the answer.

We knew then only a handful of things about him: he was born in 1953 in Casablanca, the son of a colonial-era banker; said he was once a diplomat with friends in high places; that his Berger family blood flowed back to the Holy Roman Empire. Yet we'd also heard he got by in a flat in Nice, was dining out on the royal title, and had done since the last white king of tropical Tanna abdicated in 1999.

Such rumours didn't dampen his followers' fervour. When word went round that Majesty was in the hotel, a hush descended.

The gentry were herded into the conference room where three rows of chairs had been arranged in a semi circle. In the centre was a plumped pillow with an appliquéd design of prancing lords and horses. On a fold-out table draped in black velvet was a ceremonial sword and, against the back wall, a flag the colour of the Pacific Ocean, propped up precariously in a wastepaper bin.

Underwhelming as the setting was, we had seen the flag before. In fact, we first saw it in Vanuatu, being unfolded in the cool shade of a thatched hut. A local woman called Grace, whose tight curls and teeth were the same shade of yellow, carefully removed the flag from her home and held up a corner in one hand, shielding her eyes from the sun with the other.

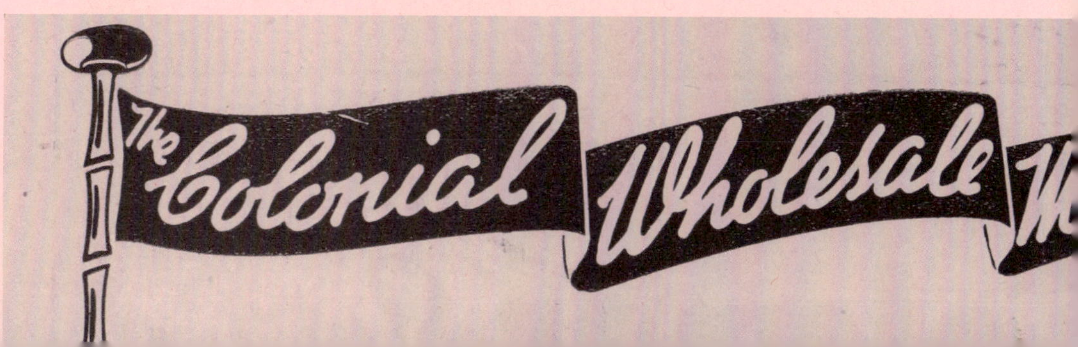

Grace explained that she and her husband put their hopes for the future not in the modern nation of Vanuatu, but in a dream of secession that began in the 1970s. That was when a Frenchman, predecessor of Claude-Philippe, was crowned the first king of the island and led a short-lived insurgency to carve out a new nation.

This all went on, of course, far from the eyes of the world. The isolation of the Pacific has long provided cover for mischief.

Captain James Cook first sailed to the South Seas in 1768, and with each successive voyage the crew returned to London with stacks of watercolours showing sunny atolls and voluptuous flora. They also came back with stories that Cook was received as a god or an ancient ancestor by various peoples around the Pacific. Whether that was true or just vanity, from that moment to today, via Colonel Kurtz and Kipling, an old colonial trope about divine white men being revered in faraway lands has not gone away. It is embedded in the Western imagination: We can all think of a cartoon in which a huddle of grass-skirted people suddenly prostrate themselves before a foreigner who has unwittingly breached a sacred taboo.

The goings-on in Vanuatu today, which are this book's subject, hold up a mirror to this fantasy. By the time of the gala in Berlin, Jon and I had been to Vanuatu and seen first-hand that there are other Westerners, like Claude, claiming or believing they are the fulfilment of a local prophecy about a divine figure who will come from overseas.

Surrounded by the Pacific Ocean, the horizon has been a source of great promise and greater disappointment for the Ni-Vanuatu people. European rule brought little lasting development and complex societal structures were decimated by waves of itinerant missionaries.

The cult of a coming messiah – promising riches, renewed dignity, and a return to pre-colonial ways – arose at the zenith of Vanuatu's domination at the hands of imperial powers, long before independence in 1980. The belief has endured in a multitude of forms and pantheons: These are, after all, the islands where the late Prince Philip is revered as a mountain god. However frivolously such beliefs are framed in the West, their origins lie in an anti-colonial struggle, a backlash, a desperate howl as one culture was about to be consumed by another.

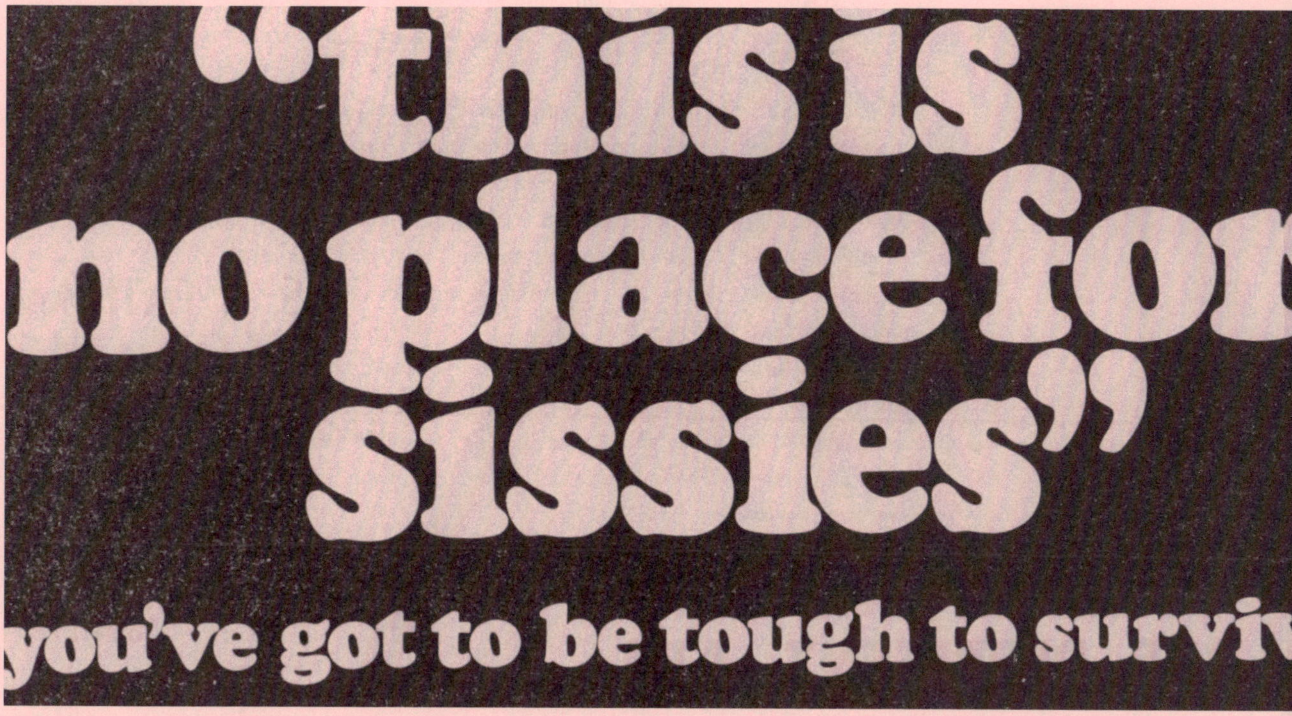
"this is
no place for
sissies"
you've got to be tough to surviv

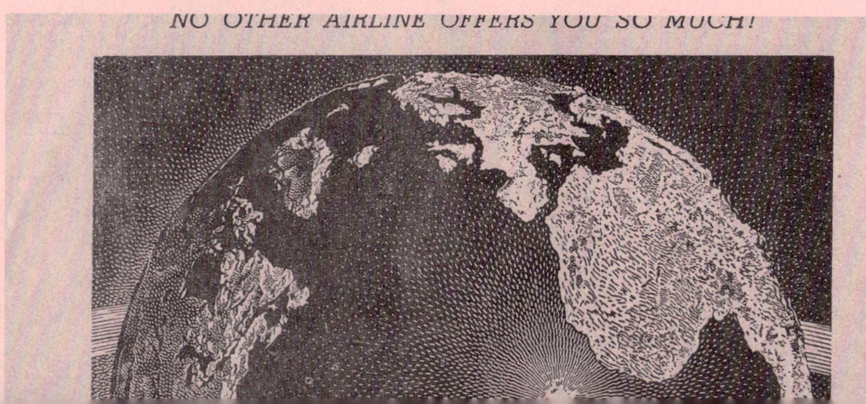
NO OTHER AIRLINE OFFERS YOU SO MUCH!

Learning that these poignant beliefs could provide a backdrop for Western fantasies was, for us, hard to believe.

In most cases, the intentions of men like Claude aren't malevolent. In fact, they believe they are doing a good thing. Like the self-proclaimed civilisers of the age of discovery, they too have a reassuring tale that it's for the betterment of a beleaguered Other. But while this could just be an age-old tale of power, of those who have it speaking over those who don't, it isn't that simple. There's a twist here, which fascinated Jon and I, and led us to spend years trying to understand the truth of it all. What amazed us is that there are islanders, like Grace, willing to make room in their beliefs for newcomers; they turn the situation to their advantage, and in doing so, realise their own prophecy.

That can be a dangerous fruit for the foreigners – like creepers crafted of hallucinatory jungle juice and biblical details whispered in the dark, they become snared in their own myth-making, unable to fully extract themselves, sometimes sacrificing large sums of money or ties with home to keep the dream alive.

We quickly learned that for the pale prophets and kings who come to Vanuatu, life back home tends not to be quite so regal. Which is what brought us to the Tetris motif carpets of Berlin's Steigenberger Hotel.

Claude-Philippe strode into the conference room with a magnanimous grin and a full white beard – the sea captain kind, used to market rum or cigarettes. His military tunic was made taut by too many medals and a row of polished buttons.

The counts all creaked to their feet to greet the royal convoy: the consort of the king, Princess Sylvaine, edged into the room steadying her tiara, followed by an eager-faced bishop, clad in long white robes with a tiny metal cross on the top of his headdress, who stood solemnly next to the tea and coffee-making facilities.

Over the course of the next hour, a sheepish man was knighted, kneeling on the pillow to kiss Claude-Philippe's pudgy white hand. The king made long

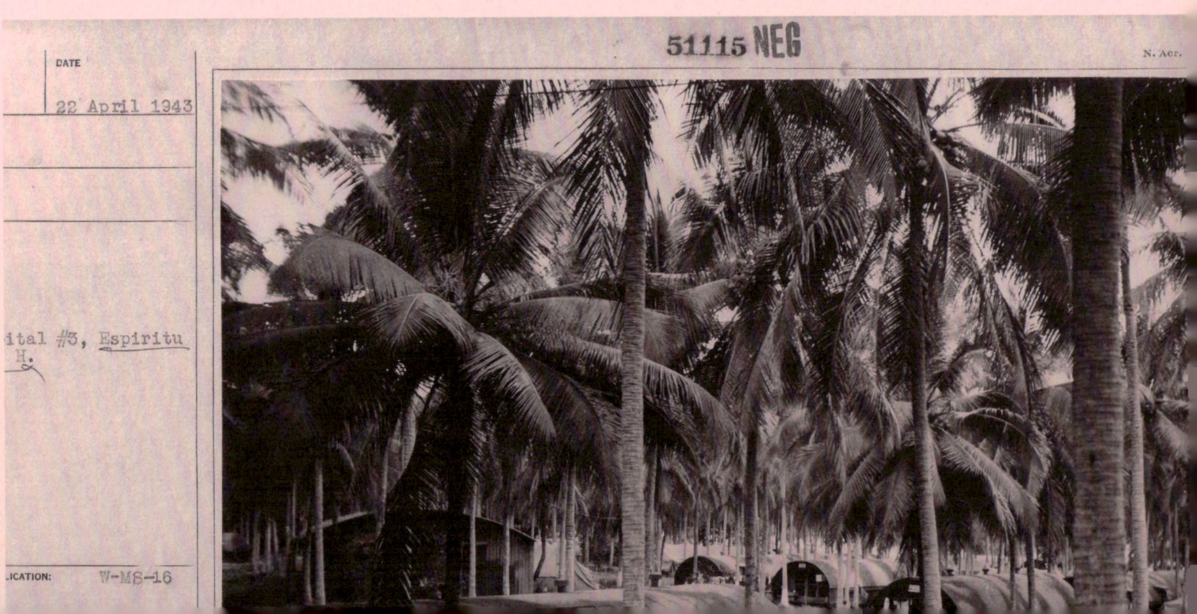

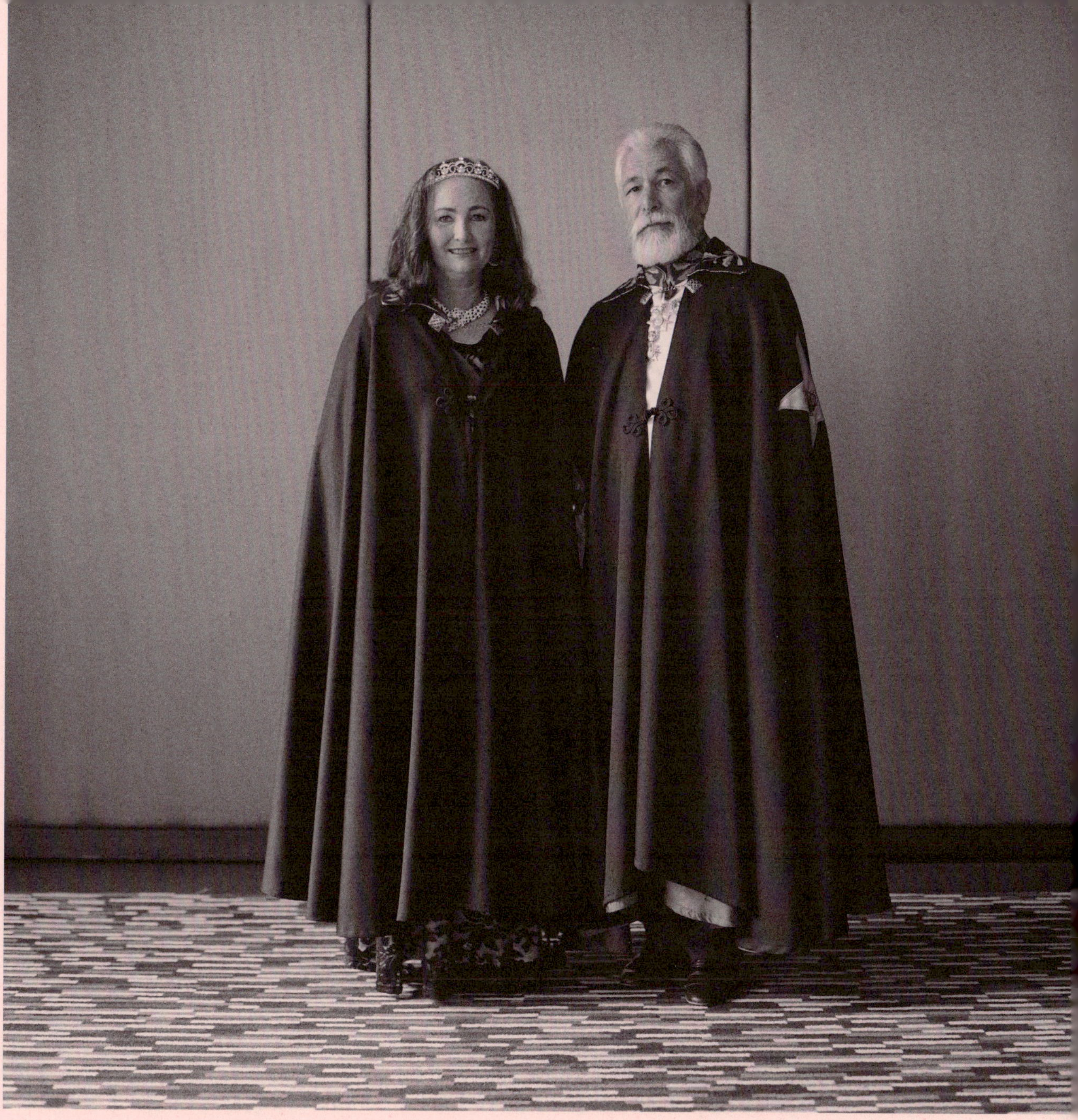

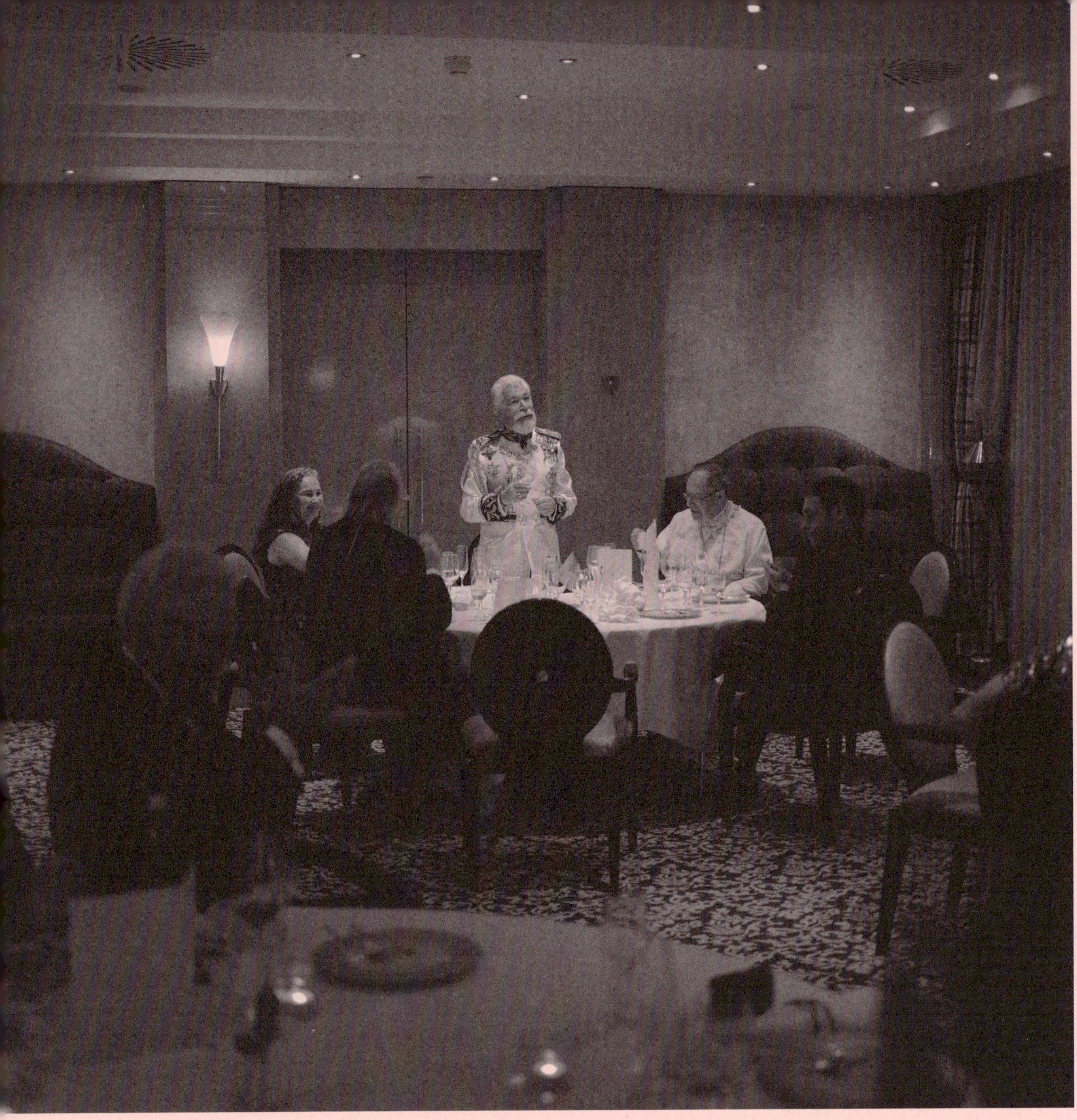

guffawing speeches in French; thanked the house for their largesse which would go to the loyalists in Vanuatu after a cyclone ripped through their islands a year earlier. A massive novelty cheque was held aloft then quietly signed for six hundred and fifty Euros.

Few of the royal house had ever actually been to Vanuatu. Some would probably struggle to point to it on a map. The bishop led the king and princess in rounds of liturgical chant. It felt like an elaborate roleplay. *"De siécle en siécle!"* they sang, and the old German maids in the audience smiled vacantly, patting their laps: "Amen!"

When the ceremony ended they all piled off to the hotel bar. But Claude-Philippe was left behind in the corridor, trying to unhook his cloak which had snagged on his medals. Unfortunately, his white silk gloves got in the way. "Can you help me?" Claude said, in hiccupy English.

Up close, one could see his collar was threading and white whiskers tumbled from his ears. The princess translated as the king outlined how his island should one day be an independent country in its own right, with him installed as its traditional ruler.

"It's not just me - the people, they want this!" Claude interrupted, switching to English in his excitement. Jon and I got our first taste of his boundless, if not entirely baseless, hubris: The last time he went to Vanuatu, Majesty explained, great crowds of people met his plane on the runway and several pigs were slaughtered in his honour.

At the Steigenberger, an arduous gala dinner followed. A man on a keyboard in the corner struck up the tune of God Save The King, cueing everyone to their feet and glasses of fizzy wine to be raised. Claude and Sylvaine sauntered in, arm in arm, to the Casio's digital fugue.

We were seated top table, which was scandalous apparently for one dedicated subject who took umbrage that he was relegated to a table of Bavarians. The Princess soon lost interest in translating our questions for the king. He, after a drink or two, cracked jokes about *le Ros bif*.

Our table mates - an Englishman and an American, both counts - were men of considerable but conceivable wealth. One owned a tower block in an average town, the other a string of car dealerships. It was the wealth of the upper middle class who never had the blood for aristocracy. They were wry about the pageantry but had coughed up to cover Claude-Philippe's visit to Vanuatu. They saw for themselves the royal reception he'd received.

"The king talks a good game," said one of the men, forking a prawn cocktail. "But none of us know who he *really* is."

Yet the longer we spent amongst the Maison Royale de Tanna, the more their rigmarole seeped into our minds. We called Claude Majesty, inquired about the brass on his chest. And when the Princess ordered Jon and I to the dancefloor we politely obliged. Before the night was over, we had each taken turns to teeter her around the carpet to a plinky rendition of 'Come Fly With Me'.

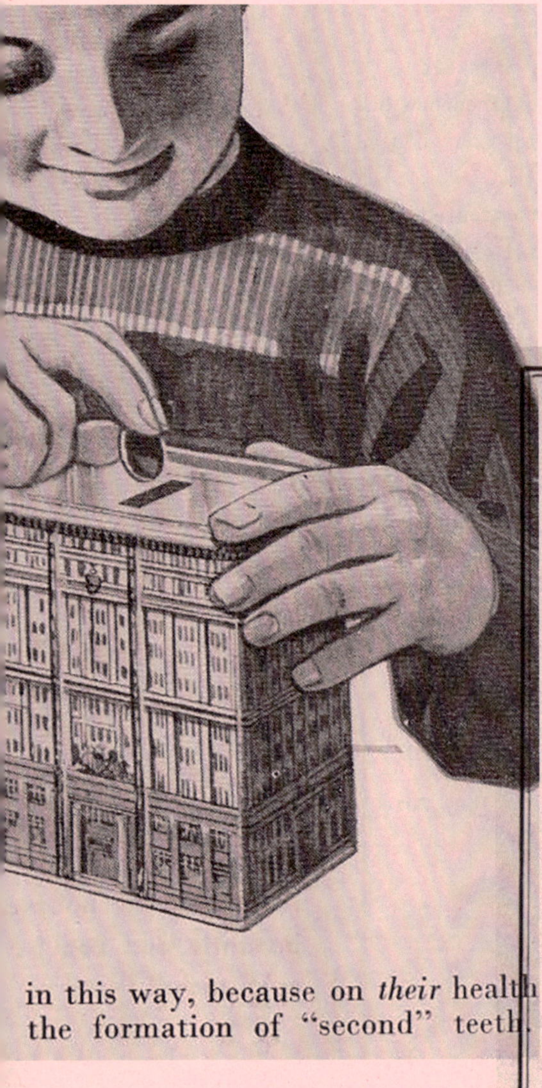

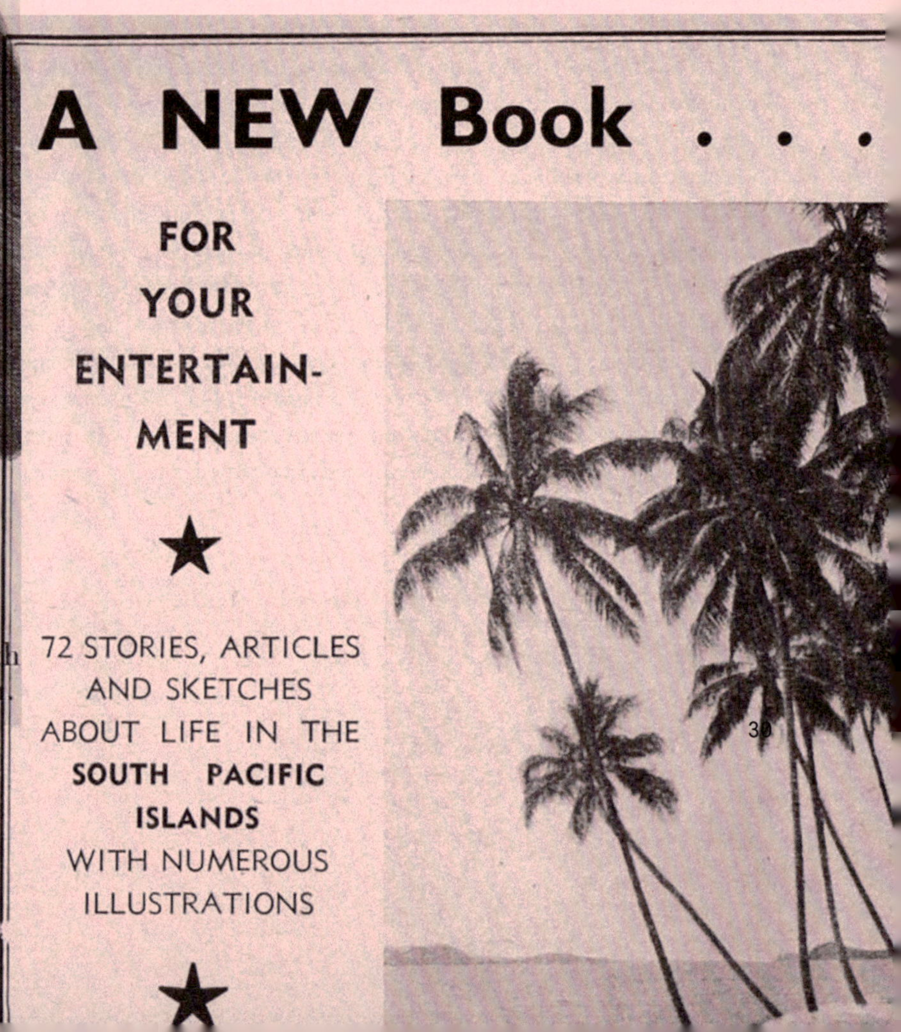

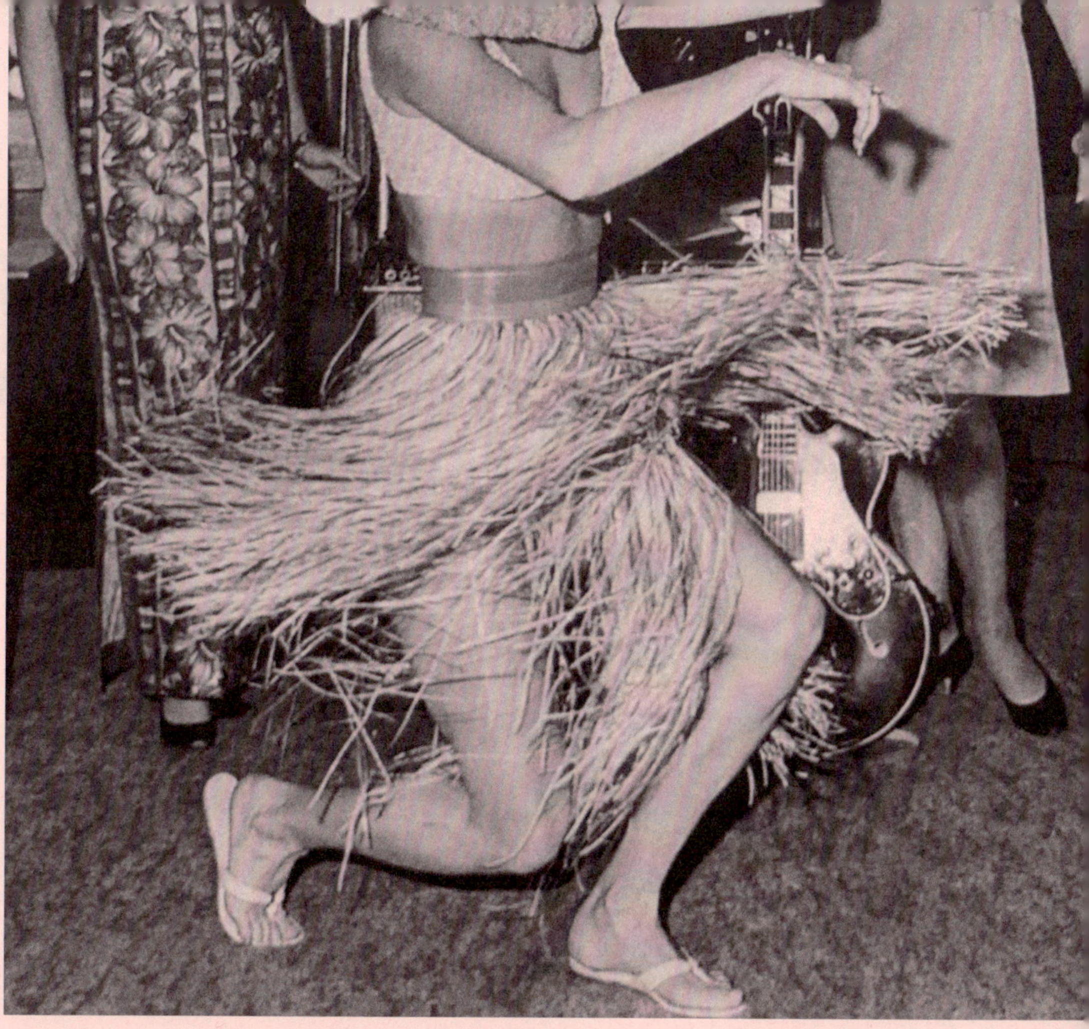

329256 NEG

NAVAER- 452

31

Sept. 1944

aval ammuni-
itu Santo,

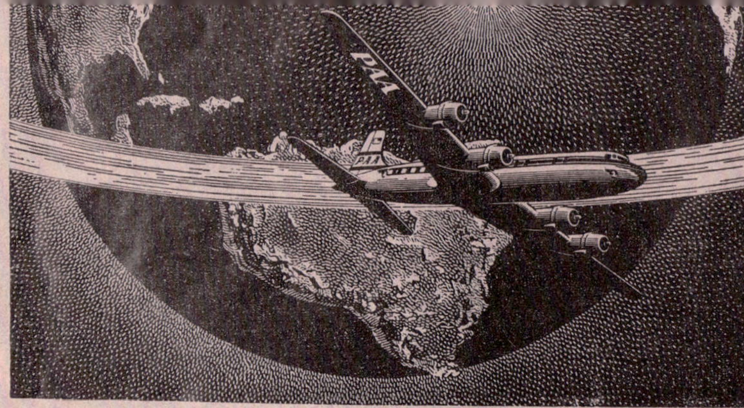

For example:

WORLD-WIDE LEADERSHIP

Wherever in the world you're going, go Pan American — the

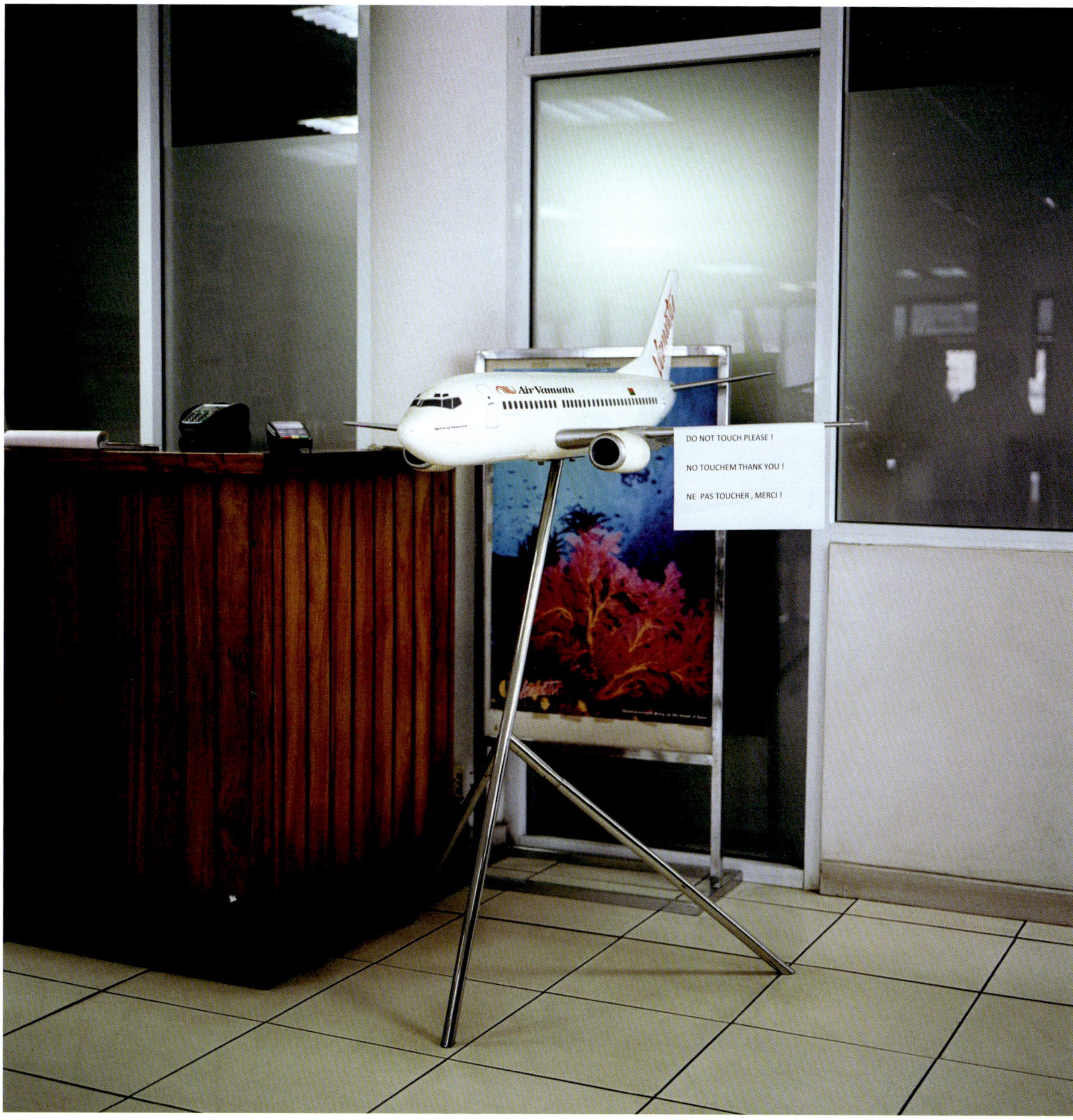
Air Vanuatu
DO NOT TOUCH PLEASE !
NO TOUCHEM THANK YOU !
NE PAS TOUCHER , MERCI !

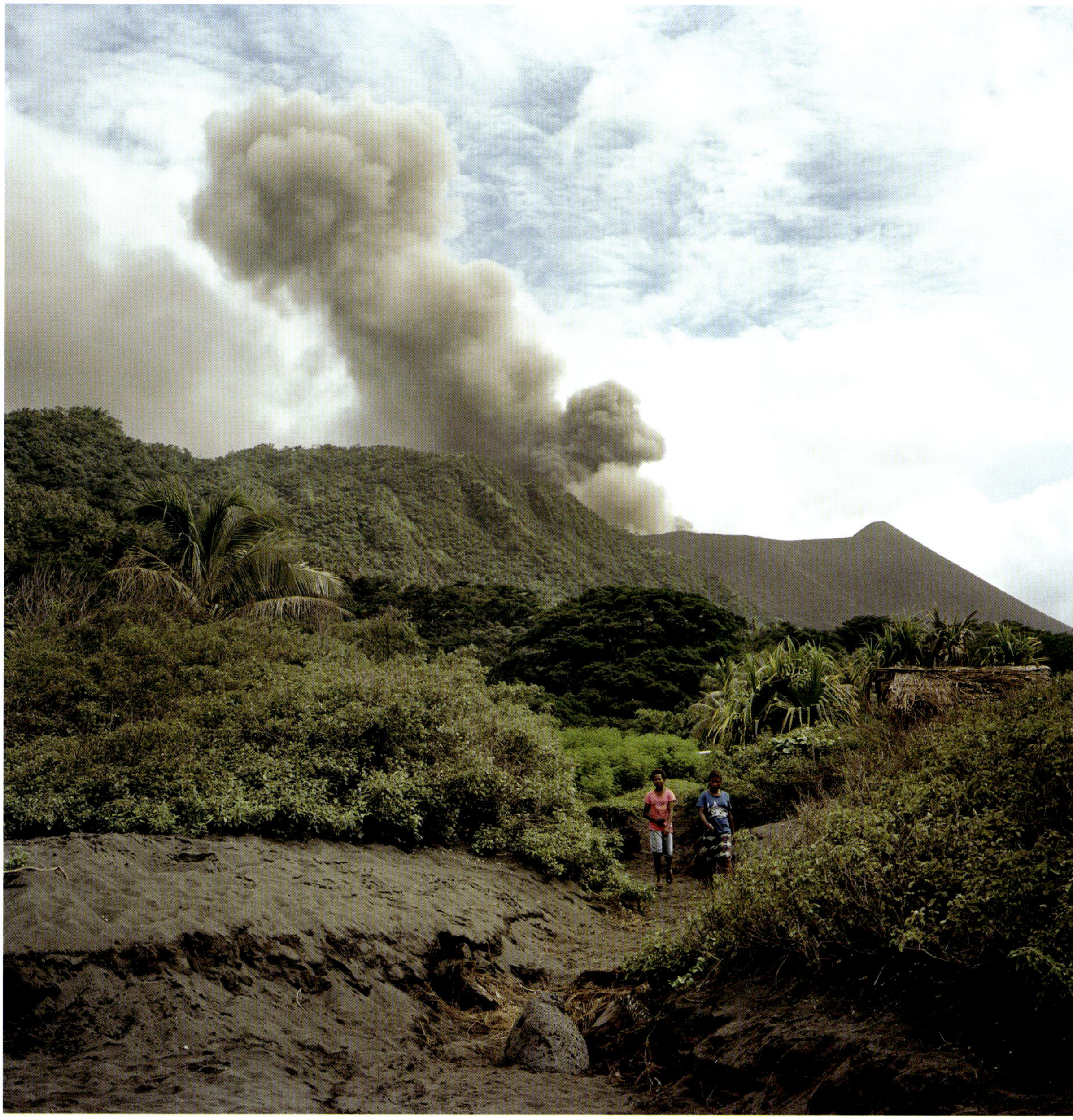

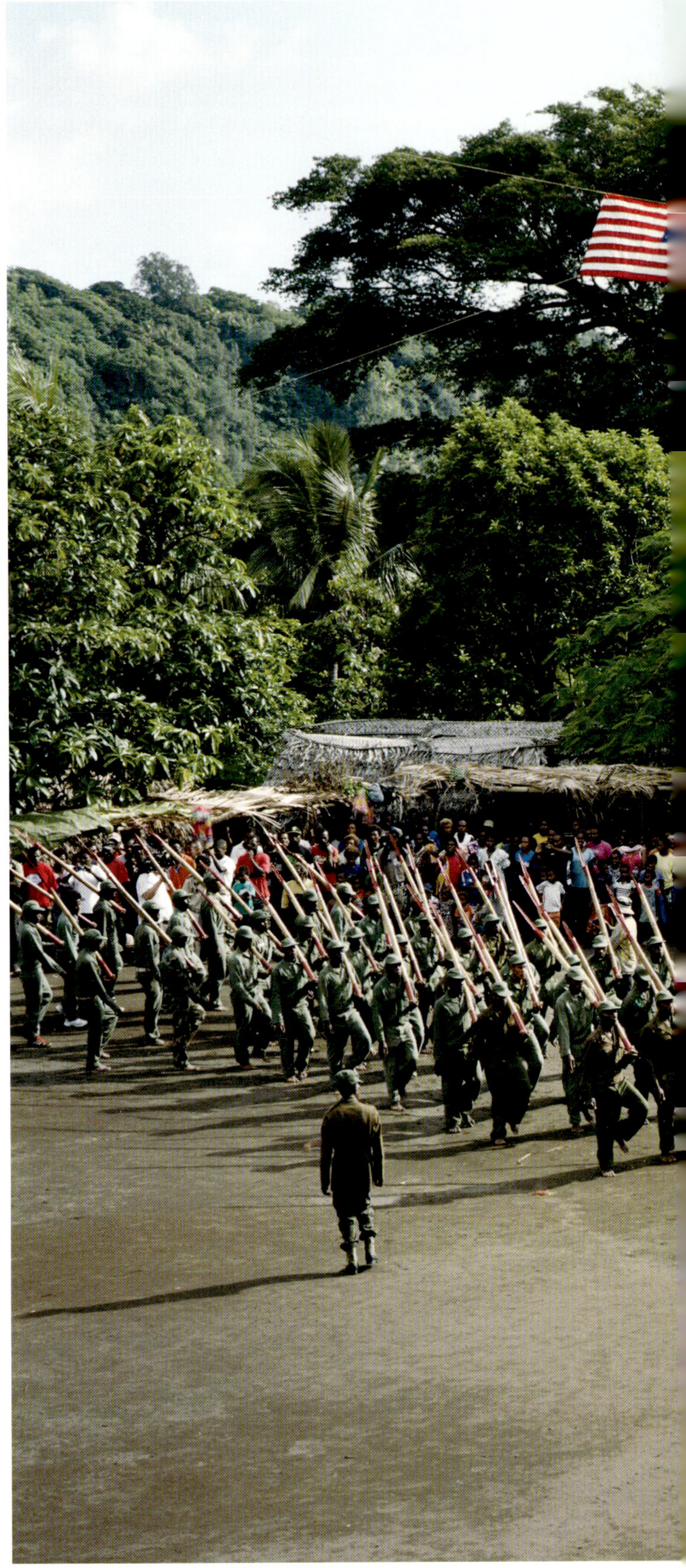

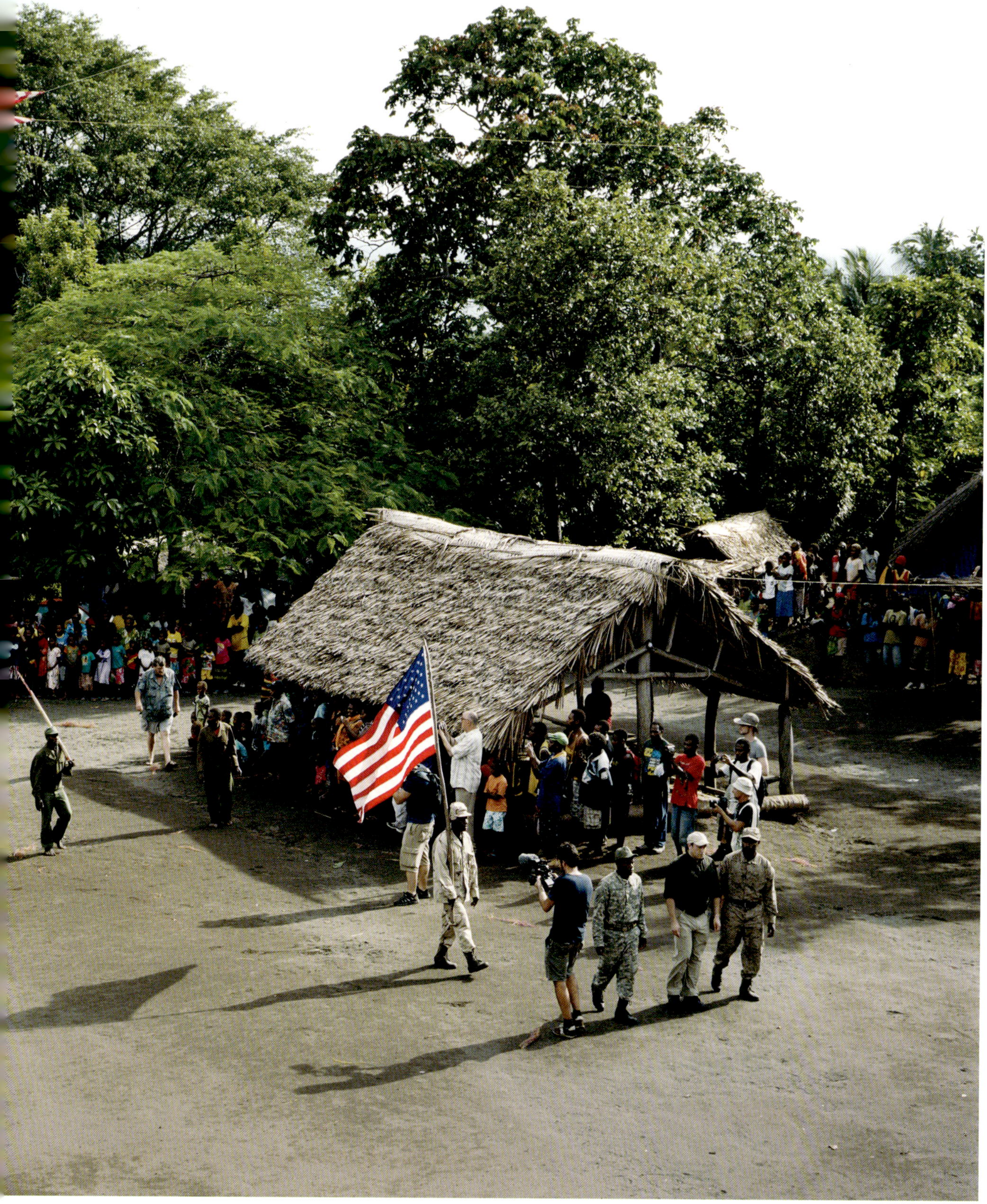

Elder Stanley and Elder Manu,
Polynesian Mormon missionaries, Tanna

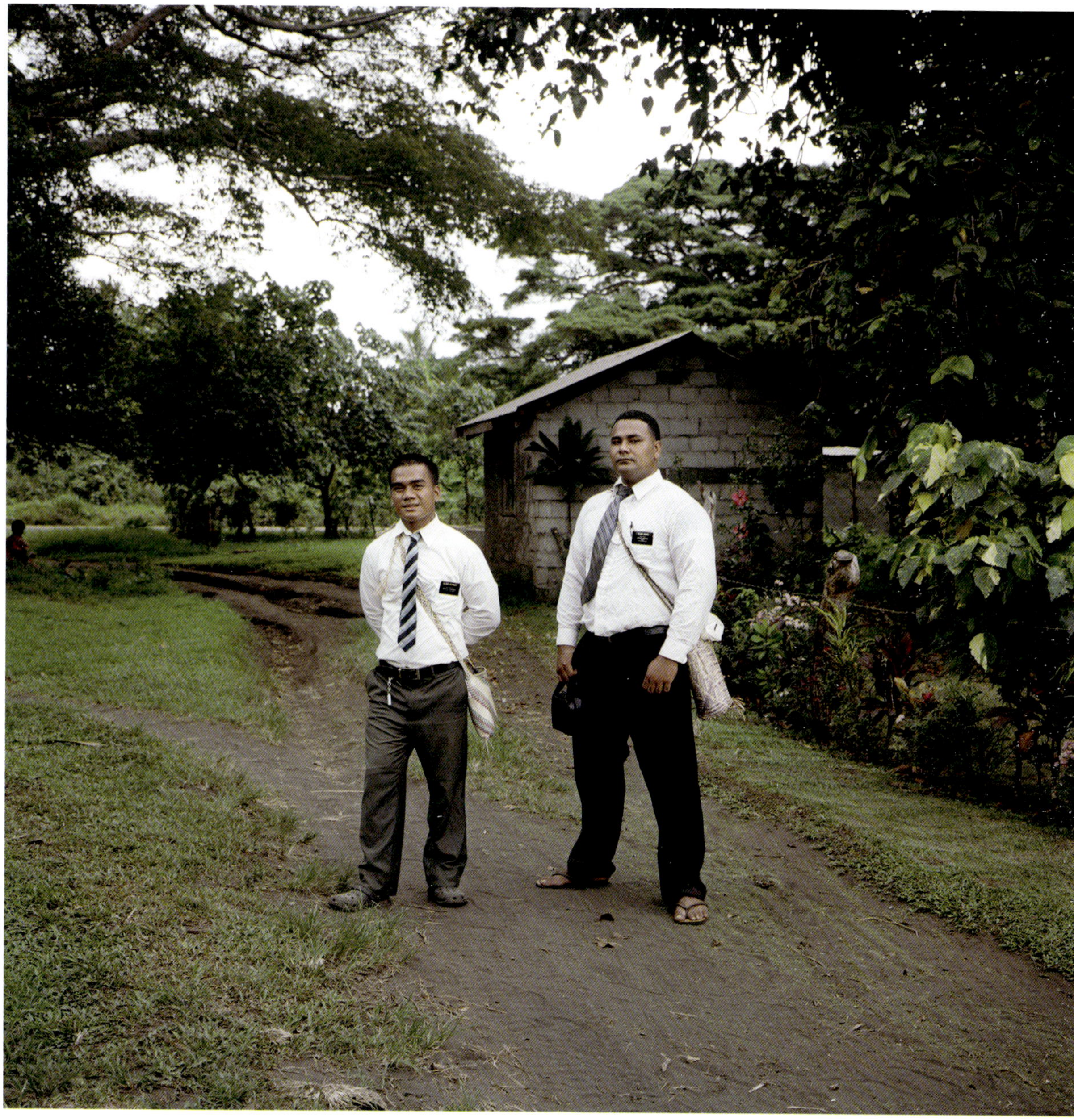

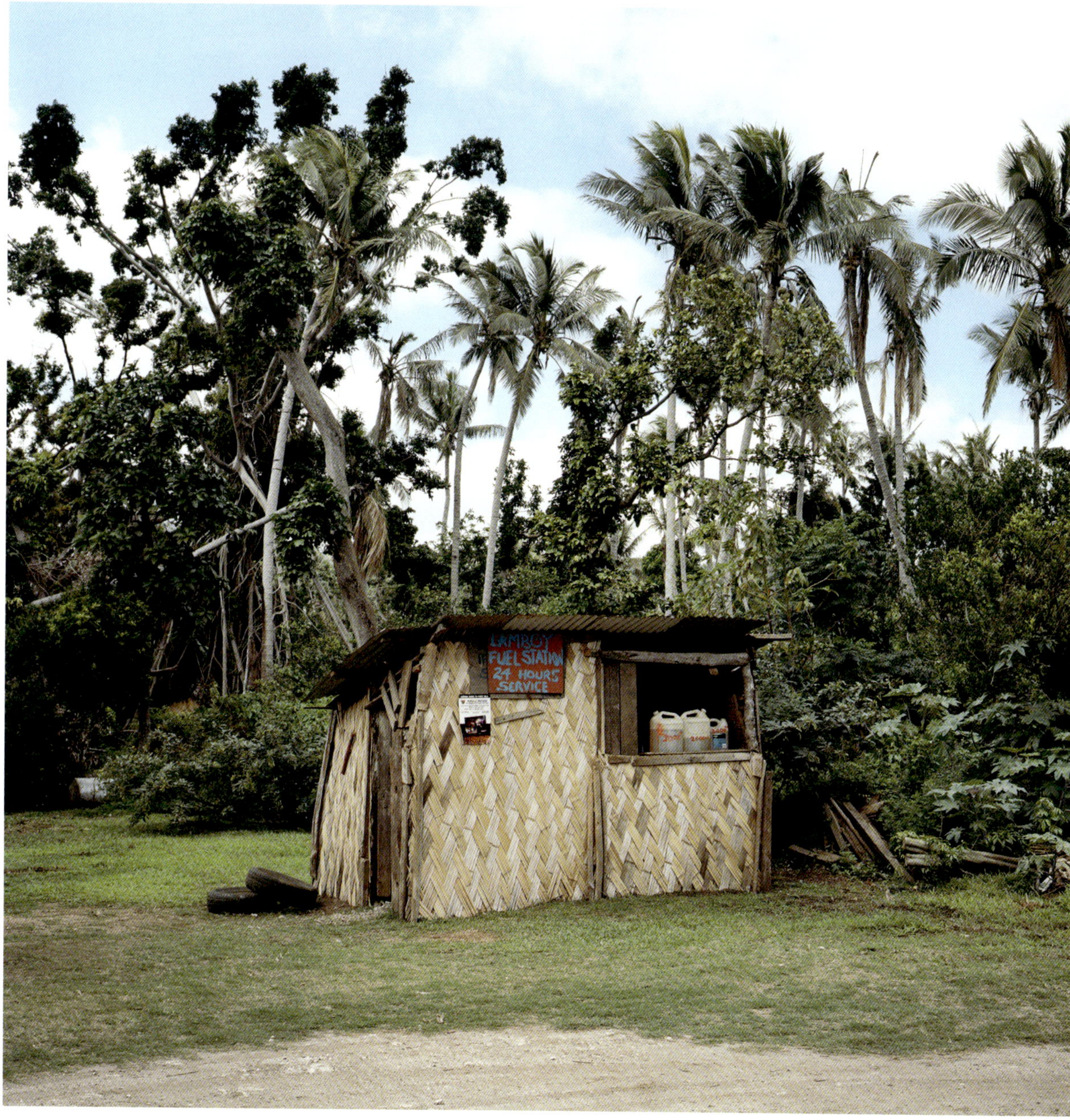
LAMBOY
FUEL STATION
24 HOURS
SERVICE

John Frum told them "I'll be back. I'm going away but I'll be back".

They asked him – "Is it true you'll be back?" He said "yes". They asked him the second time, "Is it true you will you be back?" He said "yes". After the last question, for the third time, John told them, "Since you guys doubt I'll be coming back I'll lay this stone. If I'm not coming back, this stone will disappear. But if I'll be back, this stone will remain here".

One day the old fella from Sulphur Bay came and stole it, so an old fella from Green Point woke early one morning and took it back.

They are still waiting for John to return.

John Kaurua, Green Point, Tanna

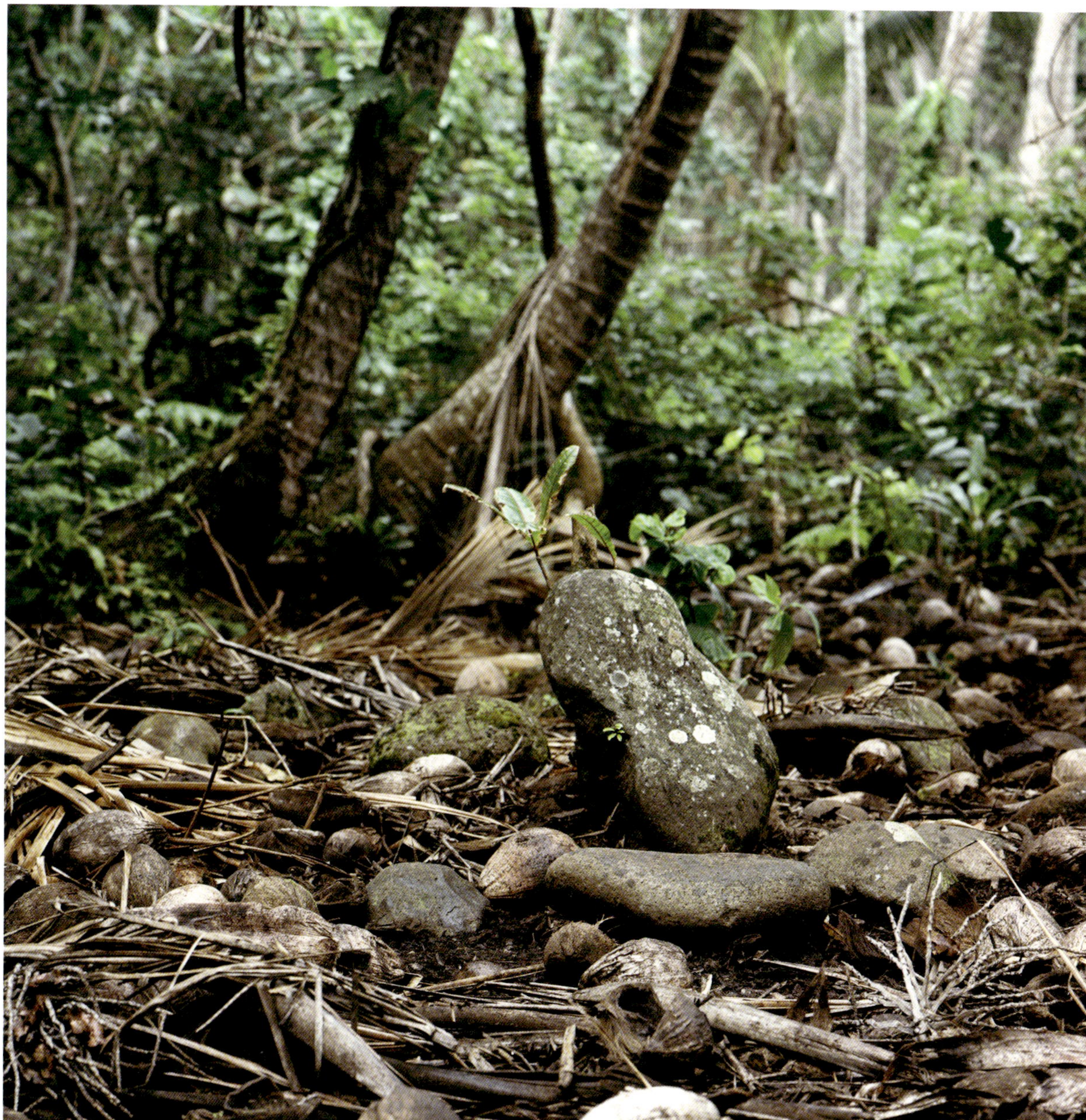

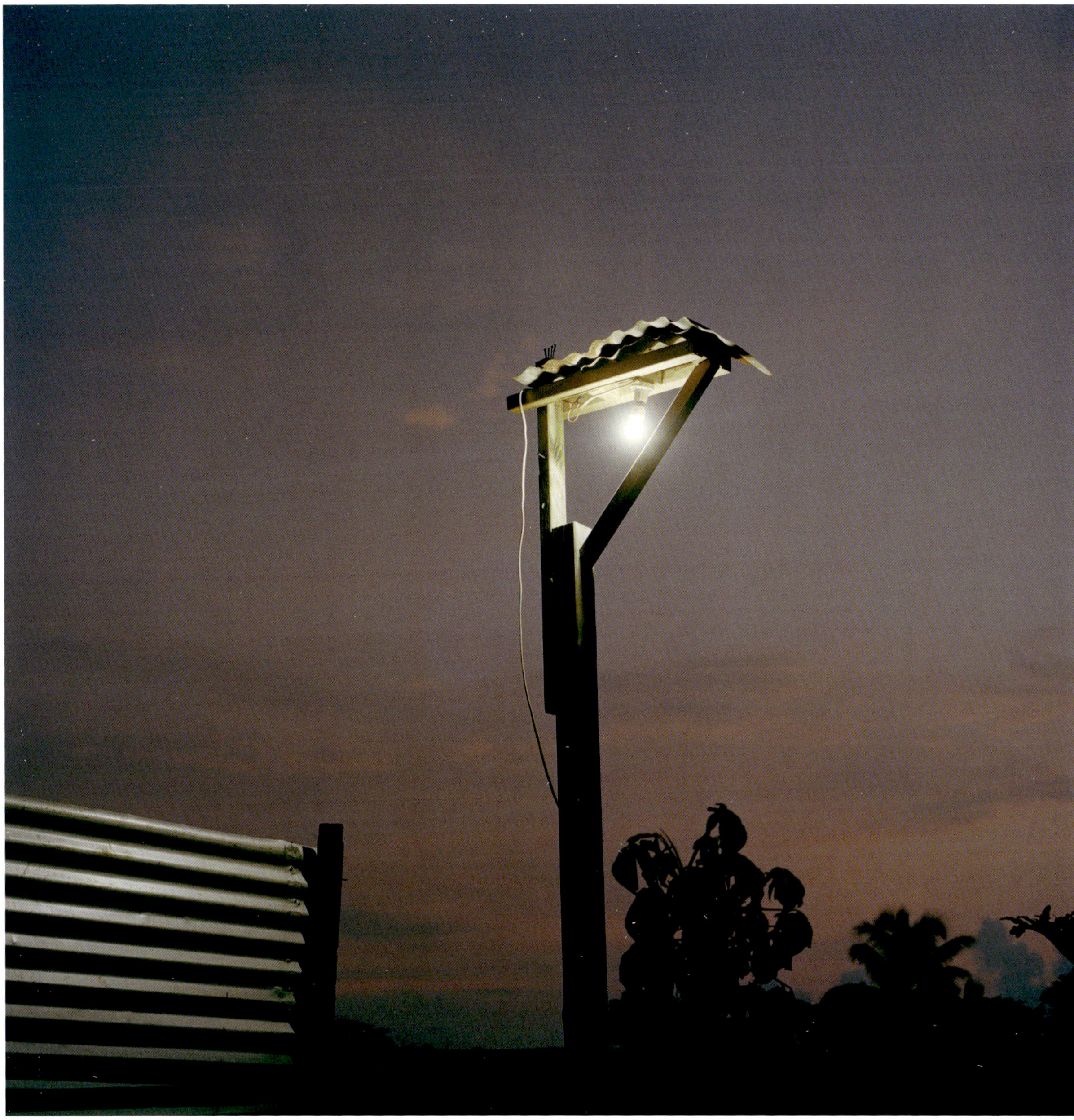

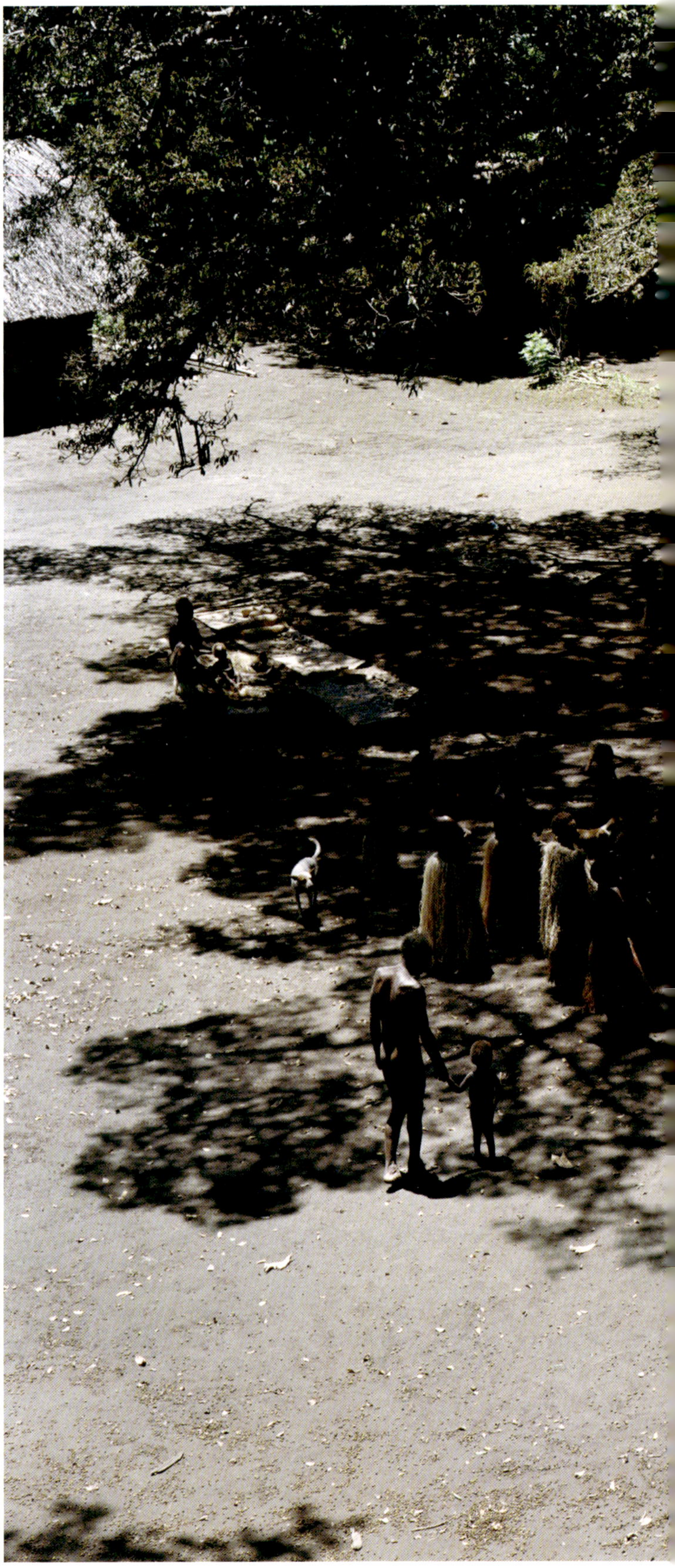

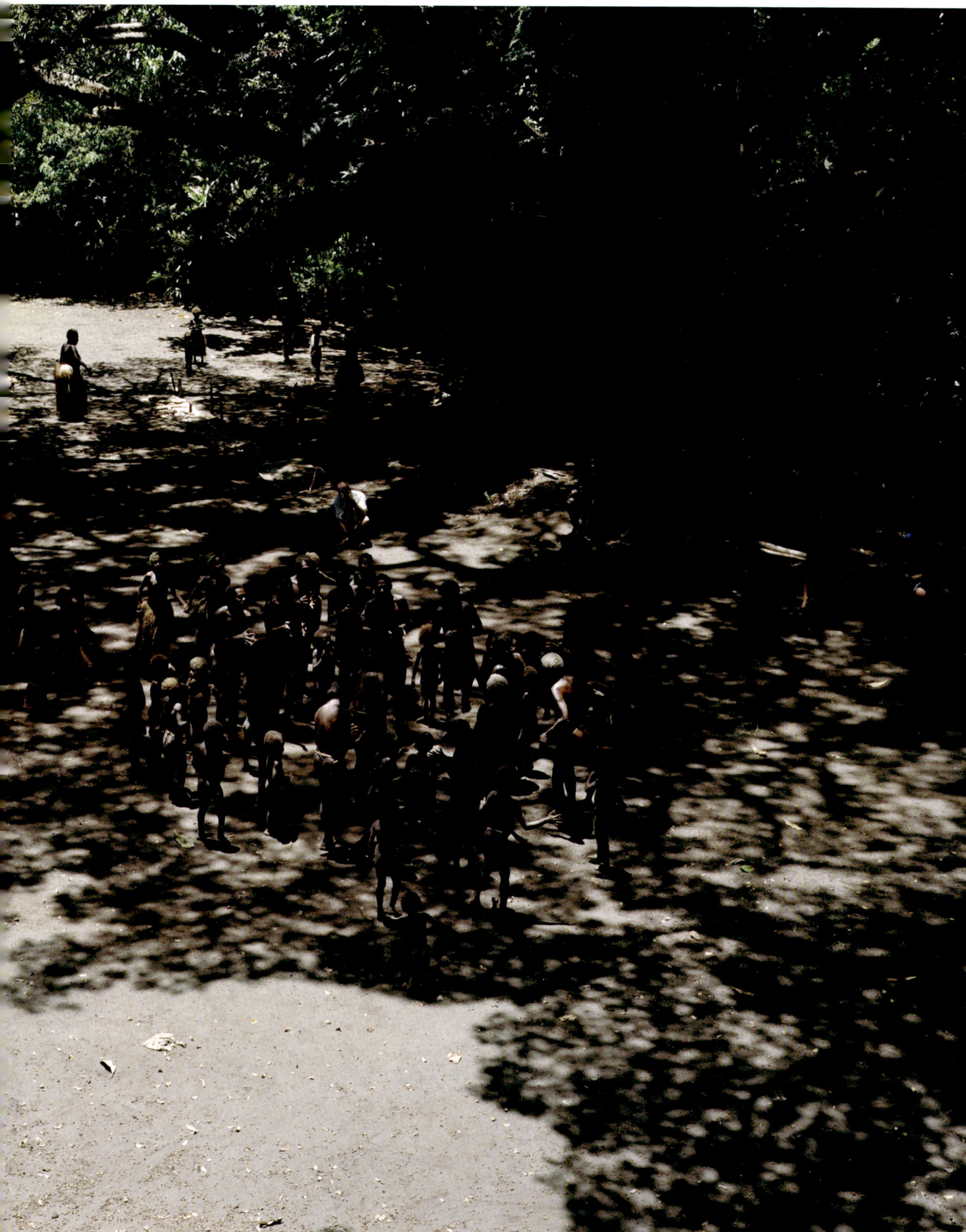

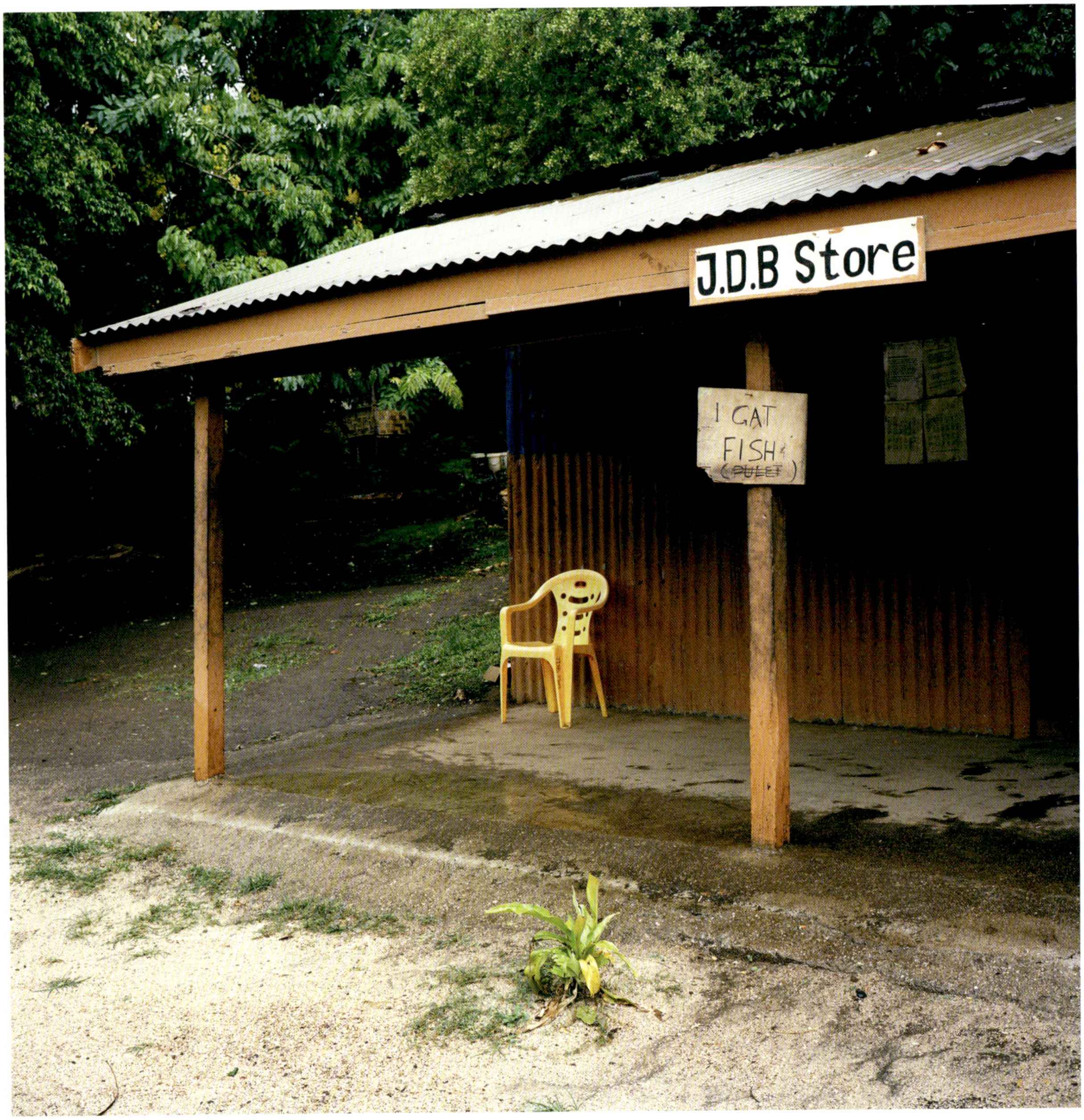
J.D.B Store
I GAT
FISH
(PULET)

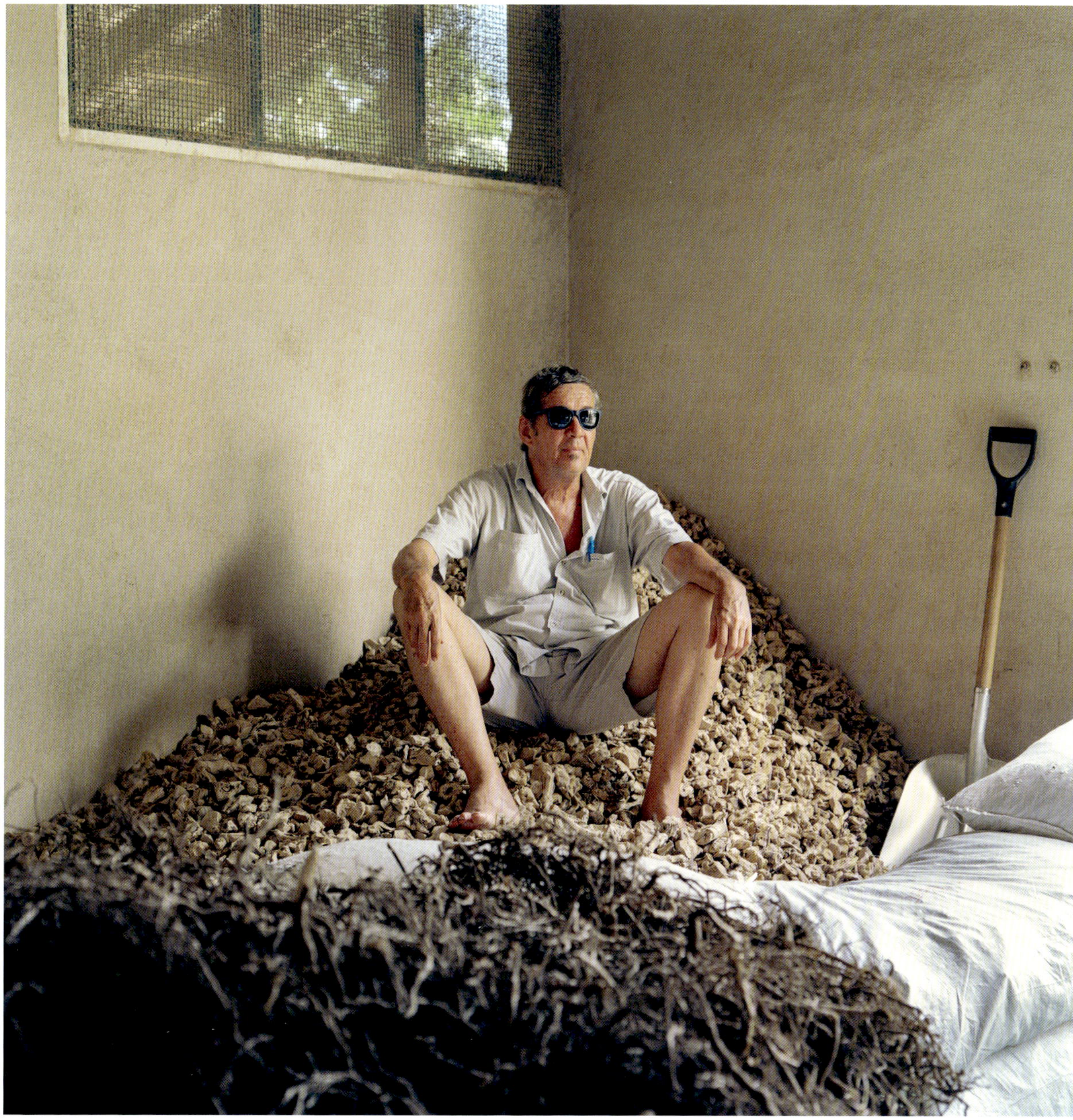

Peter Colmar, sitting on dried kava root which he exports worldwide, Espiritu Santo

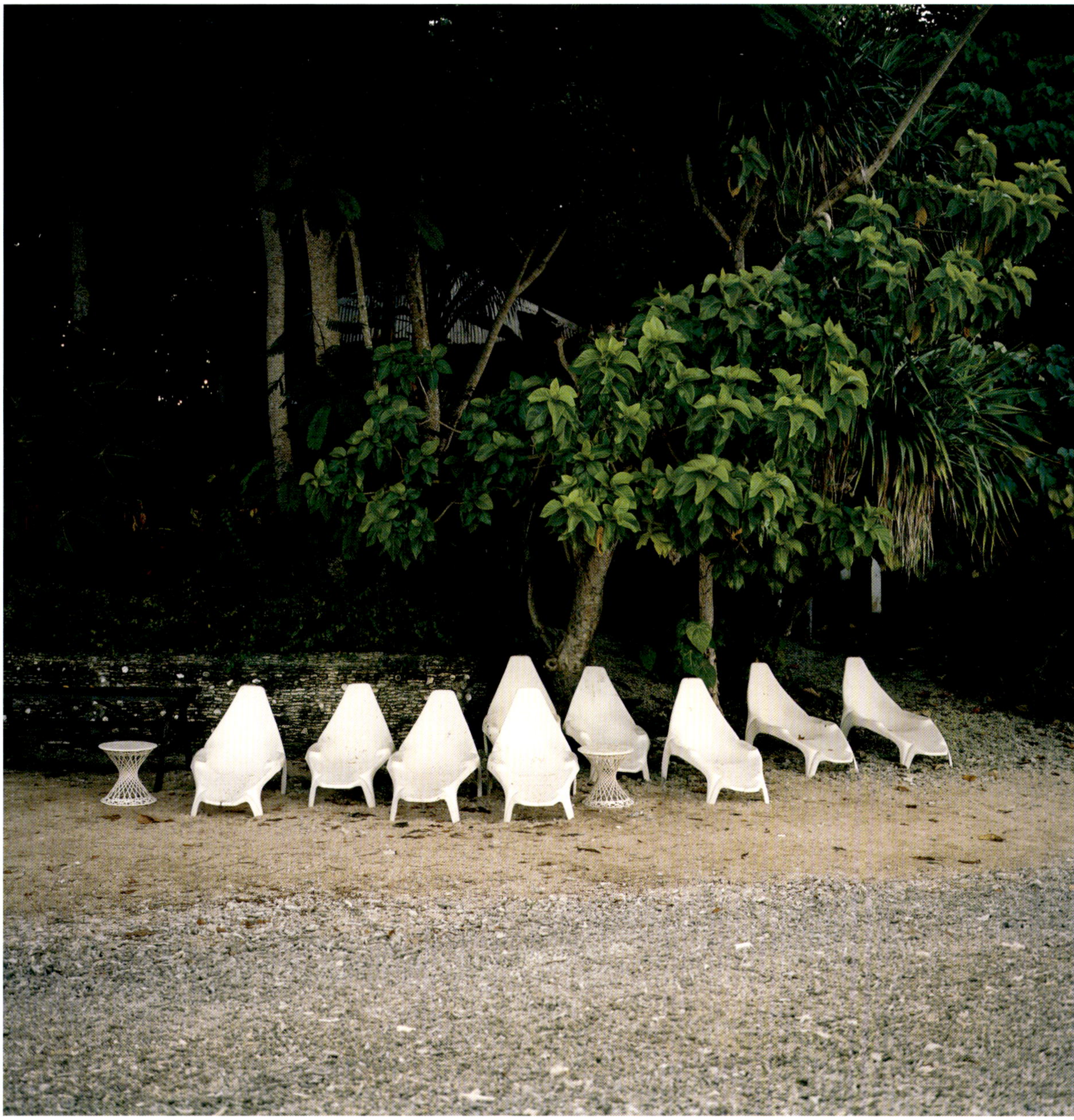

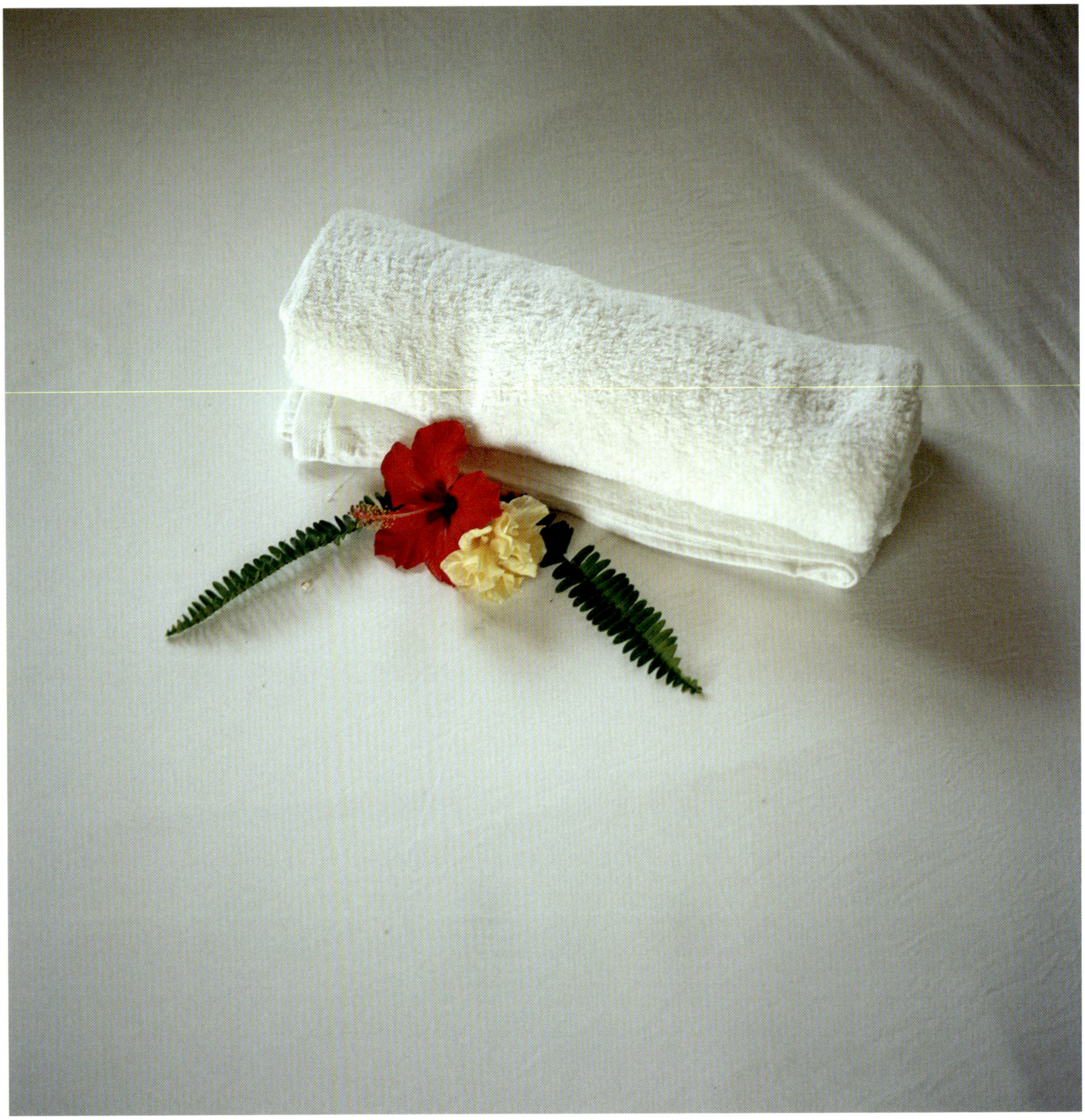

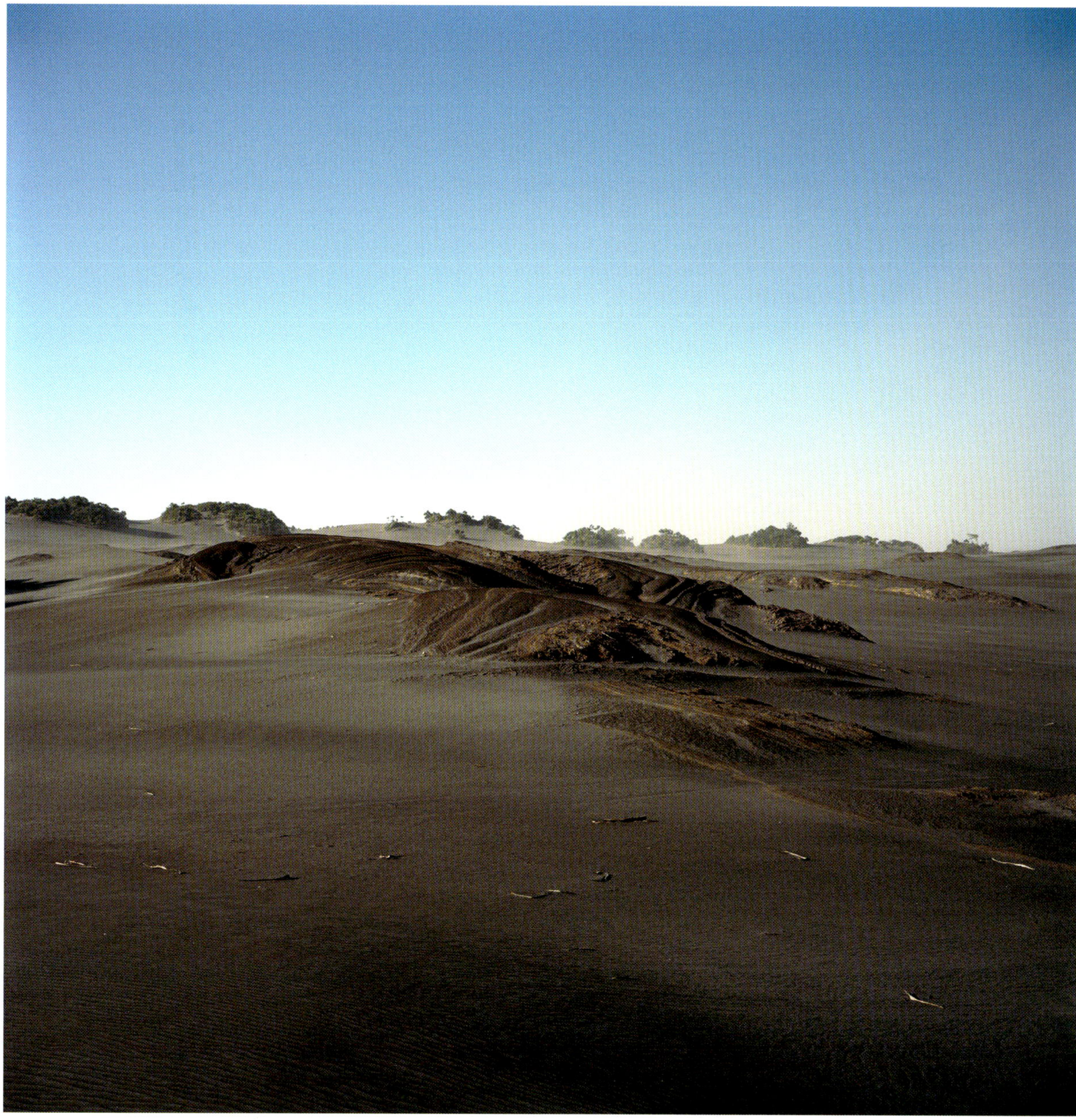

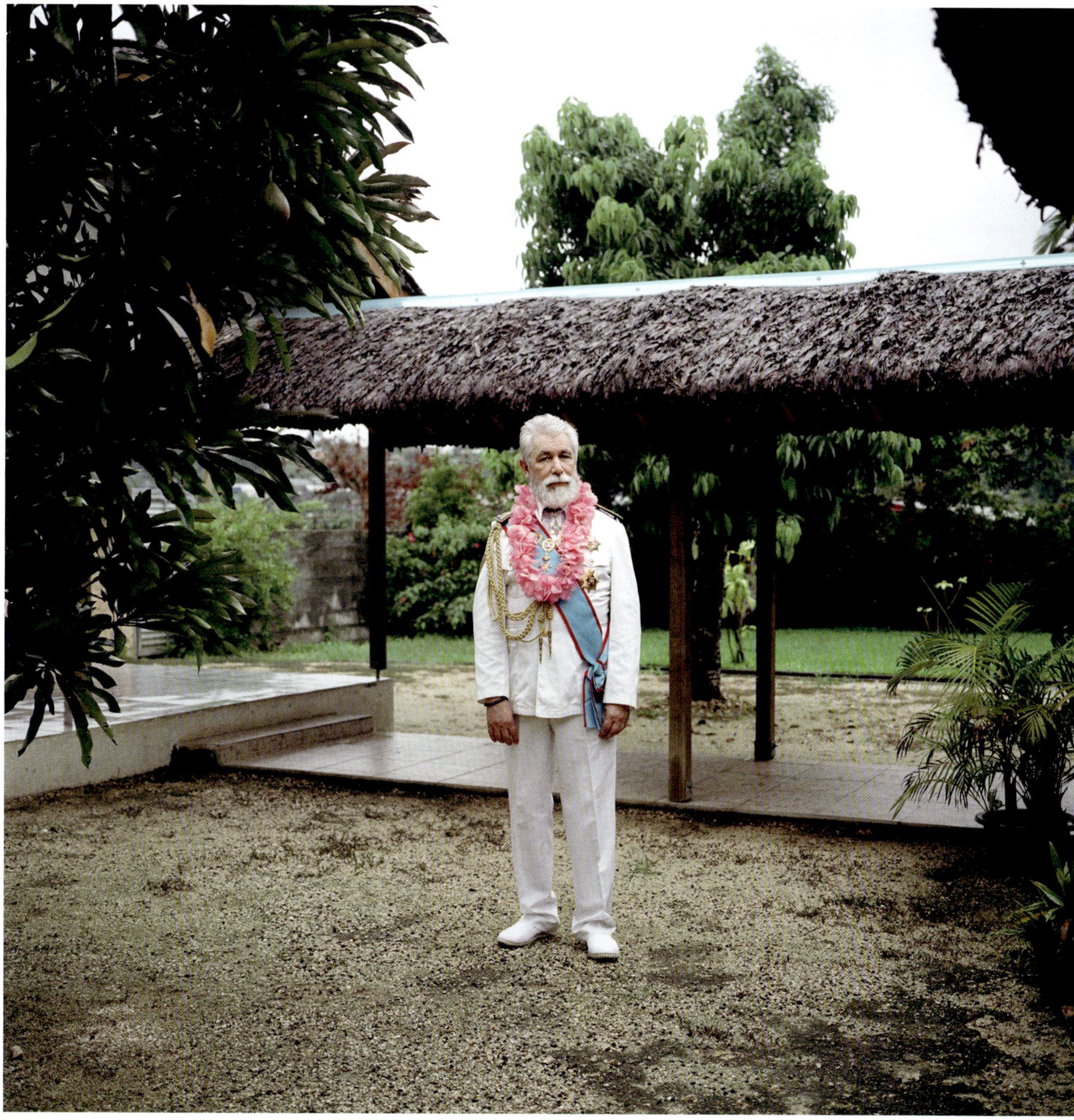

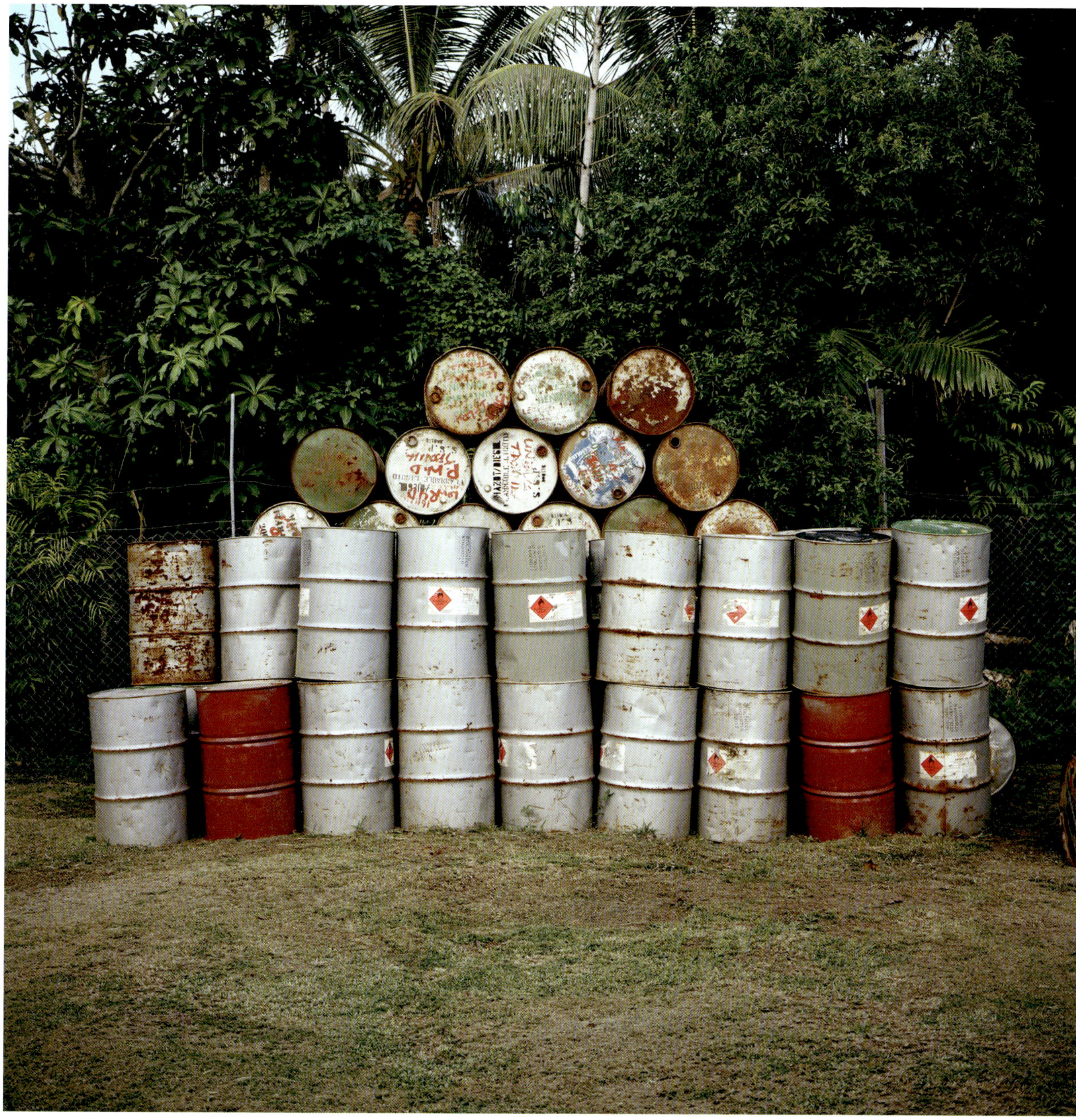

Sister Mary Alexia Kombe,
Lowanatom Catholic Church, Tanna

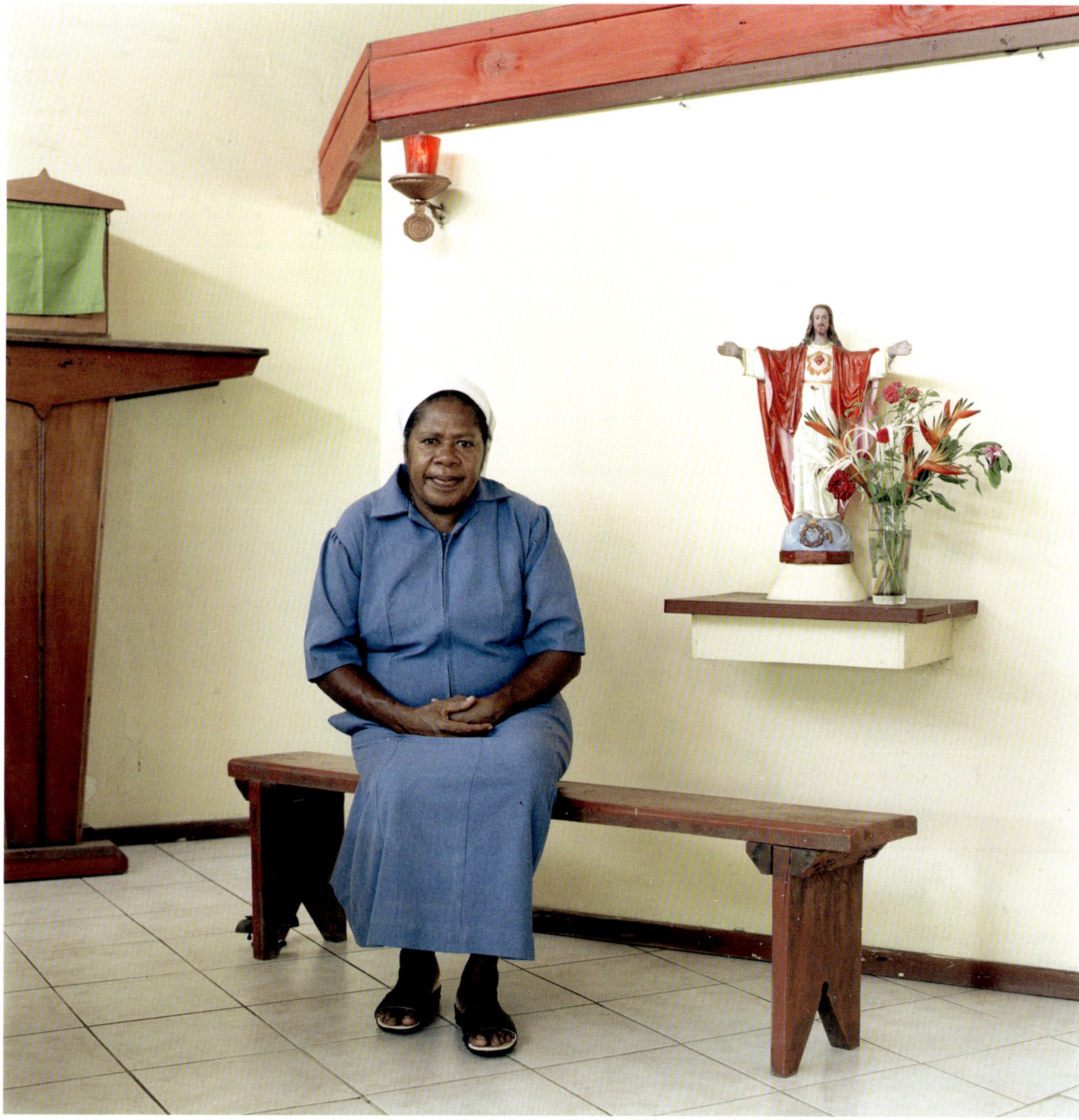

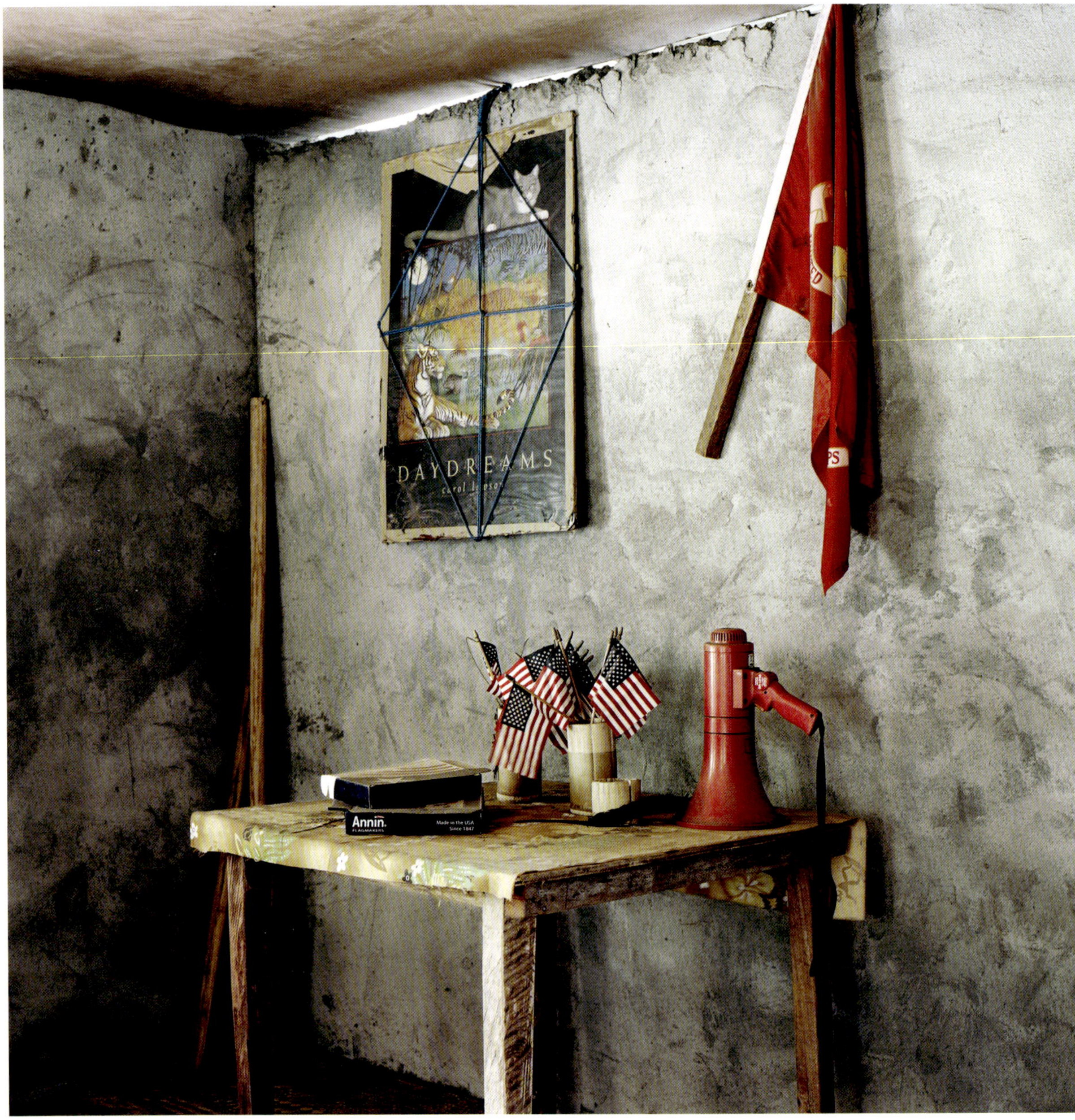
DAYDREAMS
Annin.
FLAGMAKERS
Made in the USA
Since 1847

A STEAMBOAT FROM HEAVEN

Jon and I knew nothing about French royals or German counts the first time we went to Vanuatu. All we knew was that prior to independence the country was called the New Hebrides, named by Captain Cook after the barren islands north of Scotland, and that there were people there who thought God is an American soldier.

We knew this was called a 'cargo cult' but had no real understanding of what that meant.

The words conjure a Boys Own adventure plot: A wartime care parcel with a little parachute is blown off course - it lands on a tropical island where villagers crowd around this alien cargo, wrapped in brown paper and twine, piecing through the contents to fathom what it all means. Flash forward decades later and a group of khaki-clad men are making first contact with the villagers, only to find they have built an elaborate religion around the contents of the package with iconography lifted from bully beef tins, rituals based on semaphores, and headphones whittled out of sandalwood hoping to communicate with the great flying ship.

Reductive as that is, it's not entirely wrong.

At the start of the 20th century the New Hebrides were jointly ruled by Britain and France. The Condominium government - or 'Pandemonium' as it was derided - built some infrastructure but left much of the day-to-day governance to the vast missionary corps that flocked to the islands.

Legions of Presbyterians and Catholics used the Bible, the schoolhouse, and the cane to turn the islands off traditional beliefs and onto Christ. This went on all across the Pacific and tore through indigenous societies like a cyclone.

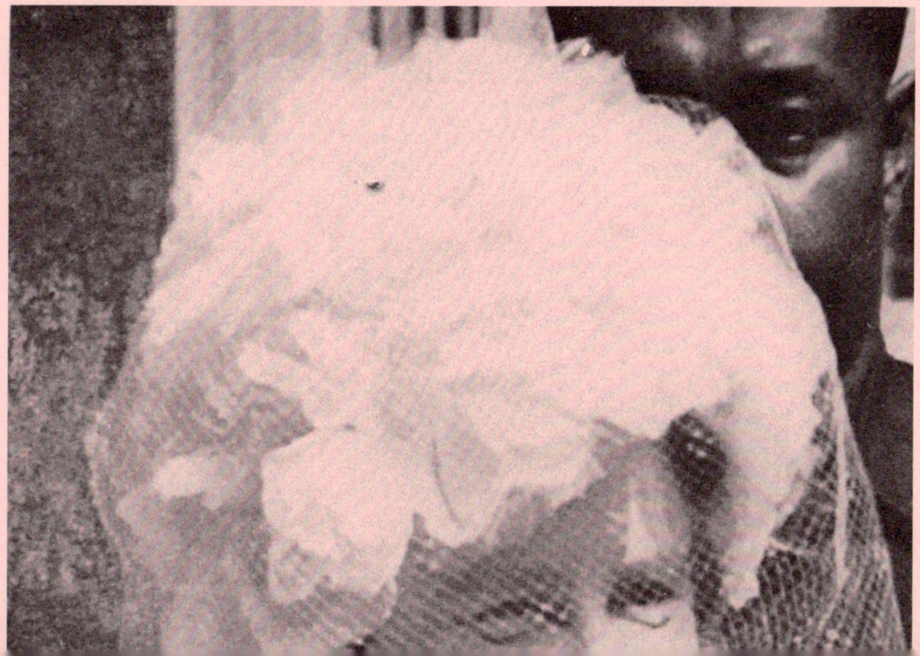

In response, a spiritual movement developed with an anti-colonial character. Starting in Papua New Guinea, men would report being visited in the night by long-dead ancestors. These visitors came with a message: the cargo coming and going to the islands on European boats had always been intended for the indigenous people of the Pacific but the cunning colonials were siphoning it off. The ancestors said their descendants should be braced for the imminent arrival of a steamboat from Heaven, weighted down with wealth, cloth, and tobacco. It would come to right an historic wrong.

Soon, plantation owners around the Western Pacific were saying that a 'madness' had gripped their once God-fearing workforce – collective hallucinations, frothing at the mouth, talking in tongues.

By 1940, the ancestral visitations had drifted to the New Hebrides and evolved into a full-blown uprising. A man called John appeared on a beach saying he would one day return to kick out the foreigners. He would bring the cargo to its rightful owners and reinstate traditional ways, or *kastom* as it was called in local parlance. Initially it was said John Broom would come, a force powerful enough to sweep away the whites. But the surname softened over time to John Frum.

John Frum had the power to reunite warring villages: to bridge some of the sectarian divides that had been wrought by the missionaries.

Yet just as the movement was gathering pace, enough to worry the Brits and the French who were busy locking up the faithful, something else came over the horizon.

The US Army arrived in 1942. During the Second World War, the largest island in the New Hebrides was commandeered for a vast Allied military base. Soon, fighter planes were roaring over smoky villages. Exotic and plentiful goods flooded into the harbours. Wide roads for tanks were carved through virgin bush.

It impressed a sense of American might and extravagance on the islanders. What particularly struck them was the sight of black and white US soldiers marching together.

The Americans regarded themselves as benevolent protectors. Cigarettes were shared with islanders, Coca-Colas were clinked, swigged, and then flung with abandon into the sea. The American author James Michener, then a young

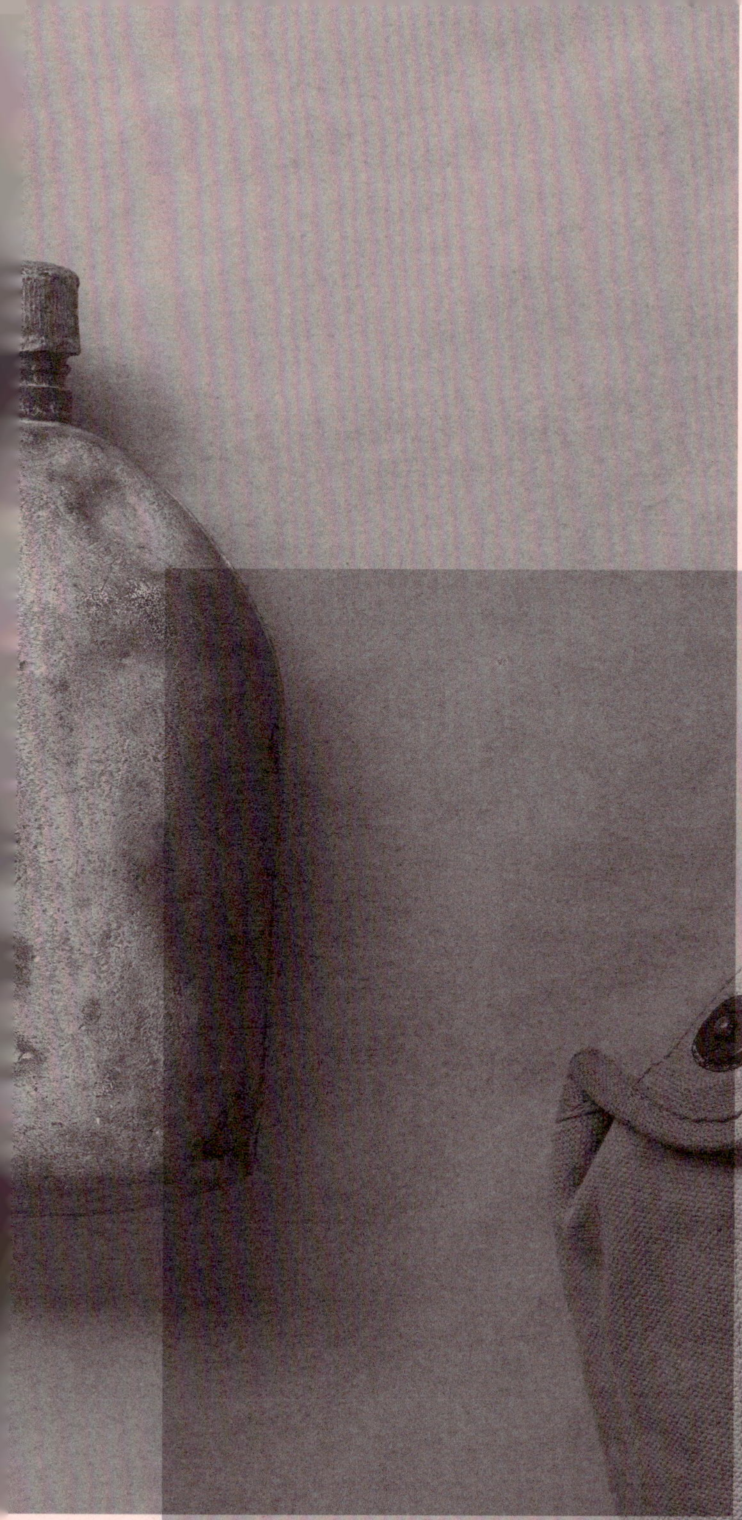

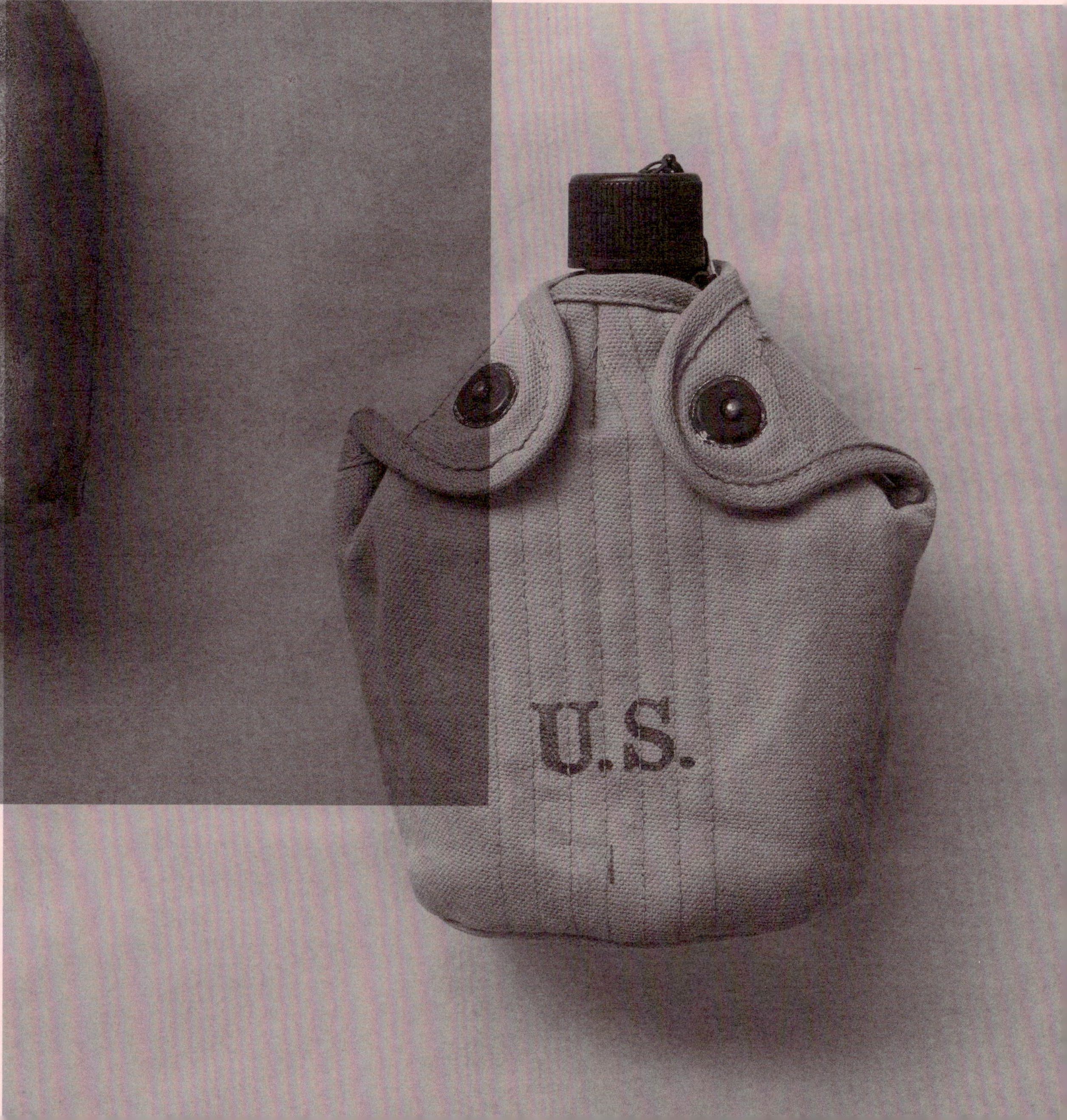

U.S.

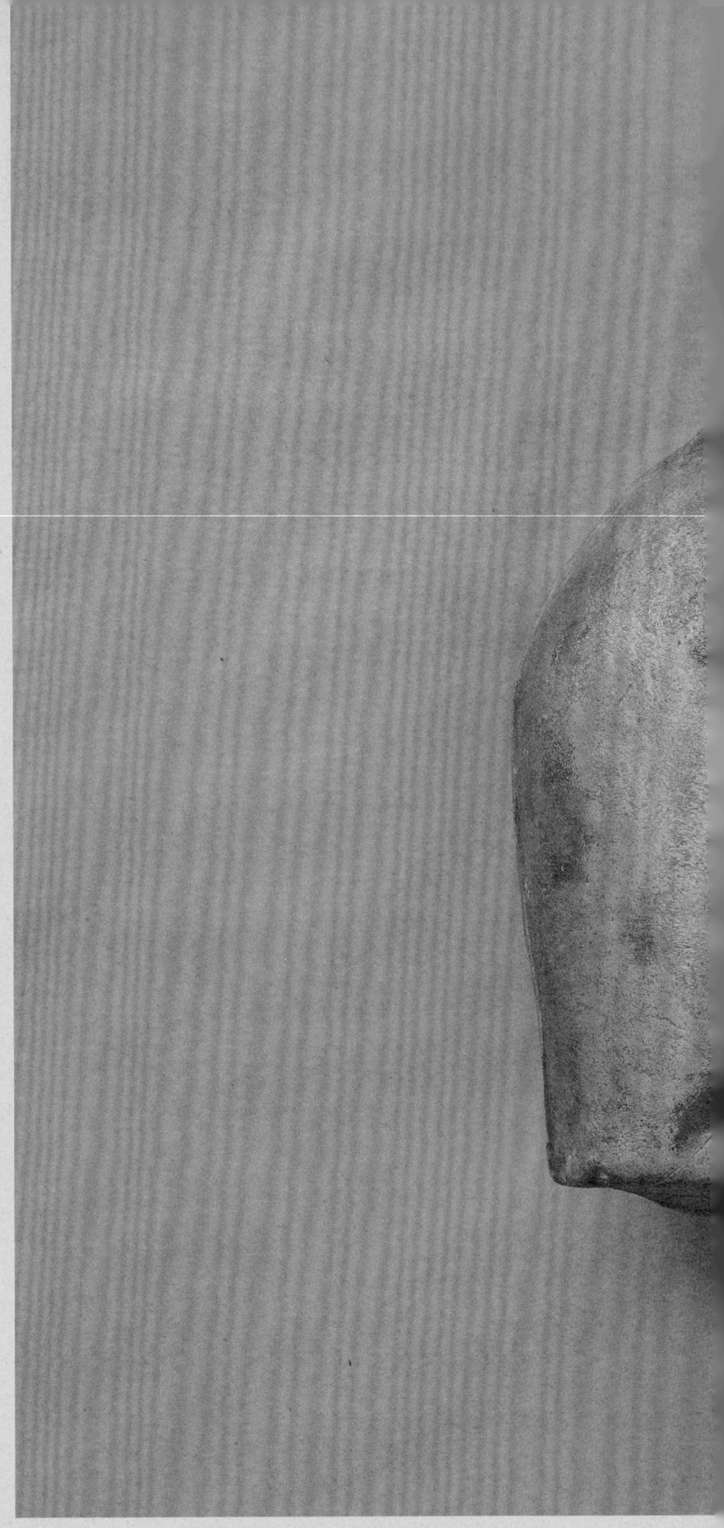

army recruit posted to the New Hebrides, sketched out an account of his life among these happy people in their grass skirts and his memoir would form the basis for the Broadway musical *South Pacific*.

By the end of the war, rumours that the Americans would someday return were already drifting on the leeward wind. And when they did - so said the whispers - the Yanks would cast off the colonials and careen the islands into modernity and plenitude, all the while restoring traditional, *kastom* society.

Enigmatic John Frum, it turned out, was actually an American G.I.

In their gardens, faithful villages planted red crosses like the ones seen on US ambulances. Every February their men would don military fatigues, carry bamboo muskets and march around their villages as the Star-Spangled

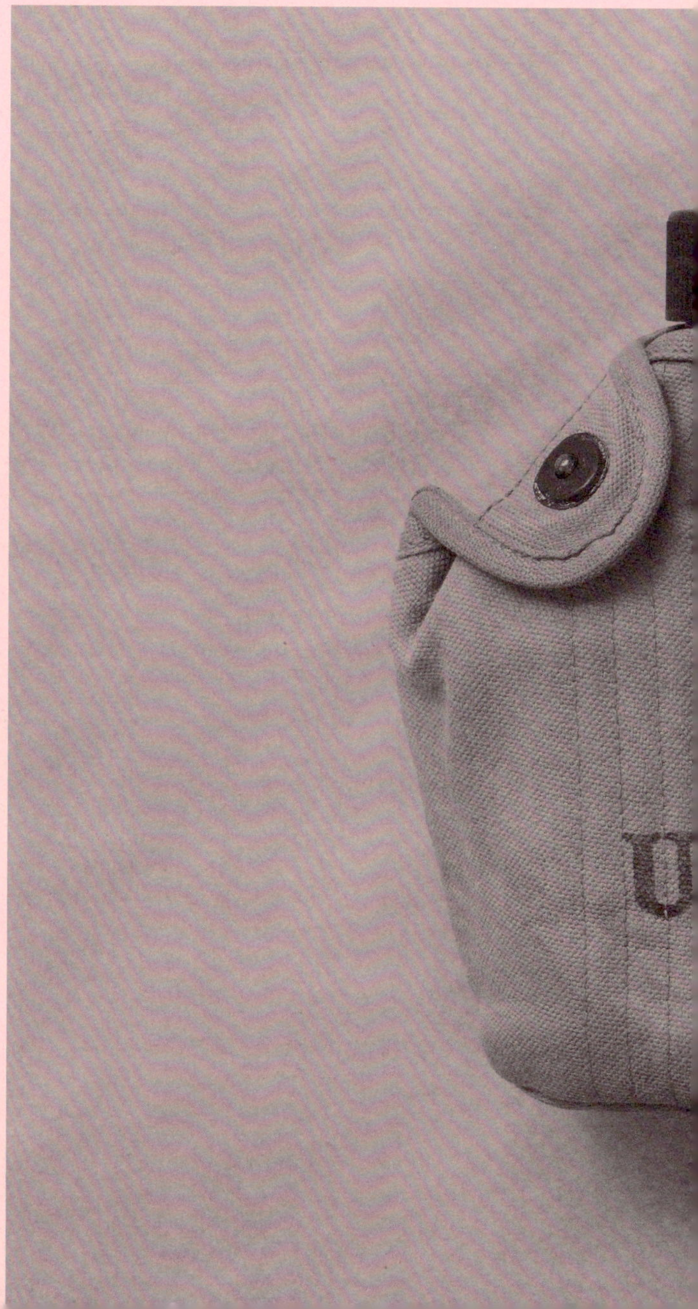

Banner fluttered overhead – a reenactment of the old army drills once seen on the islands. This ritual happened every February after 1950, almost without interruption, in the belief that it would entice the Americans back.

Today, the physical remnants of the American presence are few: Quonset huts overtaken by grasslands so they now resemble Saxon burial mounds, a few wrecked bombers in the bush, and a reef made of twisted metal after they bulldozed tanks and machinery into the sea at the war's end.

Even though independence from the colonial Condominium finally came in 1980, and the New Hebrides were renamed Vanuatu, faith in John Frum's return and cargo promise endured. This we found hard to believe. Fantastical as it was, the story seemed to offer an embryonic outline for how a religion is formed.

Could there really be people thousands of miles away marching in the belief that the messiah will come from the USA? The thought was fascinating but hard to square. The modern reality of John Frum, we reasoned, must be that it had lost its teeth nowadays. Surely it was just a show put on for tourists.

The trouble, also, was that John Frum and cargo cults have attracted plenty of sensationalist journalism over the years, in which fact and fiction are interwoven. Even 'cargo cult' is now a derogatory term in the West; it's used by Richard Dawkins, for instance, to sketch out how religions "spring up from almost nothing" in his book, *The God Delusion*. Bad science or bogus New Age-ism gets dismissed as 'cargo cultish' – with the accusation that acting out a desired outcome does not necessarily make it come true. In 2014, shortly before our first trip to Vanuatu, those beating the drum for Brexit were being labelled cargo cult by their opponents.

Yet we were fascinated by the possibility that such a profound belief could still exist. On his first journey to the Pacific, Robert Louis Stevenson admitted his ignorance about the peoples and beliefs of the South Seas, and said it was like looking at "a picture book without a text". The same was true as we tried to fathom the truth of John Frum from its lurid depictions.

So we booked tickets and learned that Tanna island, host to Vanuatu's annual John Frum ceremony, couldn't be any further away from London. It took

36 hours in the air before our plane bounced onto the runway in Port Vila, the capital of the archipelago.

We arrived in the middle of the night. Unwittingly I had booked us a hotel on its own small seashell island in a bay just outside the city limits: This would be ideal for newlyweds, less so for those due to catch another plane to Tanna the next morning. Before dawn we were strolling about again like castaways, examining the hotel sun loungers as if they were alien life forms.

The coconut palms began to rattle in the morning breeze and as the wind rose the sun surfaced too. Robert Louis Stevenson, on glimpsing his first Pacific island, raptured on 'fifty modulations in a scale of pearl and rose and olive'. He wrote of its great 'opalescent clouds'. But on that morning the world began in a fibrous pink haze. Jon and I watched in drowsy amazement as knotty green hills were chiselled out of the darkness.

Vanuatu is at first glance a South Pacific of the imagination. It has champagne-coloured sand and is carpeted in bright lichen bushland speckled with pink hibiscus.

Yet it is a volcanic archipelago. Much of what grows there is foreign. The ever-present bush germinated from hardy seeds that survived the great slosh across the Pacific. The insects came tucked in the feathers of migratory birds. Cyclones and driftwood brought the termites as well as the ominous long-legged spiders that now suspend themselves between forked trees. Even the mynah birds chattering overhead supposedly came from a wrecked British steamer – the Pikanini – that crashed at the end of the nineteenth century and expunged onto the beach its cargo of exotic Indian birds.

The common language of the islands, called Bislama, is equally itinerant. The first time we heard Bislama spoken was by the security guard who'd kindly slept aboard the hotel's skiff knowing we had a flight to catch the next morning. He was holding a mobile phone to his ear with two fingers and speaking insistently. "Mi no savvy toktok Fransis" – he didn't know or speak much French.

The name, Bislama, supposedly comes from Beche De Mer after the local sea cucumbers that were once traded to be sold in China, but the language itself has roots in a tortuous period starting in the 1840s when large numbers of

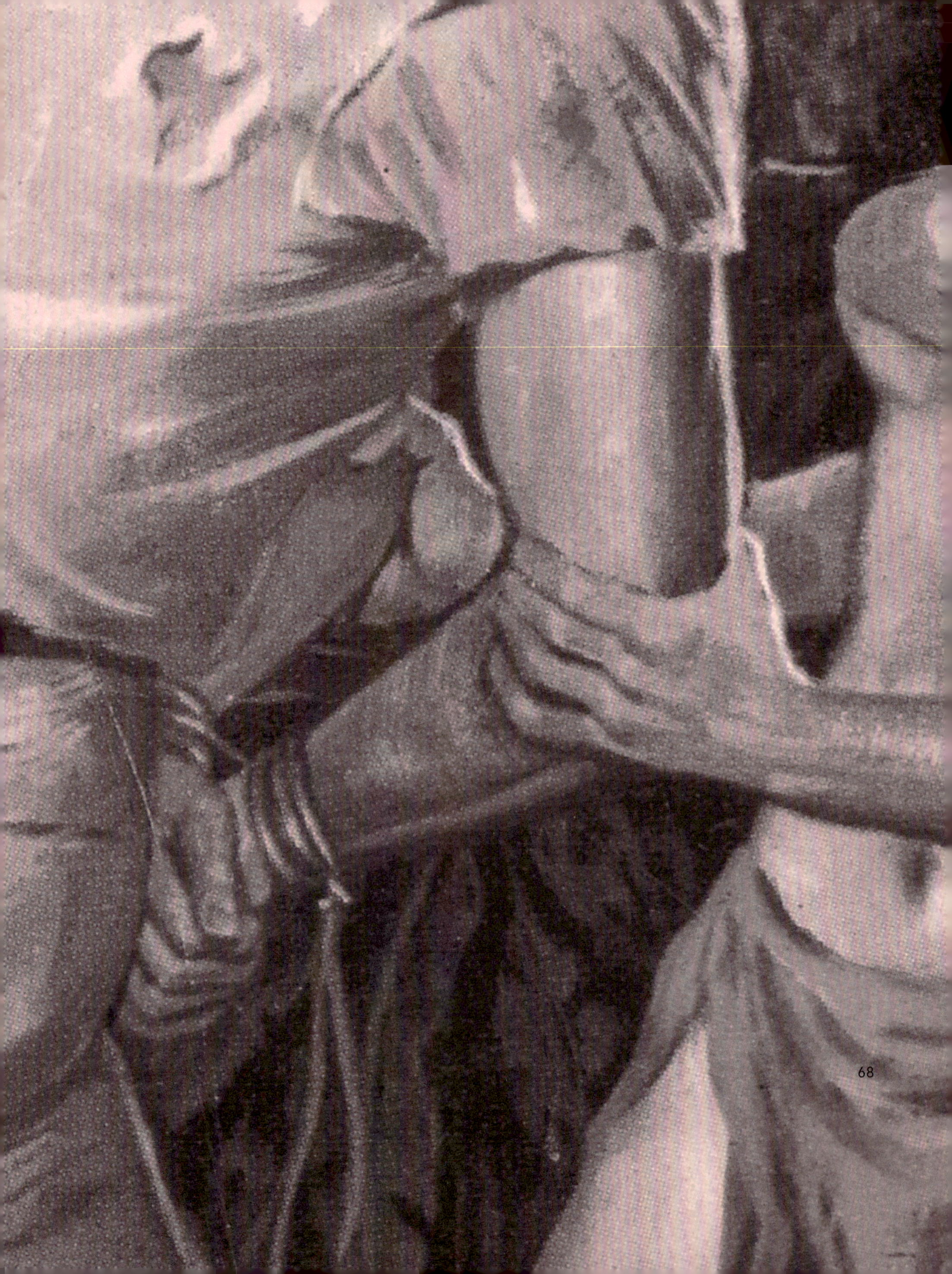

islanders were tricked or strong-armed into undertaking plantation work in Australia; this was indentured labour, poorly paid if at all, and the practice – known as 'blackbirding' – was little more than slavery.

Bislama is today called a creole, implying that it's a mixture of English and indigenous tongues. But it is more like a claimed, commandeered tongue: Bislama can sound like English that's been hard-boiled for centuries, dried out in the sun and then had its more strange and delicious words picked out for fresh emphasis.

The most common word is 'blong' – as in 'belong', which sounds clunking in a Western tongue but in Bislama is the oil that greases syntax. Blong can mean to be, to have, to come from and, of course, to belong. (Mi blong Inglan means 'I come from England.') There's a literal, logical inventiveness to Bislama: savvy is to know; tok sweet means to flatter somebody and tok small is to whisper. A bra is called a titibasket. The language has claimed colonial slurs for itself too – pikanini is an acceptable way to refer to small children.

David Attenborough caught the cadence when he filmed there, looking for John Frum, in 1959: "But Sam, it is nineteen years since John say that the cargo will come," says Attenborough to one ardent believer. "He promise and he promise, but still the cargo does not come. Isn't nineteen years a long time to wait?"

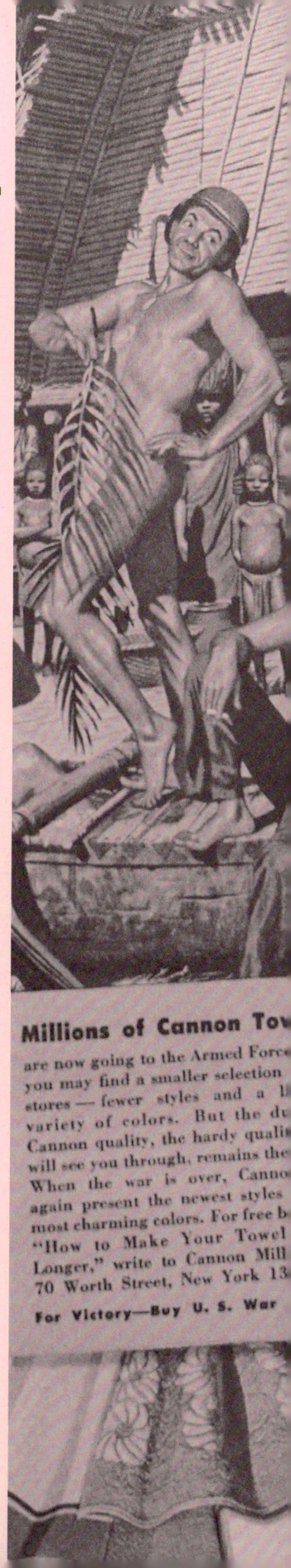

Tanna is an hour south of Port Vila by propellor plane.

Where the capital Vila has paved roads, pastel-pink bakeries selling hot cross buns, and a string of supermarkets called Au Bon Marche, Tanna has the occasional roadside rattan hut that announces it's open for business with a sign: "I gat fish."

The island's thick bushland is riven with hazily-hewn paths. There are no billboards, few telephone poles, fewer streetlights. Between tall grasses, you might sight a family walking between villages or a group of working men, briefly halted, with their machetes dangling from their wrists. White faces still elicit a nod of surprise here, often a wave.

It comes into view like one continuous shrub. Near its eastern shore is an ashen scar – Mount Yasur, the active volcano that still fulminates with the subterranean crackle that first enticed Captain Cook.

There are also hardly any cars on Tanna's roads, except for labourers and the missionaries who speed around in gleaming white four by fours. So we'd had the good sense to book ahead for a driver. A man called Lewis met us at the airport. He was evidently high as a kite on kava: The pounded juice of the kava root that's supped all over the western Pacific to soften tongues and calm busy minds.

John Frum promised that, in his bright future, kava would be drunk every day. That daily libation wouldn't be interfered with as it was under missionary law.

Kava numbs the throat and lips. It sharpens the drinker's senses – especially to noise. So after a few perfunctory questions to Lewis, making it absolutely clear to him we didn't want to hire quad bikes, the three of us jiggered on in silence. Despite Christian prohibitions, many of the Tannese men we met were wasted on the stuff by sundown. Through the windows of the pickup, we could see only dusty mud banks and a wall of scalp-high grasses that kept the interior out of sight.

On that first trip, Jon and I stayed at a hotel called Tanna Lodge. The sign out front promised 'Barefoot luxury'.

It was run by a Kiwi called Hugh, an ex-lawyer with swept-back silver hair and handlebar moustache. We never once saw him in a shirt; he preferred

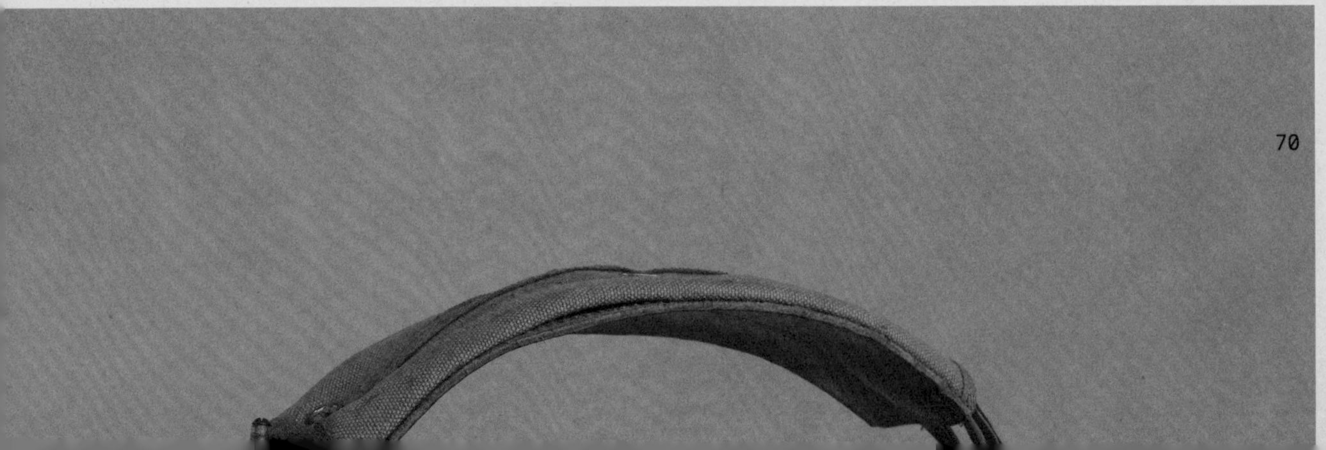

to keep his considerable belly permanently on show, regardless of the huffier guests.

Our hut was at the far end of Hugh's unruly garden, close to a black sand beach. Breakers foamed around the rocks and for an hour we each lay under our respective slow fans, letting the cymbals of the Pacific Ocean smooth out the long hours that brought us here.

It was quiet season at Tanna Lodge. We were among the only guests. The menu was steamrollered steak and peppercorn sauce. An ensemble of Hugh's friends gathered around the one set table. Polite chatter was punctuated by the occasional thwack of hand on shin.

They were all expats - doctors, aid workers and the like - except for a Ni-Vanuatu woman called Ketty Napwatt. She was an activist who had done a stint in regional politics and had a keen ear for foreigners' pretensions. She wanted to know why Jon and I had come to Tanna; we explained that we were trying to find out what remained of the John Frum movement today, and Ketty listened silently, sternly over her rectangular glasses. She chewed it over for a moment and then explained that, in her view, as a local who

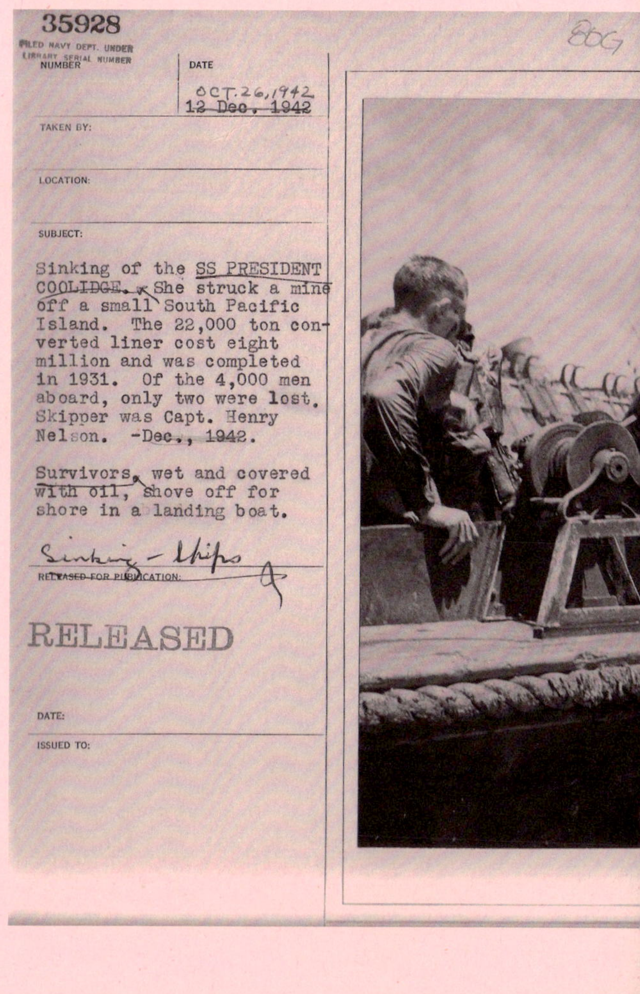
35928

FILED NAVY DEPT. UNDER LIBRARY SERIAL NUMBER
NUMBER

DATE
OCT. 26, 1942
~~12 Dec. 1942~~

TAKEN BY:

LOCATION:

SUBJECT:

Sinking of the SS PRESIDENT COOLIDGE. She struck a mine off a small South Pacific Island. The 22,000 ton converted liner cost eight million and was completed in 1931. Of the 4,000 men aboard, only two were lost. Skipper was Capt. Henry Nelson. ~~-Dec., 1942.~~

Survivors, wet and covered with oil, shove off for shore in a landing boat.

Sinking - Ships

~~RELEASED FOR PUBLICATION:~~

RELEASED

DATE:

ISSUED TO:

had grown up hearing tales of John Frum believers' fervour, the cult was an intangible facet of the rich culture of the islands. It was something the government should be better at 'recognising', she felt, and should promote as part of the *real life* of the islands.

Ketty explained that, a few years earlier, Channel Four had shown up on the island and made a documentary where they'd taken a group of Tannese men to the UK so that they could offer comment on Britain's quality of life, sense of community, and class system. That was fine, Ketty said, but she wanted to know this: "Why on earth had they called the documentary, 'Meet the Natives?'" The title was meant ironically, we offered, but Ketty wasn't convinced – she peered at the idea over her specs.

Regarding John Frum, Hugh was quick to shoot down any romance we had. "A right load of old…" he said, then paused to pour more drinks and proffer a theory: it was all a byproduct of an opium binge when bottles of medicine flooded into the island at the turn of the century. "The sort of stuff they used to give for toothache; if you took enough of it you'd believe anything. Look at this." He disappeared into the chaotic bedroom he shared with his wife – a wild-haired woman called Stella – and retrieved a mucky old vial with the name of a long-lost European pharmacy debossed in its side. "I found hundreds of these things down by the shore," Hugh said. He held the bottle up to a candle, letting the light capture its narcotic lustre.

According to Ketty, the origins of John Frum were more political. It emerged from a particularly repressive period when many traditional practices around marriage rites and kava drinking were banned in a series of diktats called 'Tanna Law'; formulated by the missionaries and enforced by the colonial authorities.

"Man Tanna wasn't ready to let go of everything the white missionary did not like," Ketty explained. From that premise John Frum, the avatar of rebellion, was born.

Purple night clouds, fat with rain, were gathering over the beach. If it chucked it down overnight, Hugh said, we'd need a four by four to reach Sulphur Bay, the centre of the John Frum movement. Despite his cynicism for the movement itself, Hugh was very happy for us to pay him to procure such a vehicle. A jeep was scheduled for eight in the morning. Soon, jet lag

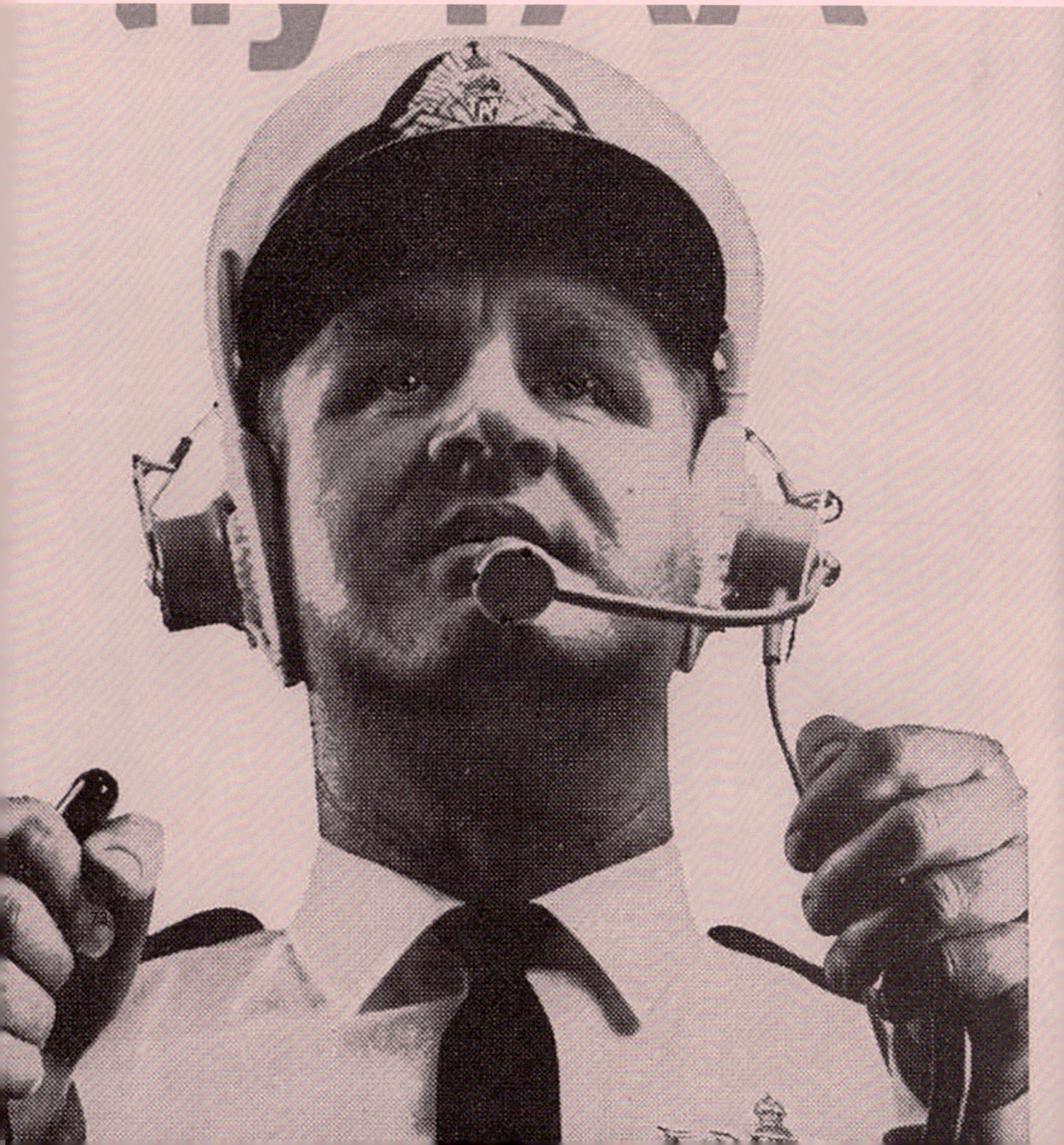

called us back to our beds, but the expats kept drinking and slapping their thighs until late. Thoughts of the mysterious foreign prophet weren't far away, however: I woke up in the middle of the night to find that I'd got out of bed and sleepwalked to the front door, believing there was an intruder outside. I was shouting "John? John?" into the downpour.

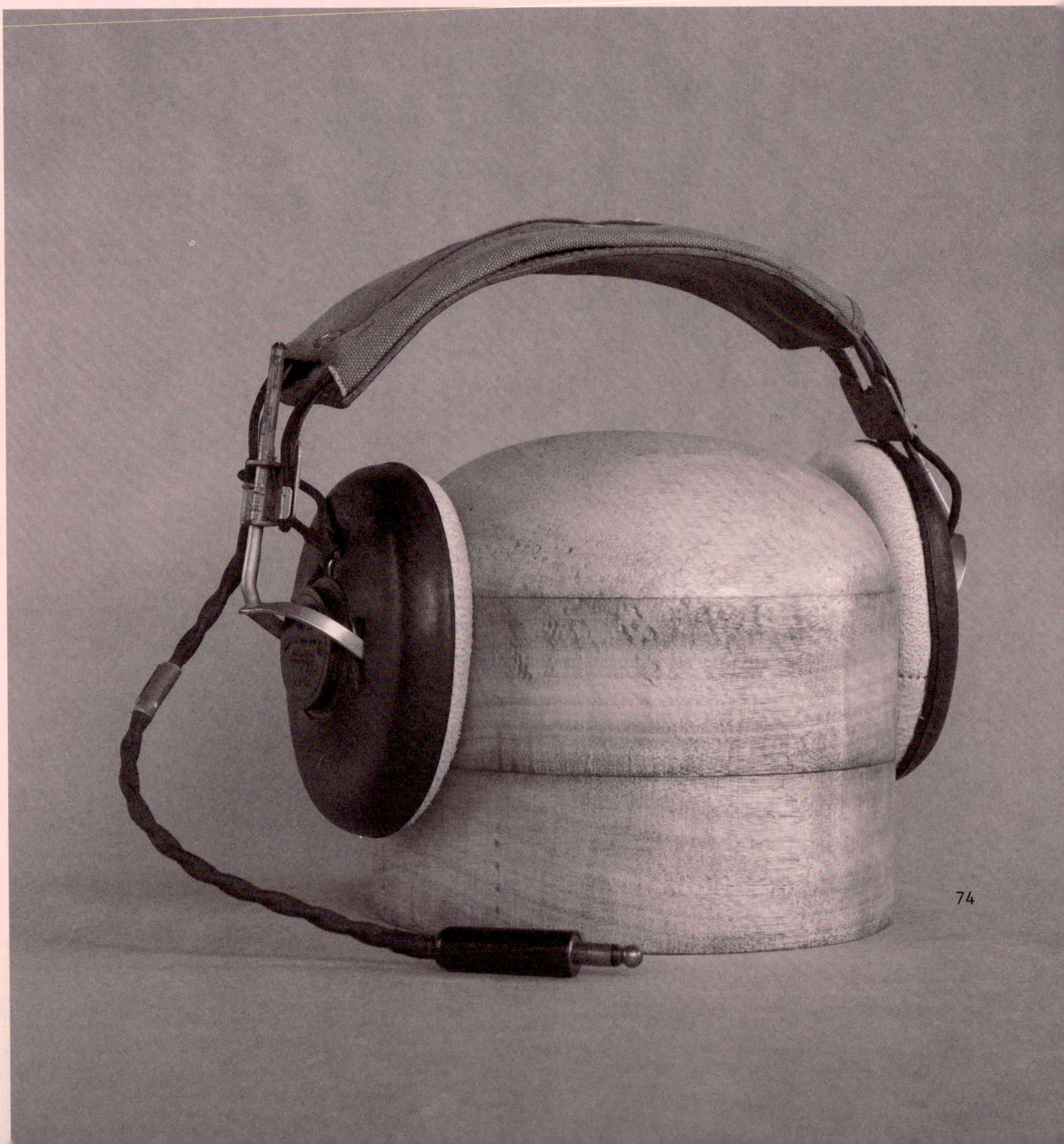

ιοι so
ength
ressed
times,
to do

The
r, who
good
'as of
ınse of
people.
l have
news-
known
in the
ome a
owner
urnals
ıs, set
news-
e over

arrow-
Cronin
arkly.

in Aus-
ustralian

sed, by
home
t that
s that
r little
So is
story
rd M.
hern

arkable
, is a
Office.
andall,
te the
natives.

For Quality
be sure it
Hell

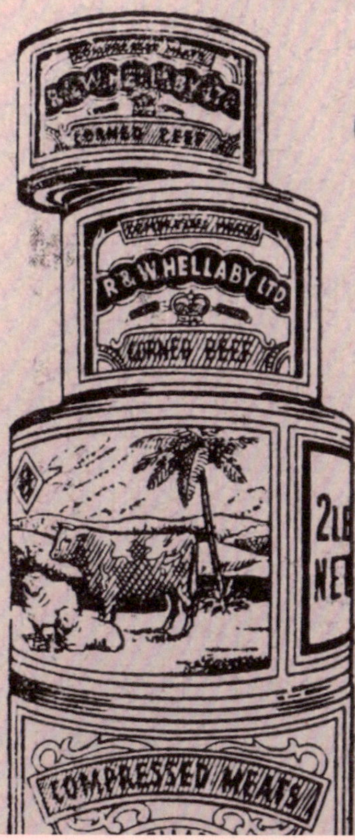

35928

35928

F

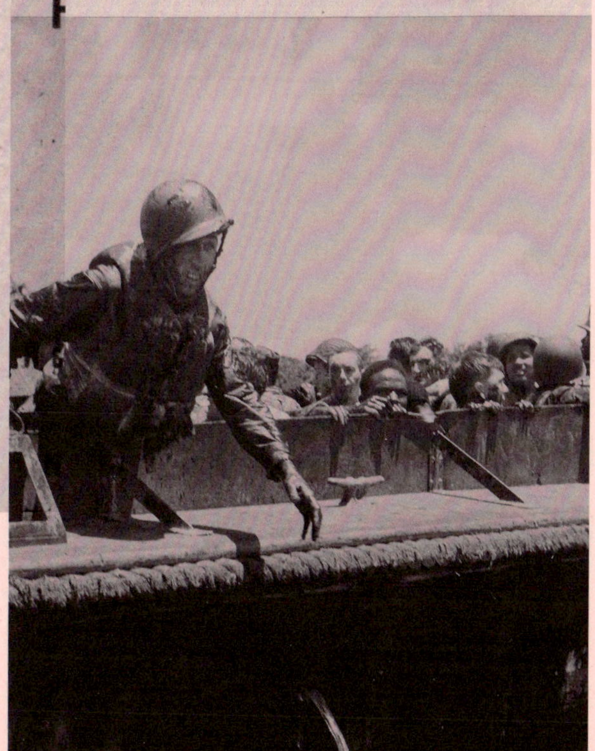

5

35925

35925

35925

UNDER
NUMBER

DATE
OCT. 26, 1942
~~12 Dec. 1942~~

N.

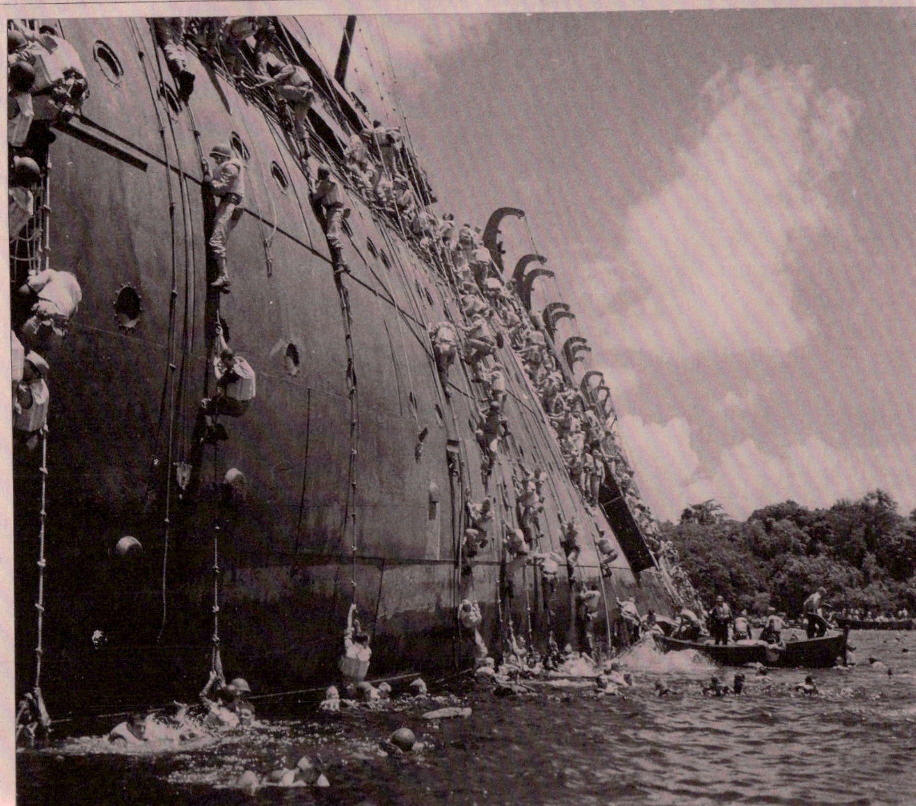

of the SS PRESIDENT
E. She struck a mine
mall South Pacific
The 22,000 ton con-
liner cost eight mil-
d was completed in
Of the 4,000 men
only two were lost.
was Capt. Henry
~~Dec., 1942~~.

s clambering down side
and net.

R PUBLICATION:

ASED

RELEASED

PUBLISHED CREDIT
BE GIVEN AS FOLLOWS
FICIAL PHOTOGRAPH
U. S. NAVY"

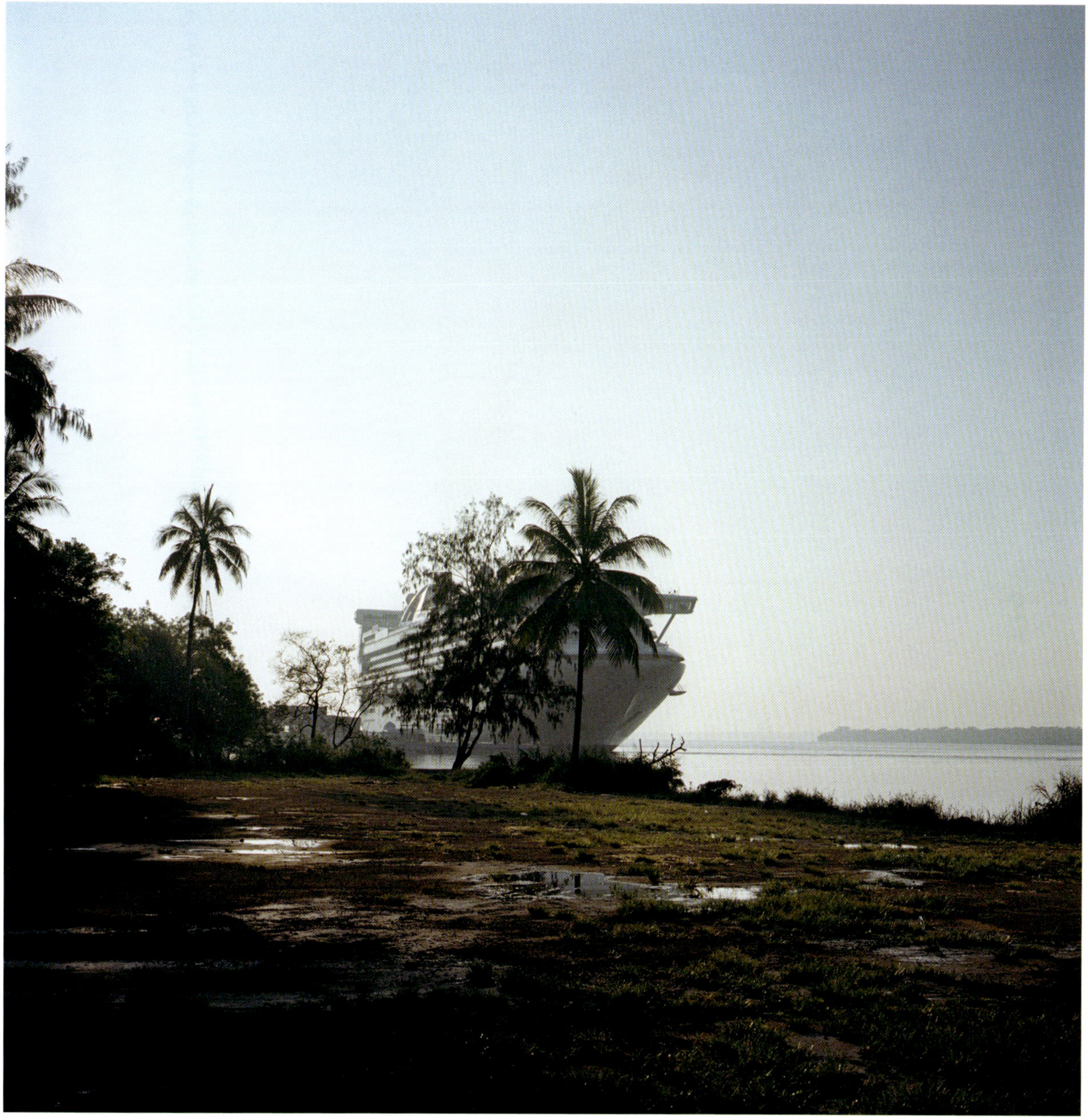

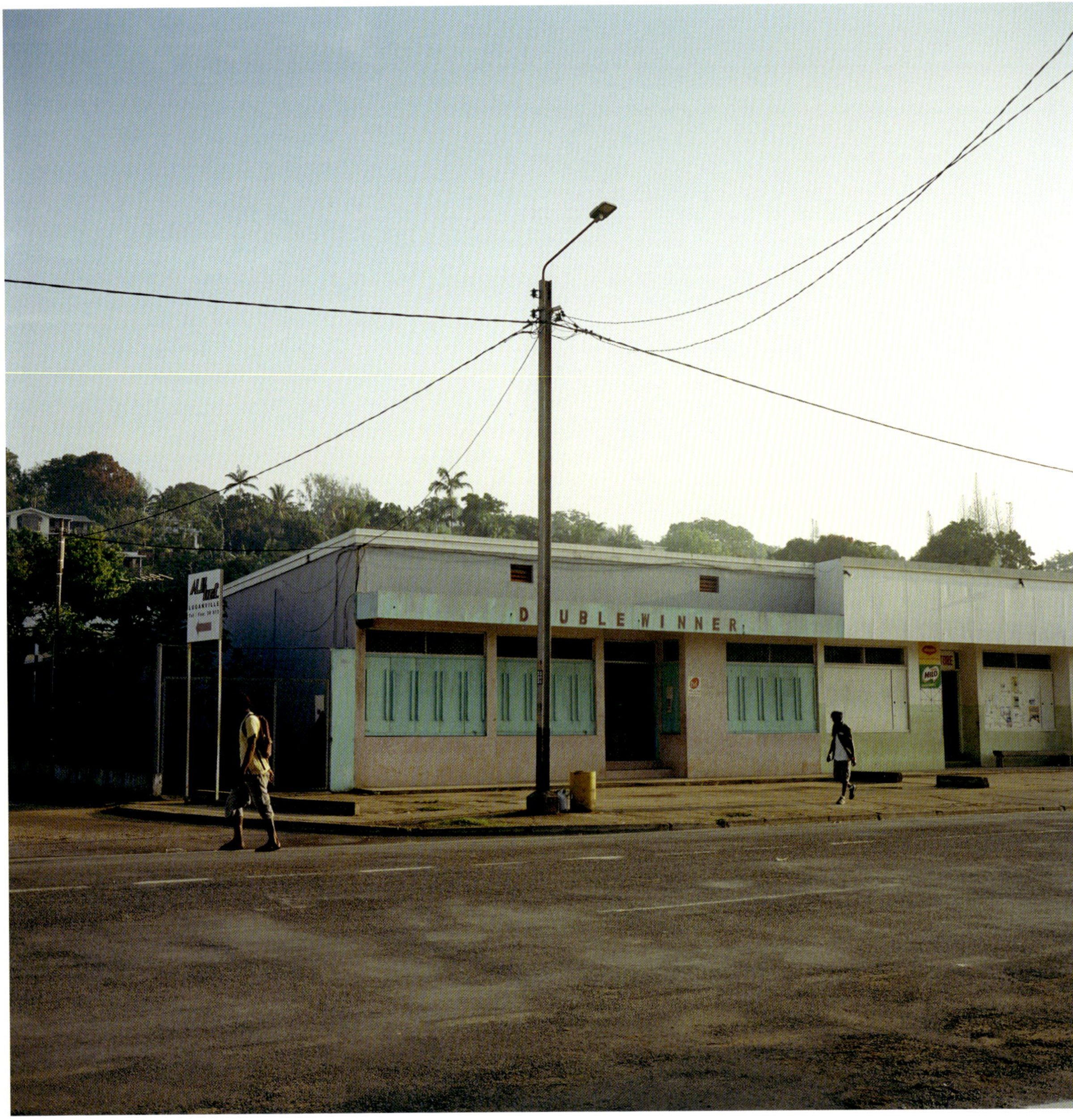
D UBLE WINNER
LUGANVILLE
MILO

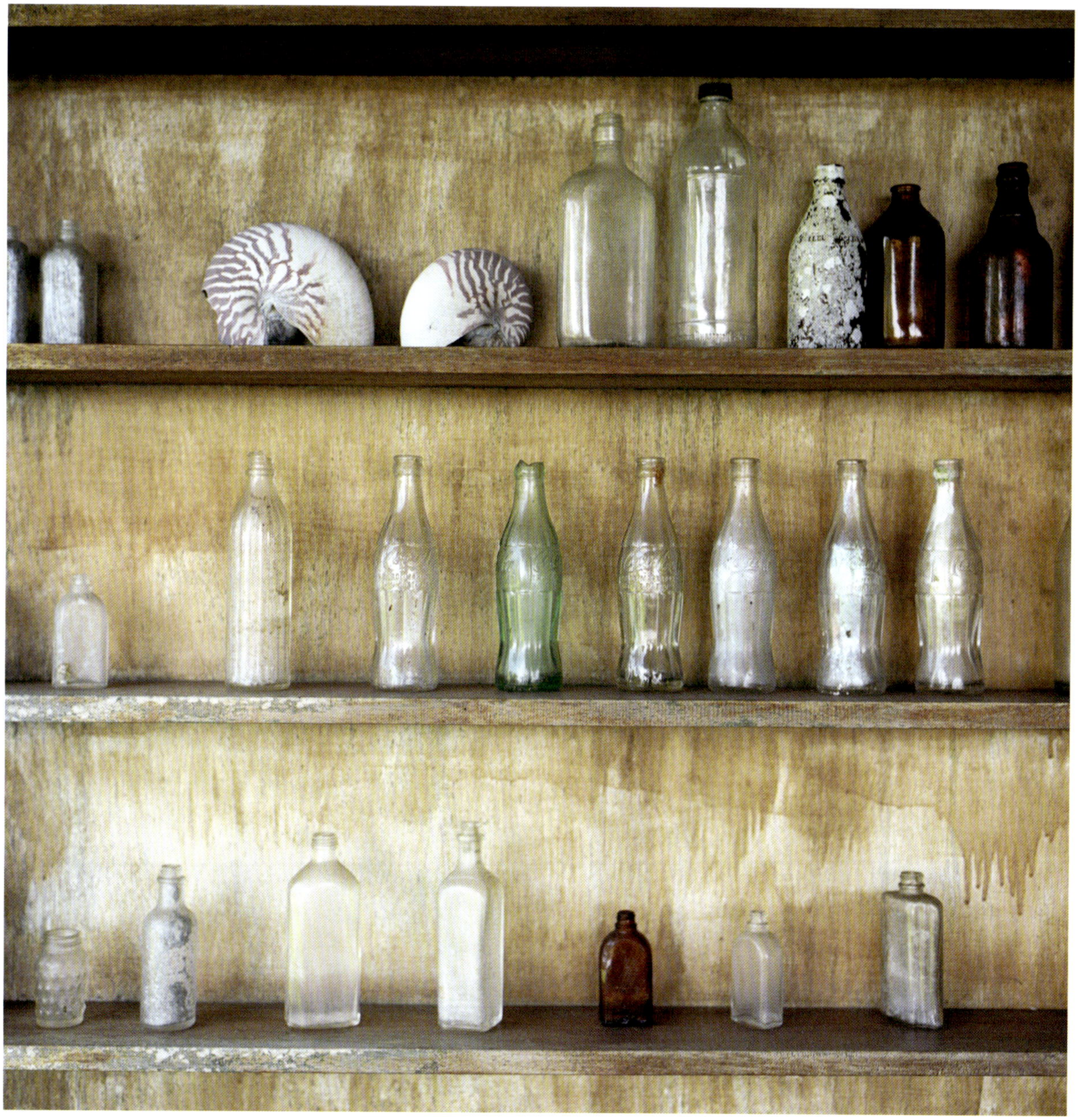

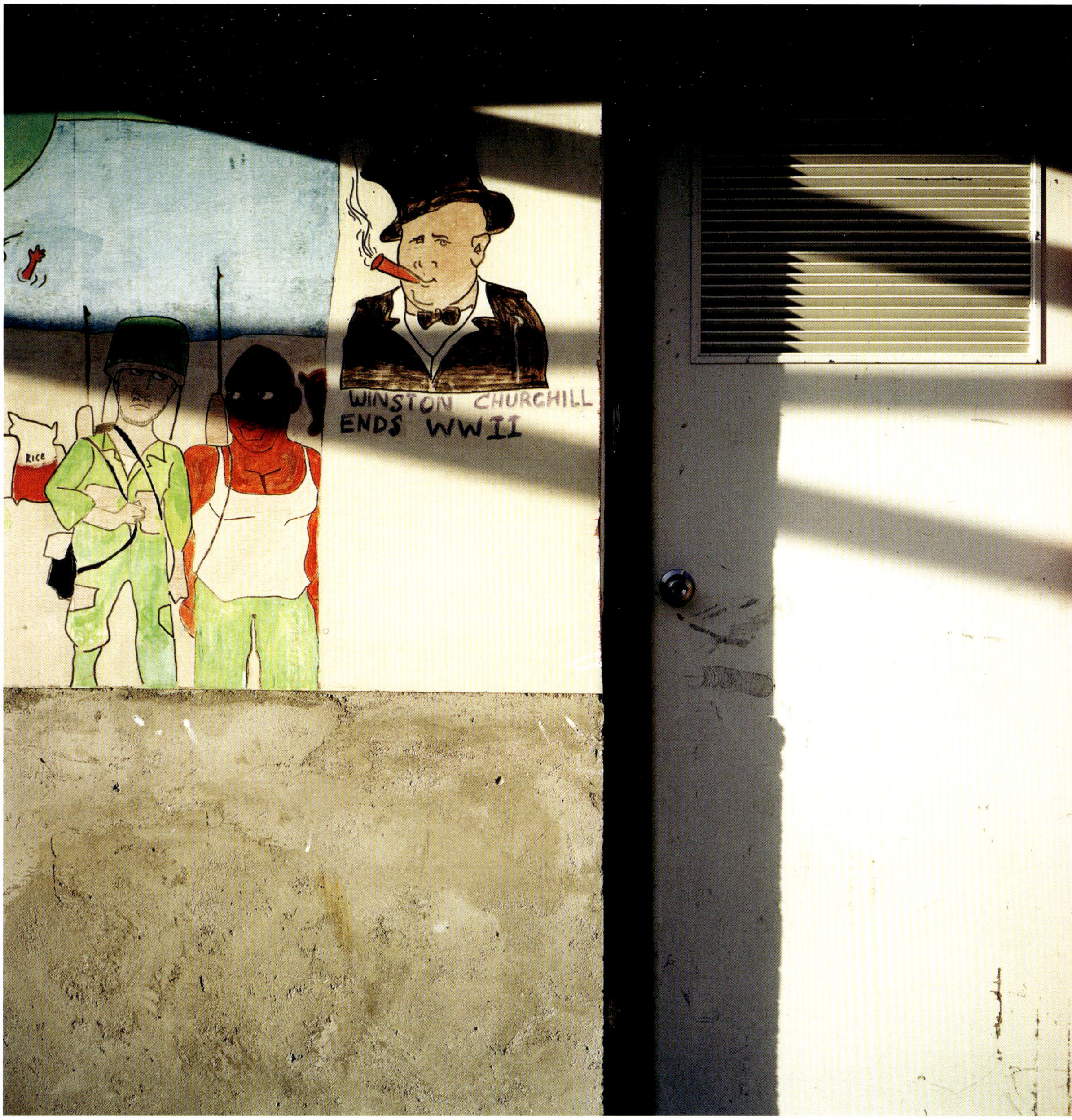
RICE
WINSTON CHURCHILL
ENDS WWII

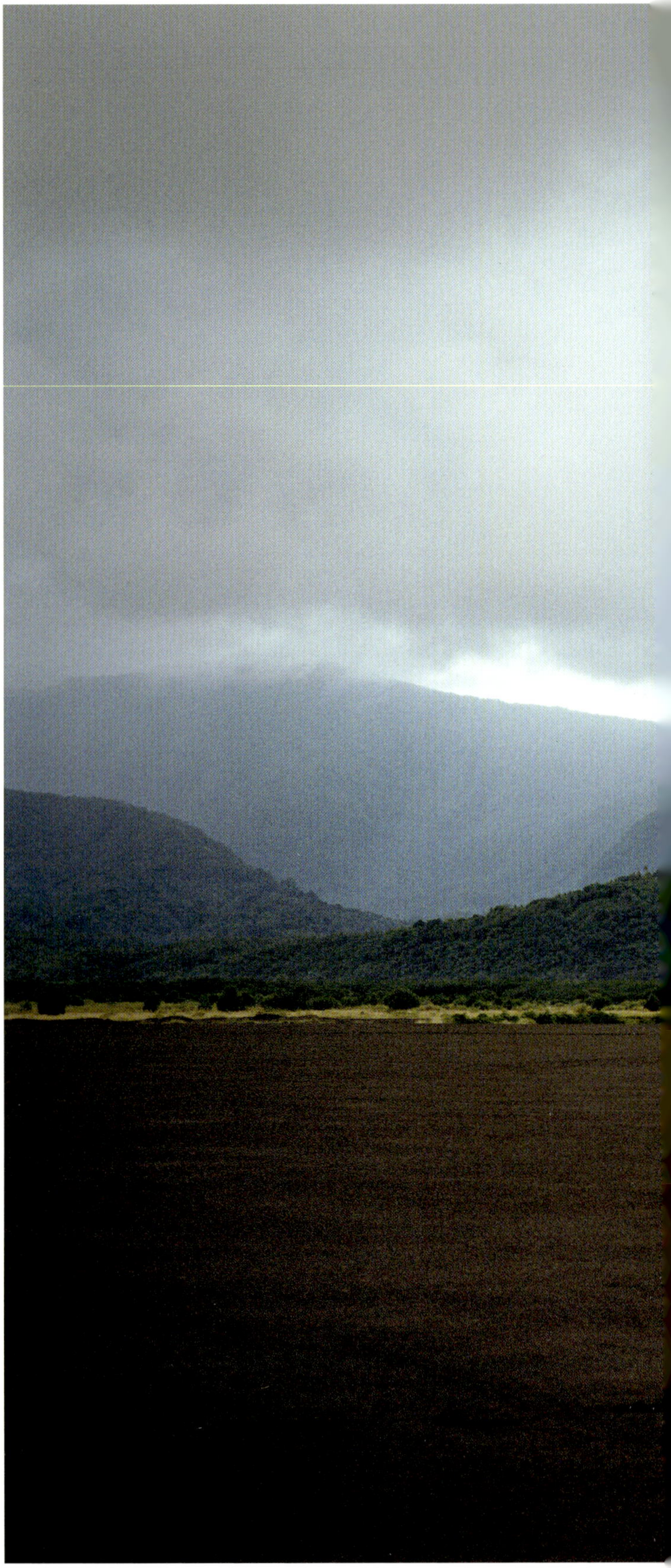

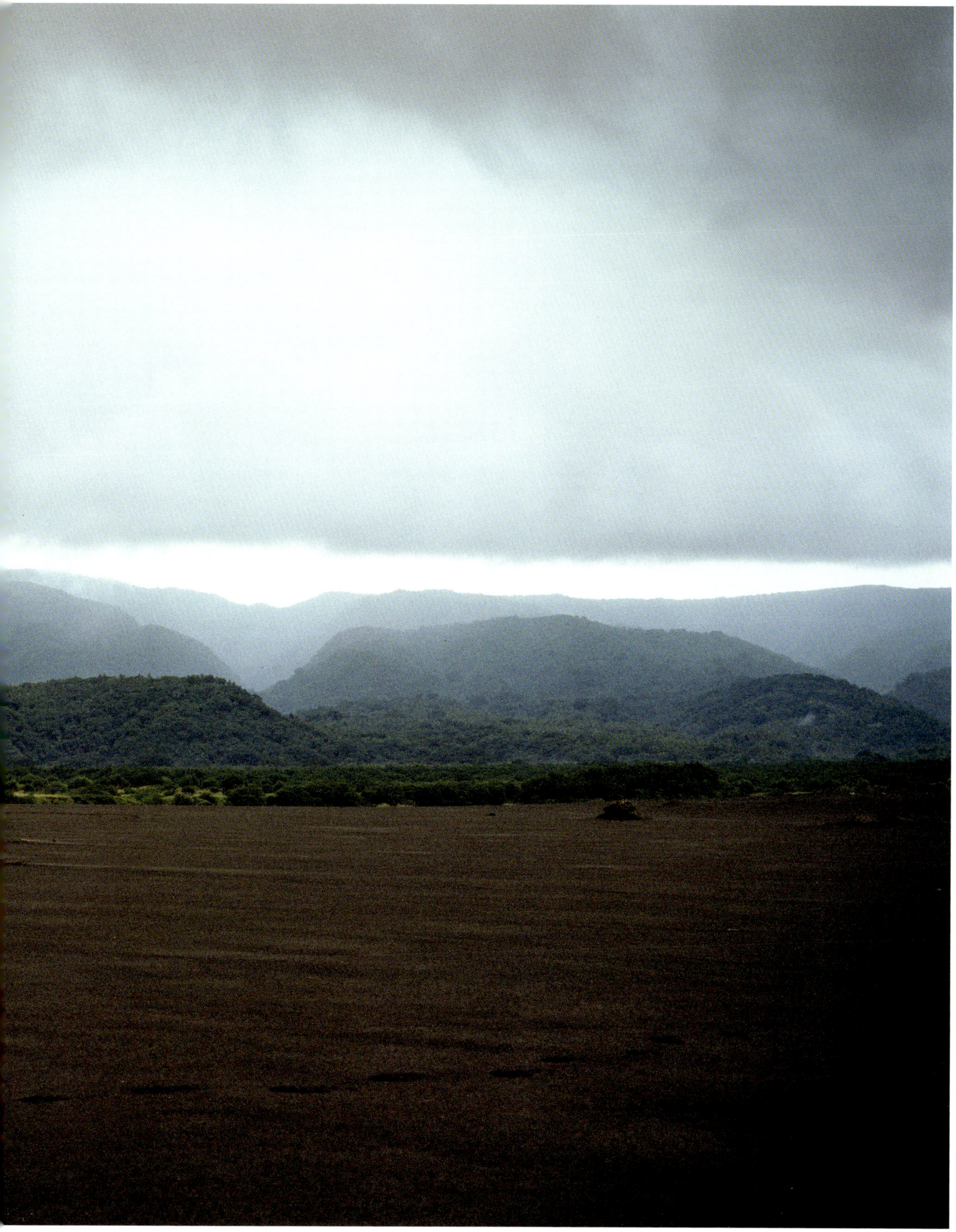

JT* - She met John Frum when she was a little girl?

JK - Yes, she did.

JT - What was John wearing when he arrived?

Discussion with elder

JK - The answer is that John was wearing clothes.

JT - Does she remember what he looked like?

Further discussion

JK - She doesn't remember.

Mary Manpina, Green Point, Tanna - translated
and told by John Kaurua
*Jon Tonks

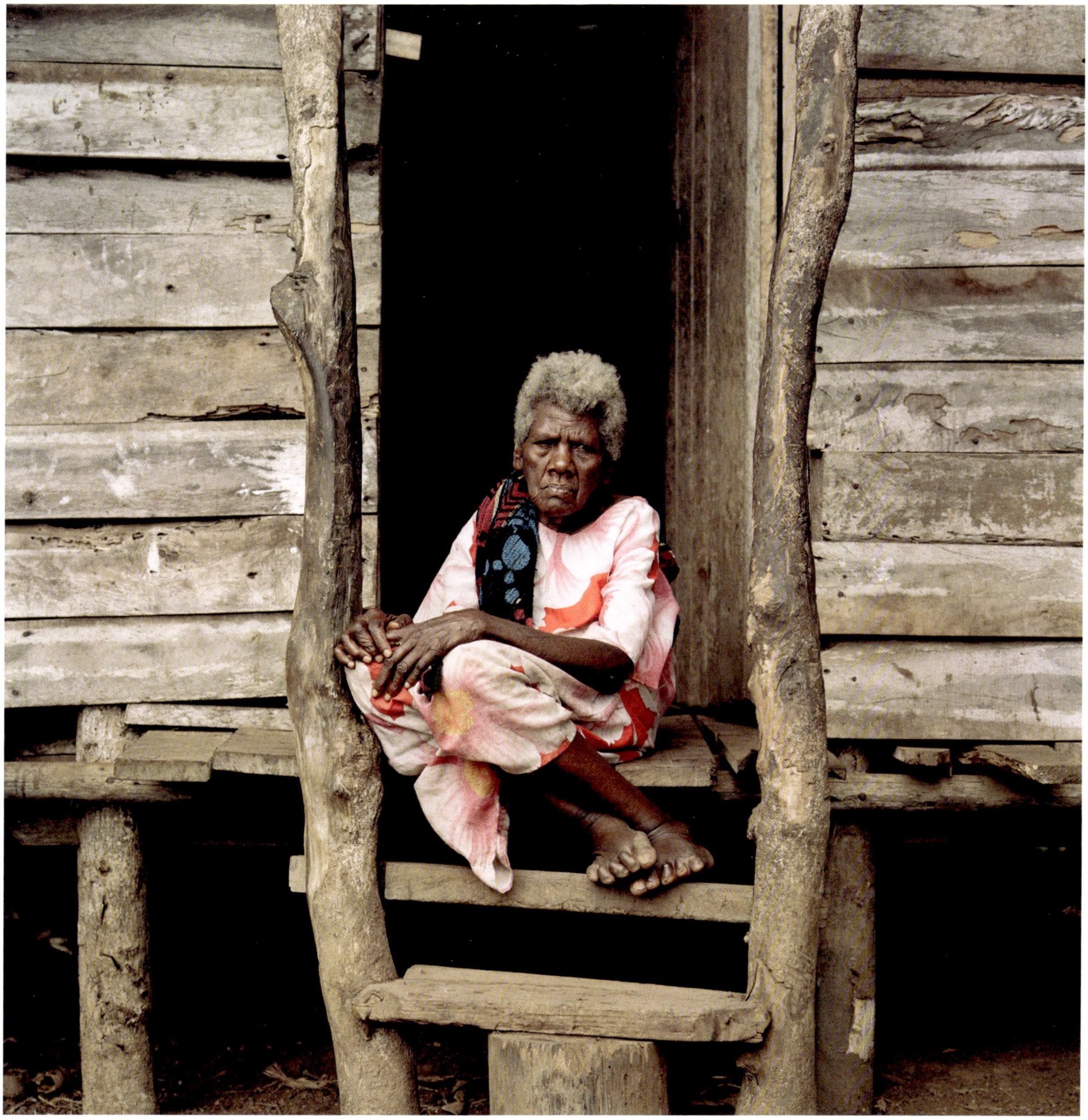

Francisca, Eva and Lyn, Million Dollar Point,
Espiritu Santo

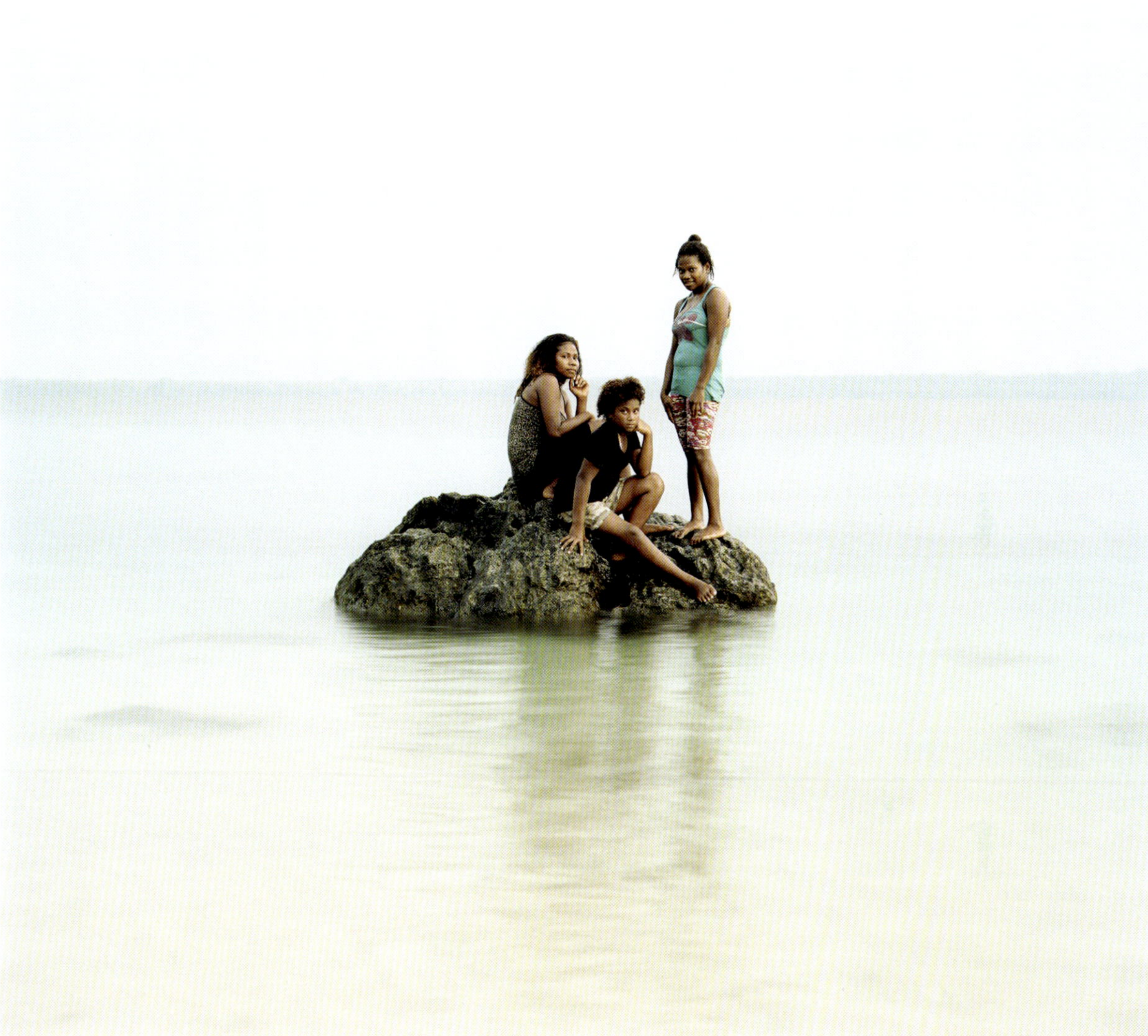

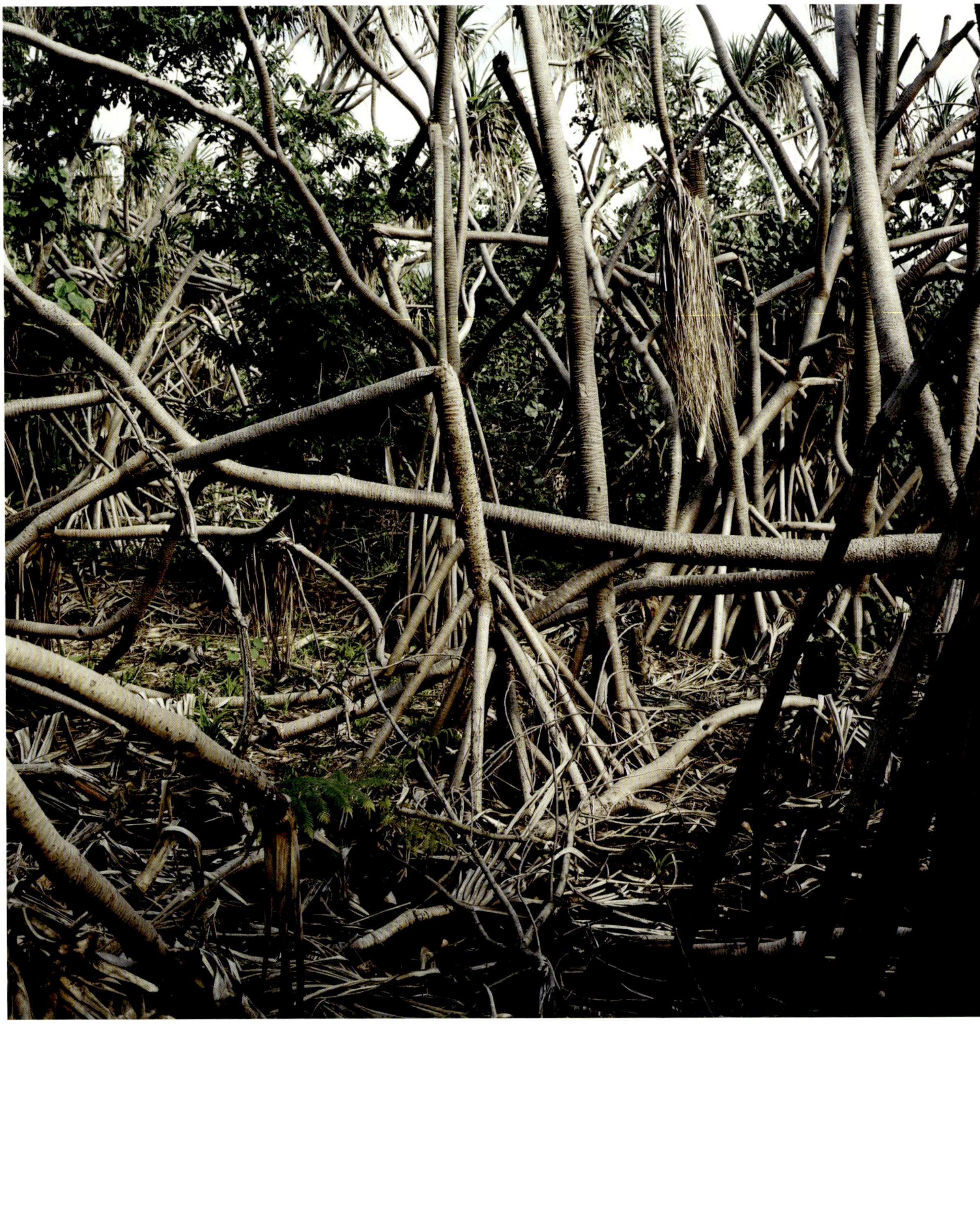

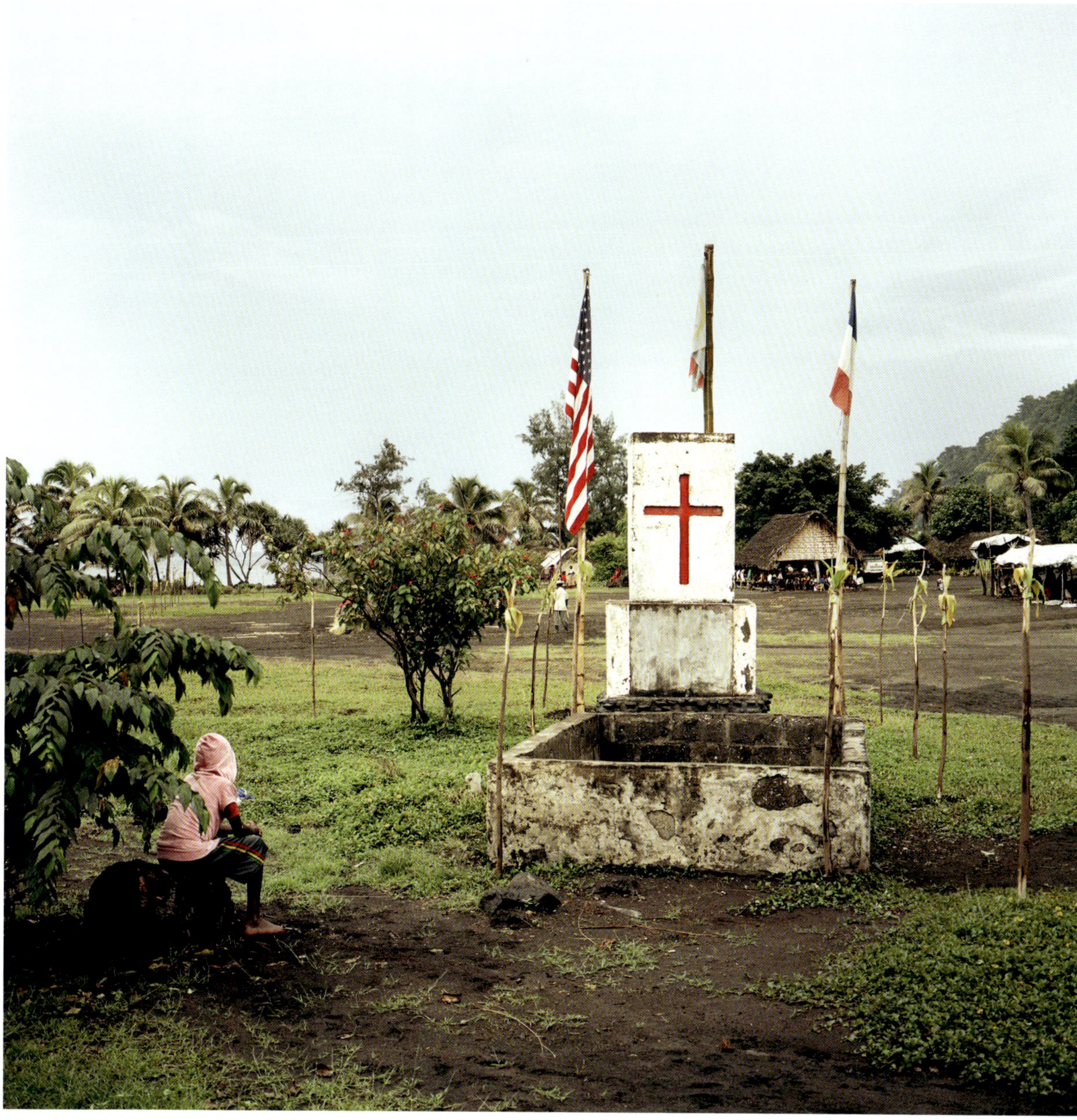

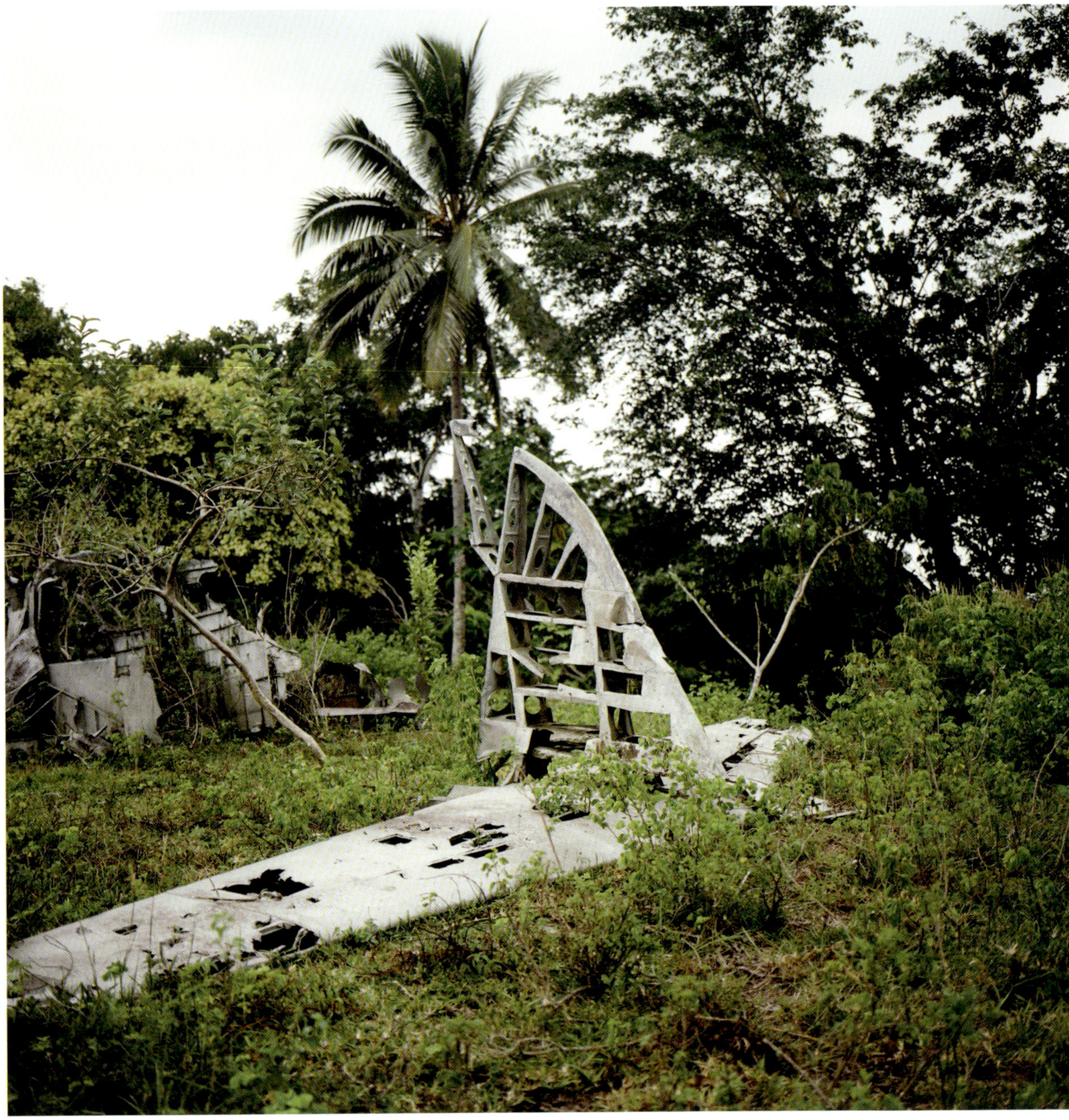

Tail of a WW2 US bomber, Espiritu Santo

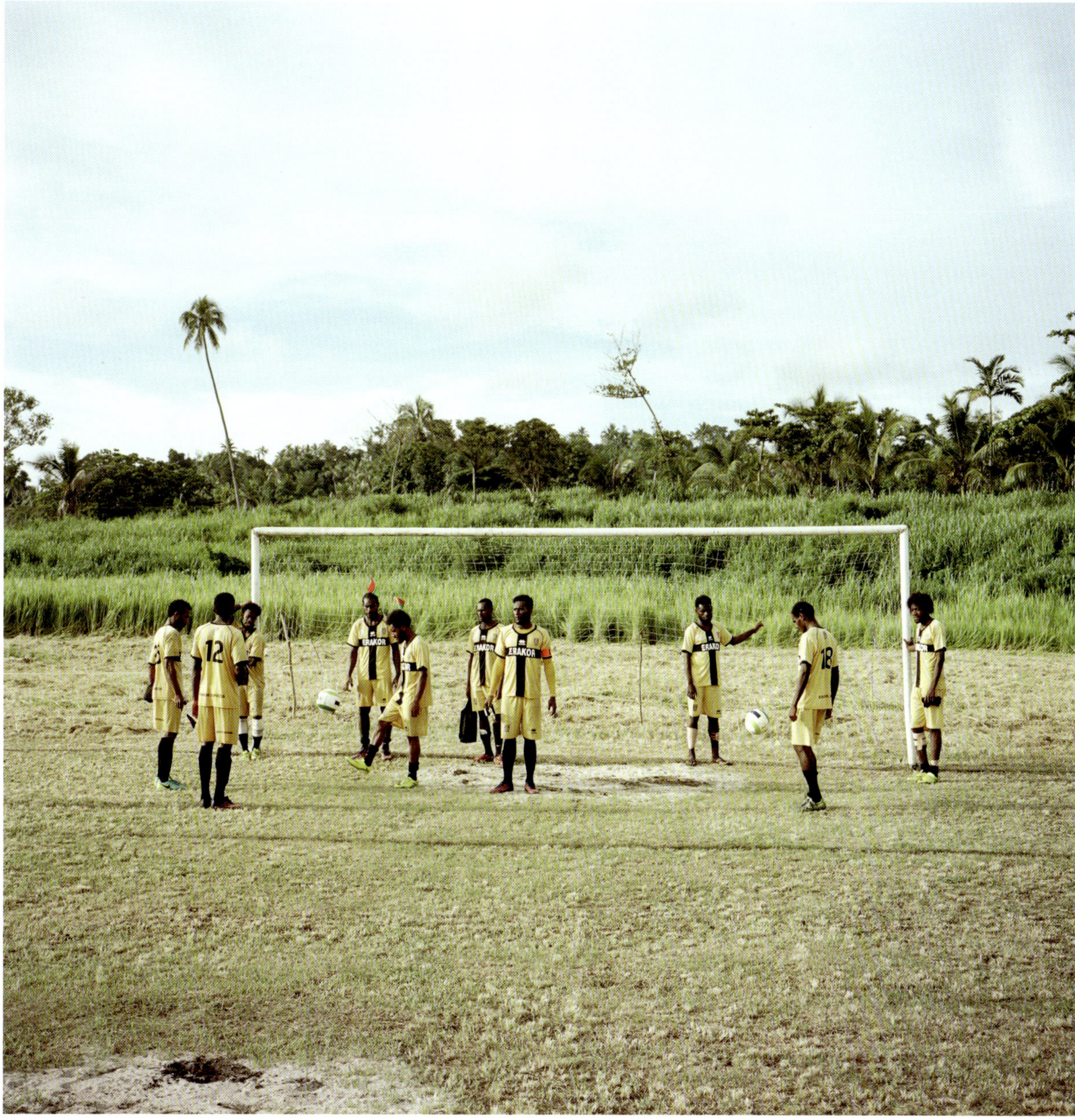
ERAKOR
12
18

Kava is drunk across the Pacific. A light on outside a bar means the sacred brew is ready

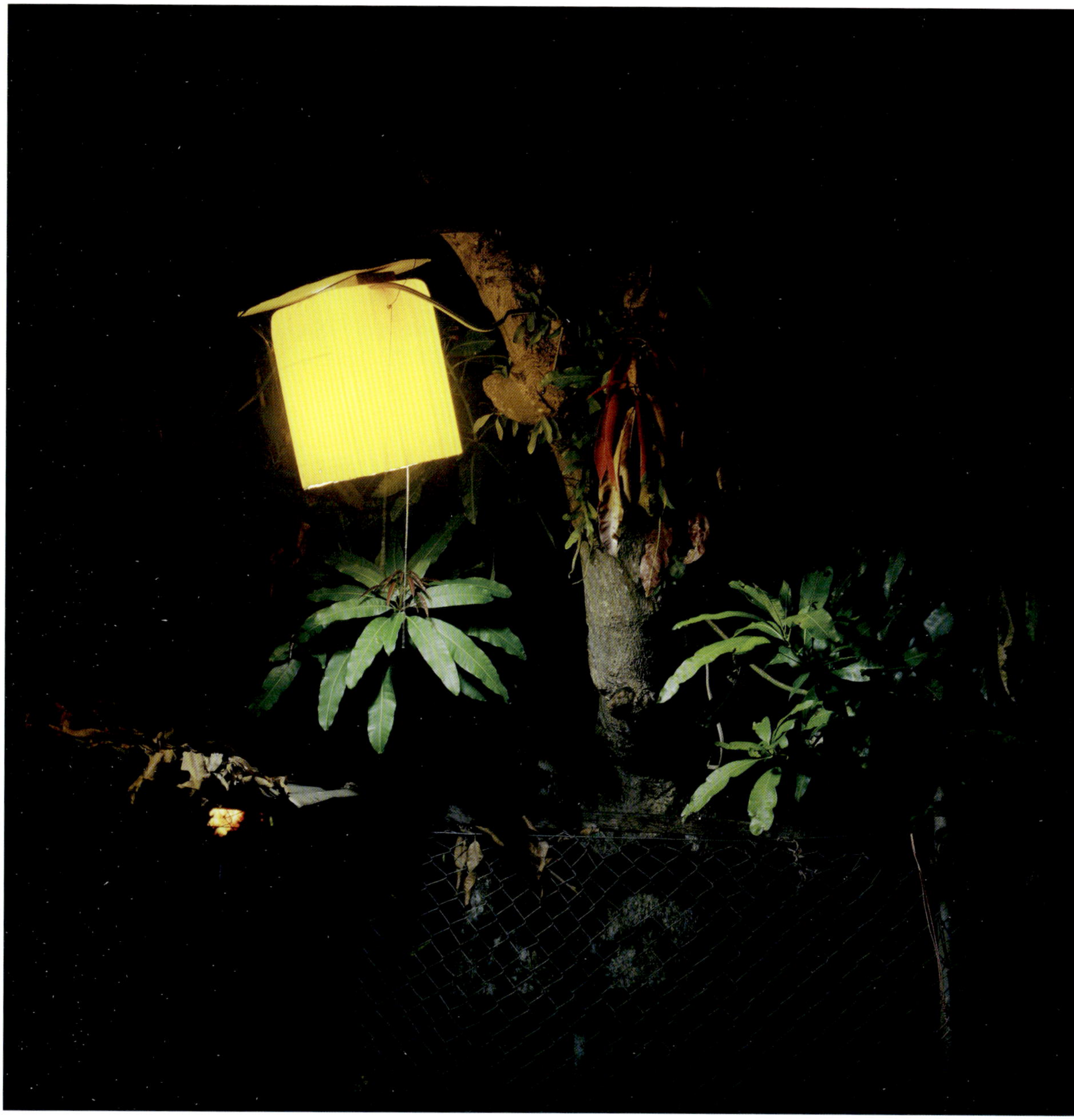

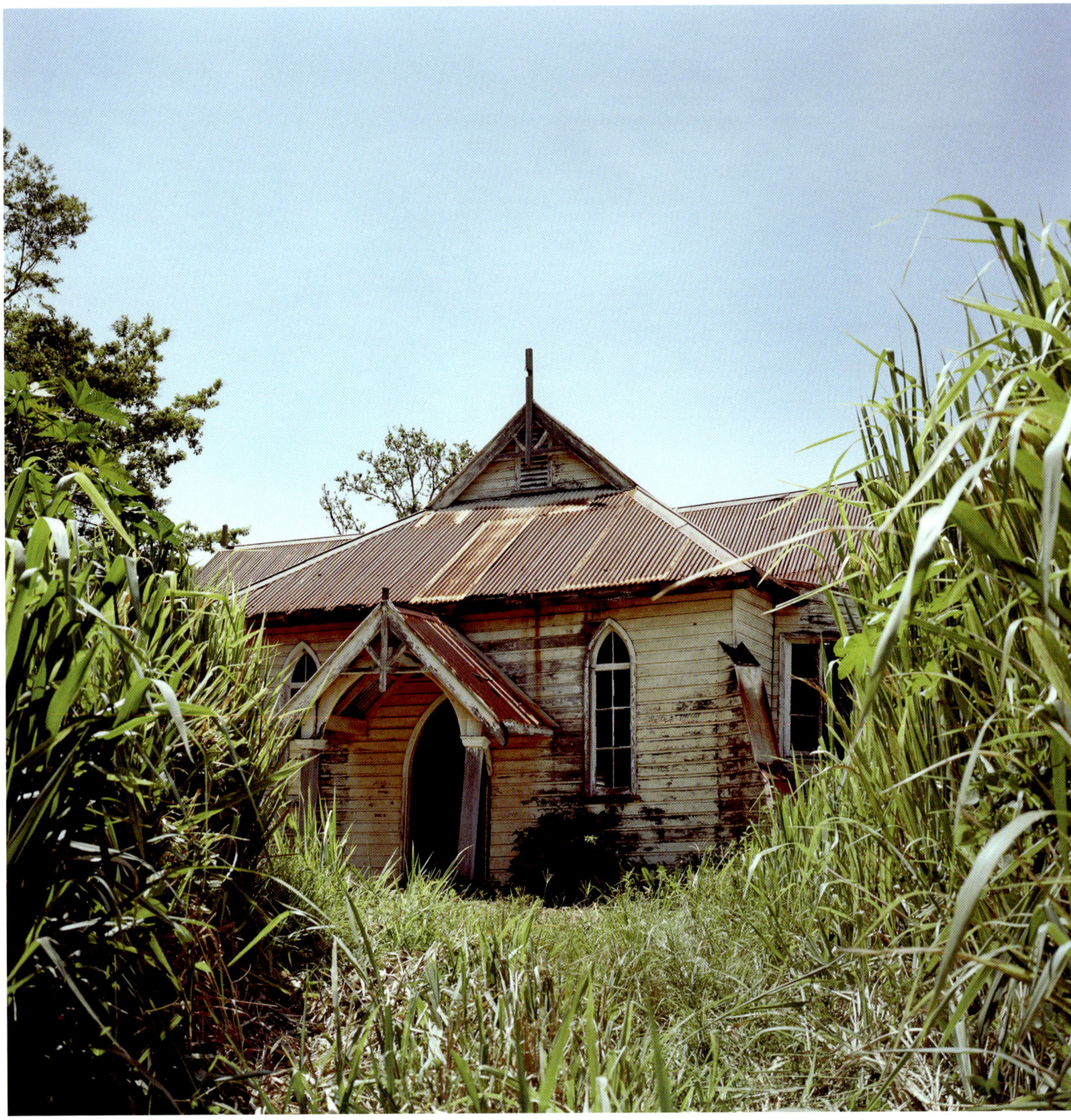

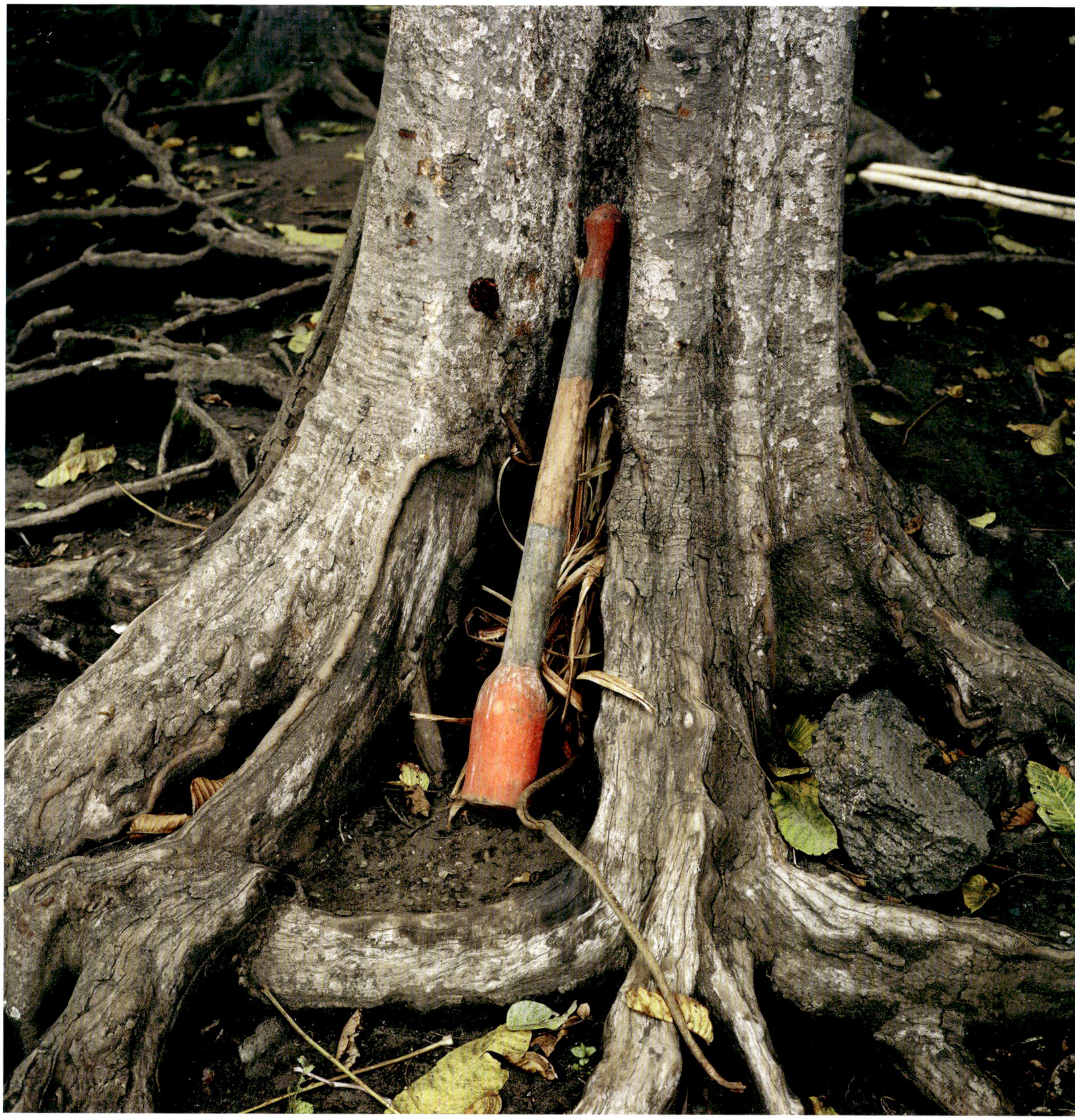

Ceremonial bludgeon used to sacrifice pigs. Lamakara
Village, Tanna

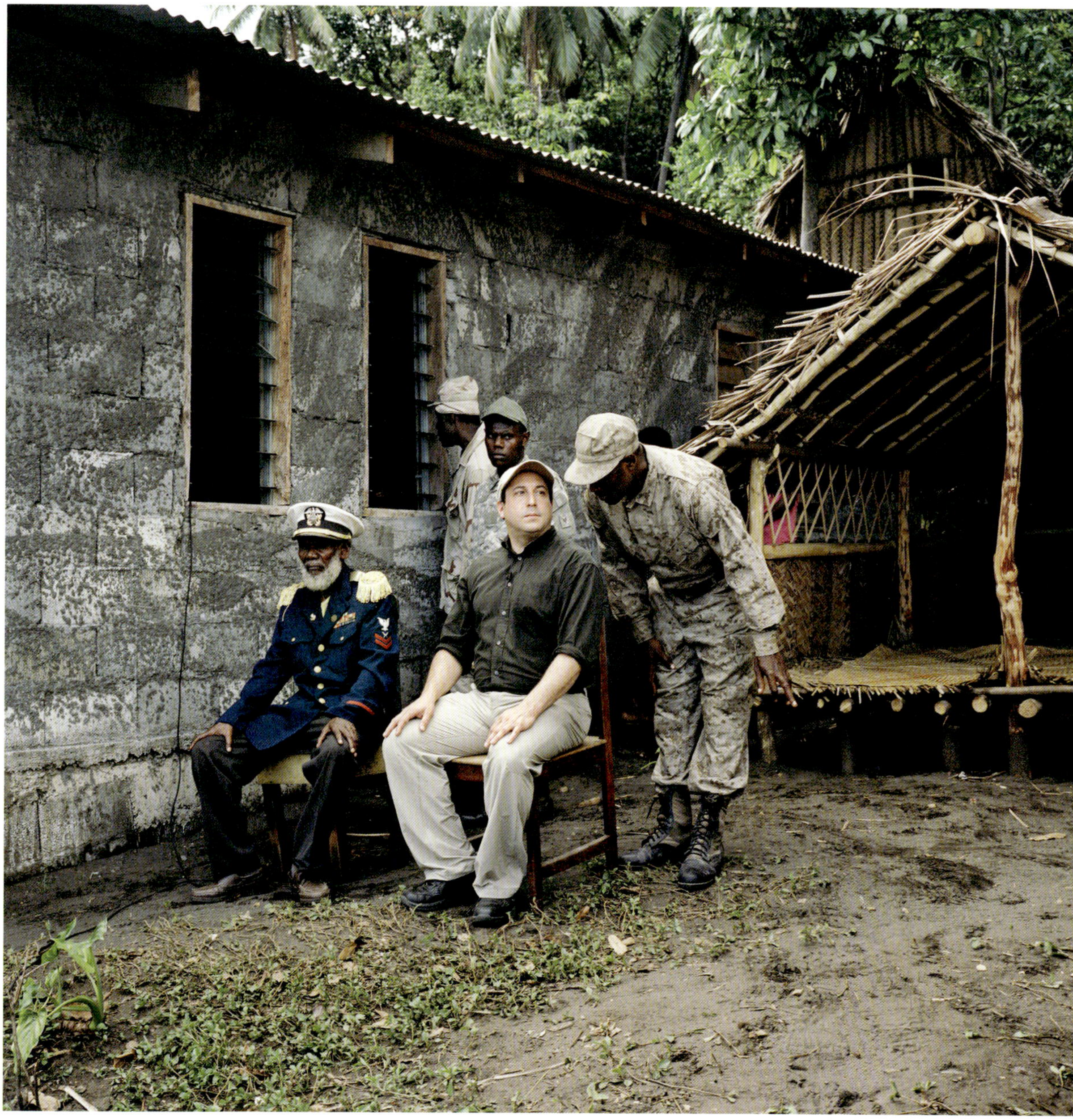

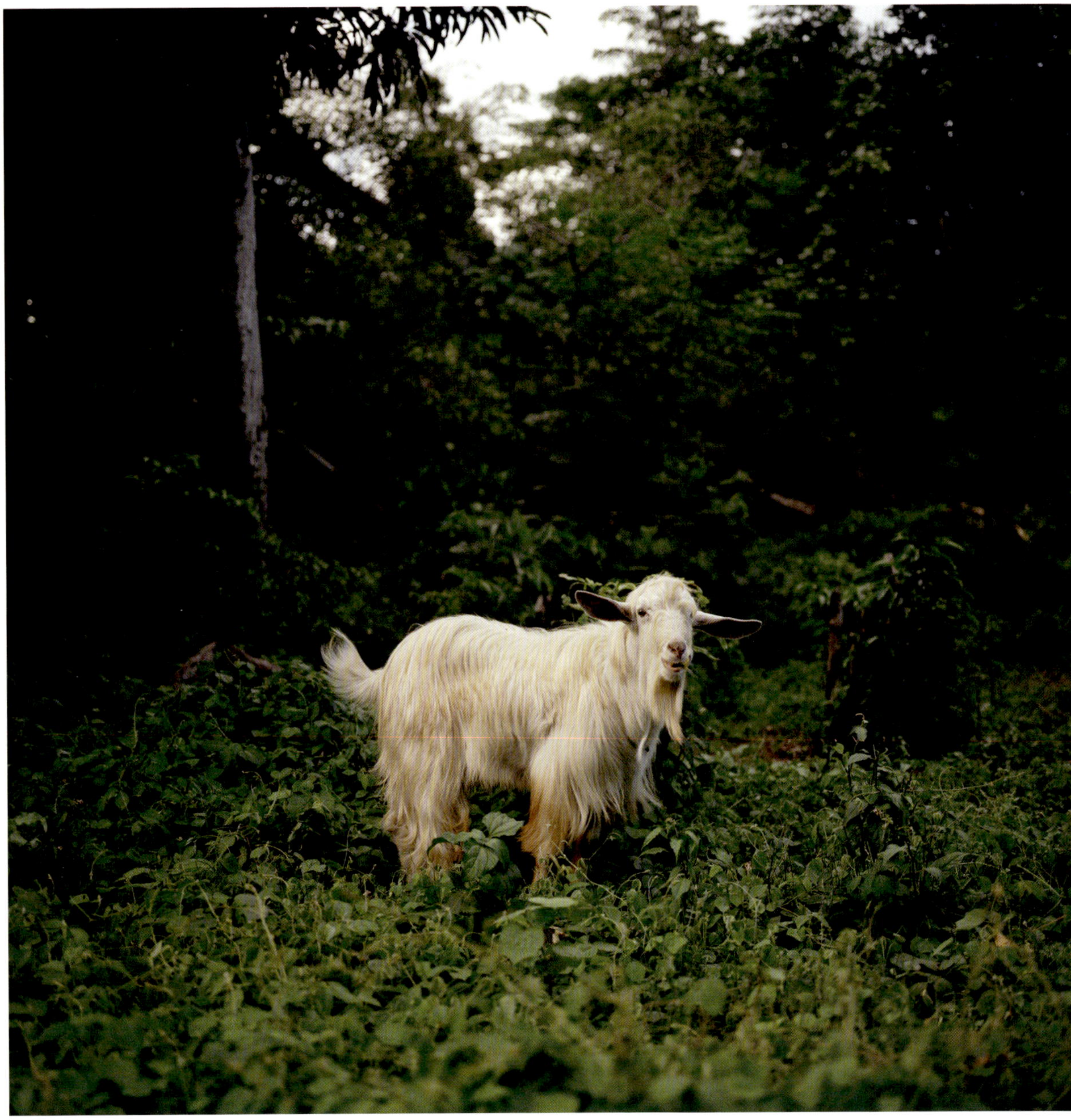

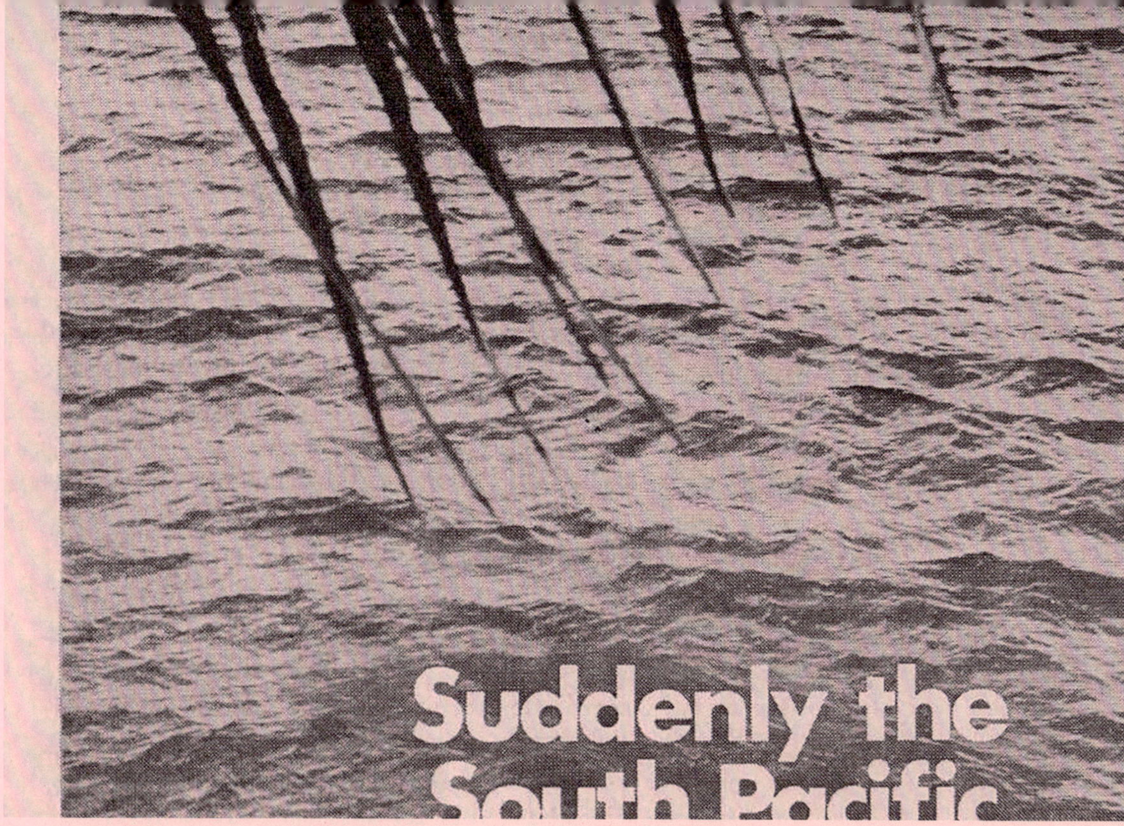
Suddenly the
South Pacific

We thought Sulphur Bay would be a small, smoky village with pigs darting about and a few locals in bedraggled army uniforms. In fact, it is a bustling settlement of several hundred people with a central parade ground and a large collection of huts down the hill sheltered by coconut palms.

On the morning of the John Frum ceremony, athletic young men with sweat-glittered faces had been stamping out dance routines on the soggy dirt for hours, as an overloaded PA system blared out jangly guitar music. The women of Sulphur Bay, meanwhile, were sat in the shade on the periphery, holding down the hems of their beige dresses and swatting at their ankles.

In the centre of the village was a large *nakamal*, a woven palm leaf structure found throughout Vanuatu where men gather to eat, drink, and tell stories. Behind it, a flagpole with the Star-Spangled Banner fluttering against the overcast sky, and a row of elders and tribal chiefs watching the dancers in silence. The chiefs wore a mishmash of military regalia: jaunty side caps, gold-brocaded jackets, green berets.

Overnight, the hills had turned sodden. We hiked up one at the edge of the parade ground. Hundreds of Ni-Vanuatus stood or squatted there, waiting for something to happen. This lot were not Frum believers but Christians from nearby villages who had come along for the spectacle. Also milling around were about 15 awkward-looking Westerners. One particularly enervating Austrian journalist in an akubra hat trailed behind Jon and I – "Who are you working for?" he asked, as if we were rival spies encountering one another in the field.

There was no answer to his question. We had travelled thousands of miles uncertain what we would find, looking for something like authenticity or belief. And now, watching the twirling dancers and the Westerners making aloof small talk with each other, pausing only to stick their iPads in a performer's face, we suspected we might actually be just like them –

gr

travelling around the world looking for something odd or original to recount back home. Quite a few of the foreigners we learned were freelancers hoping to flog a story or a picture or two. There was a sense that something solemn was about to happen, which we had no part in. What were we all doing here?

Just as Jon and I were grumbling at this, the PA system burst into life. A military drum rattle followed and a column of soldiers came marching into the parade ground. They wore pressed military fatigues and each carried over one shoulder a long shaft of bamboo with the end sharpened to a point, daubed in red paint.

Their bare feet bounced in unison on the black earth. The dancers scattered to make way.

At the same moment, a pickup truck tore into the centre of the parade ground. It swerved to avoid the soldiers and stopped in front of the flagpoles. The doors popped open and three Western men scrambled out; they had video cameras on their shoulders, with lenses trained on a short white man in beige trousers and baseball cap who shuffled out of the passenger seat.

He was met by two villagers in camo gear and jackboots. They marched the foreigner up to the row of chiefs, who each in turn shook the man's hand before he was shown to a seat at the end of the row, next to the chief of Sulphur Bay, Isaac Wan, a wiry man in a sailor's hat.

We watched all this from the grassy hillock with the other unbelievers. The Ni-vanuatus were as puzzled as we were: "We heard someone from the White House was coming," said one. Surely the ambassador wouldn't show up in khakis. There was conferral and consternation and plenty of shrugs among friends before a man exhaled in resignation. "I'm afraid we have no idea who this man is."

The marching soldiers halted. They shifted their bamboo muskets to the floor, saluted first the elders, then the American flag. Chief Isaac

A

at bunch

Wan stood and spoke Bislama into a microphone: The faithful had gathered according to 'John's Promise', he explained, and because they had kept their faith John had returned. "Born of America," the chief said, "the last man reveals the final destination of our movement."

Isaac then gestured to the white man, and explained that "Mister Cevin" had given them new uniforms. "It was known that he would come to show us the door to the last land, to lift up our movement and carry us through it."

Mister Cevin had his hands clamped to his thighs. He looked pensive, with the furtive manner of a guinea pig sniffing the air for trouble. When the chief finished speaking, one military-clad villager leaned over and thrust a mic into Cevin's hands.

The village called Sulphur Bay fell silent.

"America is a nation founded by people who left Europe to practise their beliefs and customs," said Cevin, in a slightly nasal East Coast accent. "When colonial powers tried to control the people of America, they fought back and won their independence. Since then American ideals have been based on honouring the culture and ideals of others."

He went on like this for some time. An unseen translator spelled it out line by line in Bislama. "I too am following the spirit of John Frum by coming here to strengthen the bonds between America and Tanna," Cevin said, then thanked everybody, clapped nervously and sat back down. There was just a moment too long of silence before the jangly guitar music mercifully resumed.

We couldn't believe what we'd just witnessed – had this American led the chiefs to believe he was, in fact, John Frum?

"Apparently there was a prophecy that I would come," Cevin told me.

"That you would come?"

"That I would bring cargo and this would be part of building a bond between America and Tanna."

"How were you described in the prophecy?" I asked. "Did they actually say a man called 'Cevin' would come?"

"I haven't pushed it that far to ask."

Our exchange was filmed by one of Cevin's film crew; a burly American in an Old Glory bandana. The crew had been hired to make a documentary called

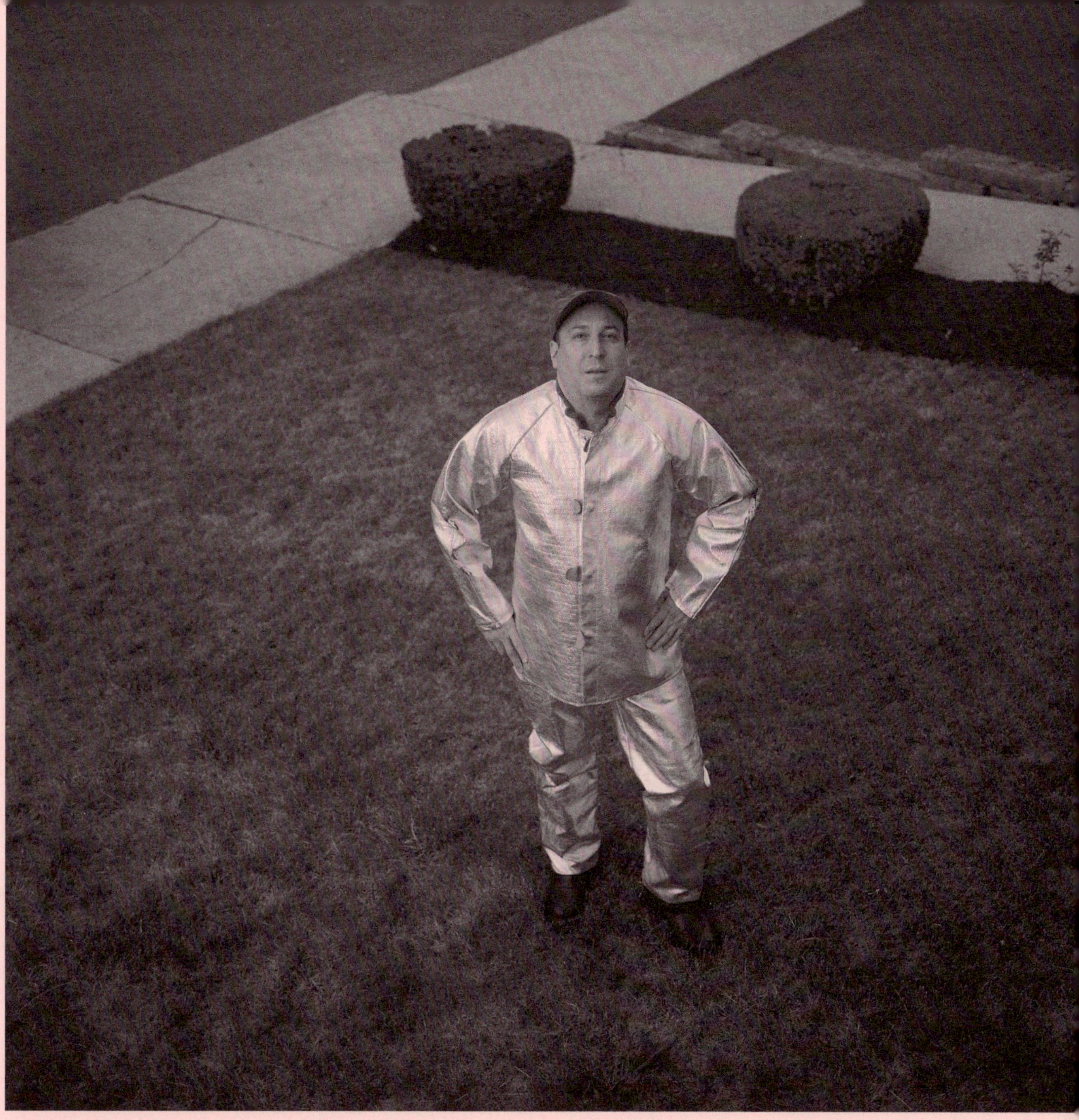

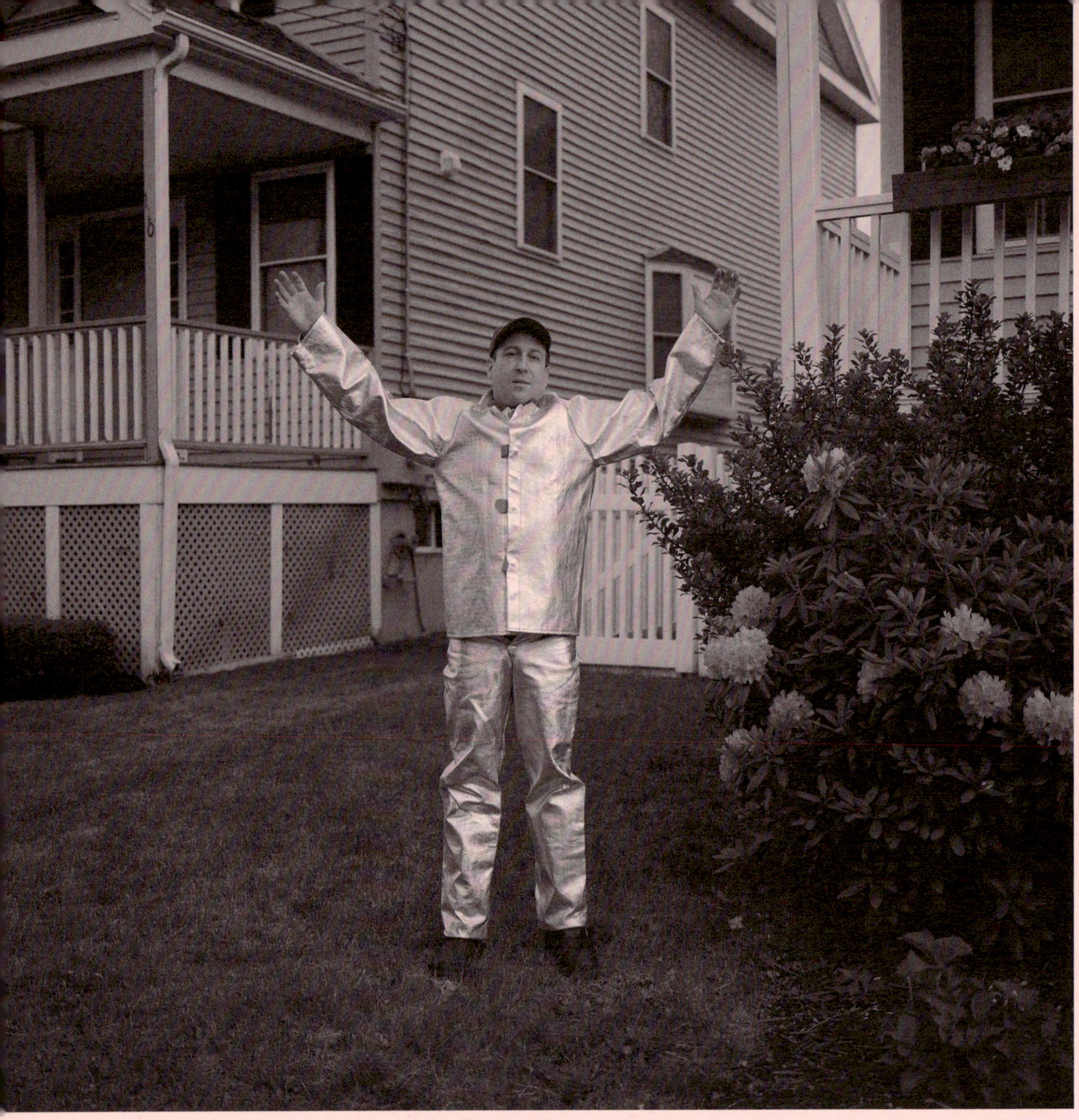

John Frum He Will Come, later described as '[Chronicling] Mr. Soling's attempt to become an island god'. Over three successive trips to Vanuatu, the cameraman explained, Cevin had brought hauls of domestic goods – the cargo! – to the local chiefs: salad spinners, gas cookers, handheld torches, fishing tackle for a community that doesn't fish.

We looked back at the chiefs, who conferred rapidly in Bislama. Cevin, meanwhile, still had his baseball cap on. He glanced between their faces, the floor, the flag. "I mean, if you're into your British awkward humour," the cameraman said, "there's your man."

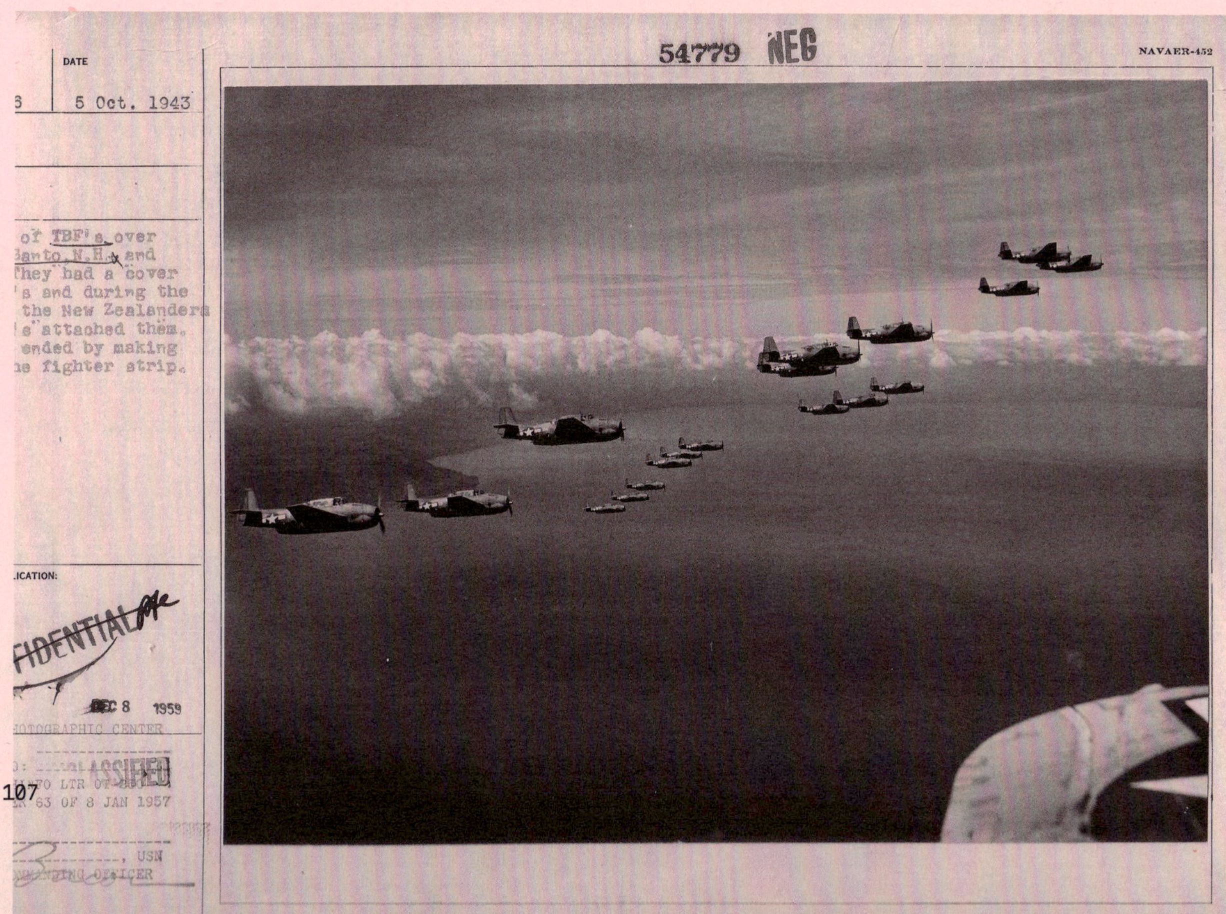

Cevin Soling lives in Boston with his wife and child on a street where the American flag hangs from most porches. He is wealthy, Harvard-educated; his father was an architect who made a fortune building in New York City. But Cevin told us he hated the uniformity of his own suburbia, which was indicative of the narrow-mindedness of contemporary America. "It looks like a big machine just spat each house out, *splat!*" he said, stood on the closely-cropped lawn. "Over and over again, street after street."

Jon and I visited Cevin at home a few years after our first encounter in Vanuatu. He had sent us a rough cut of his documentary, *John Frum He Will Come*, which had had a mixed reception. "There was some violent backlash and screaming at me when I showed the film in Arkansas," he told us. "The impulse is to infantilise the tribe and assume I was being exploitative. It was nearly a riot."

Cevin was affable, enthusiastic about his rare Beatles records and the exoticism of his adventures. He showed us photographs from when he hiked across bandit country in northern Uganda so as to film a local tribe putting on a production of A Christmas Carol, at his direction. On another trip, possibly Borneo, he said he was gifted a bag of shrunken heads by a local tribe but thought against trying to smuggle them back to America. In his stories, he was the intrepid if slightly bungling adventurer tramping through landscapes of the mind, excavating weirdness and esotericism in far-flung dangerous places, ever ready to tweak the nose of good taste.

We'd been struck by a scene from Cevin's John Frum documentary in which he's seen in Vanuatu handing out necklaces with his own face on them. There's also a long sequence of our protagonist cavorting about the lip of Mount Yasur in a fire retardant suit, demonstrating his semi-unflappability in the face of the lava's explosions.

With us, Cevin was happy to have a receptive audience but was at the same time guarded, suspicious in case we were there to hatchet job him. We took him for lunch at a Polynesian restaurant on a dusty highway outside Boston, opposite a branch of Hooters, where he ordered the lobster and after a few cocktails started to loosen up.

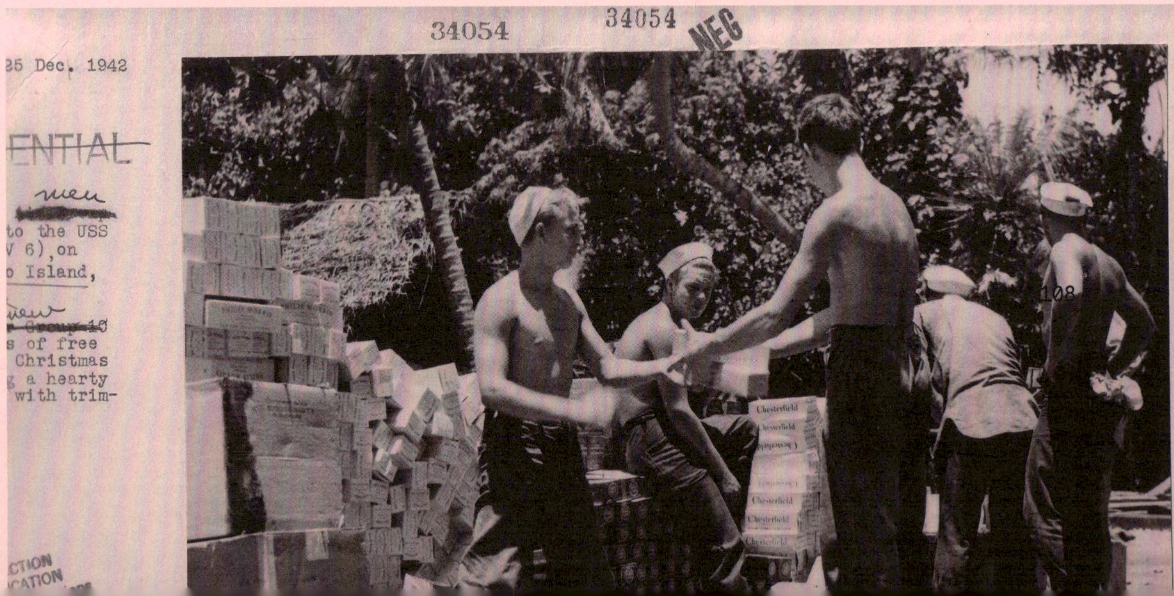

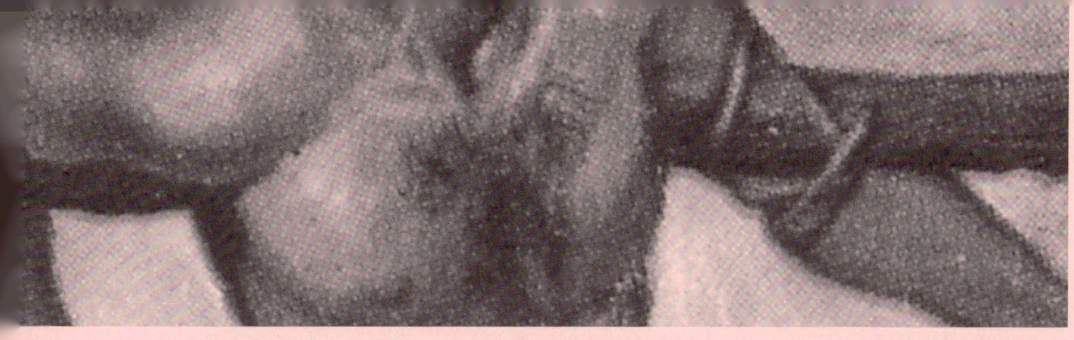

"It's a sad, sad time we're living in," Cevin said, "when status is founded on the degree of how offended you are and the greater virtue you can claim." He blamed, in part, America's 'postmodern' campus culture.

The audience for Cevin's films tends to be as niche as his subject matter. (He once made a film about the practice of drilling a hole in one's own head in pursuit of enlightenment.) But he did attract national attention in 2009 for a documentary about the evils of the US education system and was invited onto Stephen Colbert's talk show. Cevin laughed nervously at the host's irreverence and tried to get across his point that American schools indoctrinate kids and kill their creativity.

John Frum theory travels along similar lines – the missionaries brought the schoolhouse, which was the ideological apparatus for shattering Ni-Vanuatu culture. Therefore most ardent Frummers, in communities like Sulphur Bay, think kids shouldn't go to school.

Cevin said he'd stressed to the chiefs of Sulphur Bay that kids should be educated but only in the village *nakamal*, not the missionary schools. He praised the spirit of resistance that the John Frum villages showed to our deadening world.

"I'm really proud of my relationship with the people there," he told us. "I wanted to see the best outcomes for them and I believe that my contact with them was beneficial and I'm proud of that and to have my contributions recognised." He'd been honoured as a member of the tribe, and given great swathes of land, but was keen to stress that he never claimed anything divine about himself; he only helped realise some facets of the John Frum prophecy so as to see how the believers would respond. It wasn't so simple; the government regarded him as a troublemaker, and he'd had to pay off a local man who took umbrage at his quest. He also spent a sizeable amount of money sourcing and shipping the cargo out there.

Was it worth it? He equated his adventure in derring-do to climbing Everest: "If there was a specific recipe, if the rules were firm and rigid and all you had to do was XYZ then anyone could do it. But it takes someone special to do it, and I actually did it. It makes me exceptional, not divine – except in their context. But only if that's what *they* decide."

He was a man in pursuit of a story, one in which he himself was at its heart.

Scores of anthropologists have, like Cevin, dedicated study to Vanuatu's 'cargo cults' because they found in it some reflection of their own worldview.

The leftist theorist Peter Worsley saw John Frum as the last gasps of indigenous unity in the face of imperialism – the same urge, he believed, that inspired the Native American Ghost Dance in the 19th century, reviving long-dead ancestors, or the apocalyptic visions of the Taiping Revolution in China amidst its so-called Century of Humiliation by foreign powers. Cargo cults were, in Worsley's view, a plea for divine intervention, a desire to hit reset on a culture careering towards oblivion.

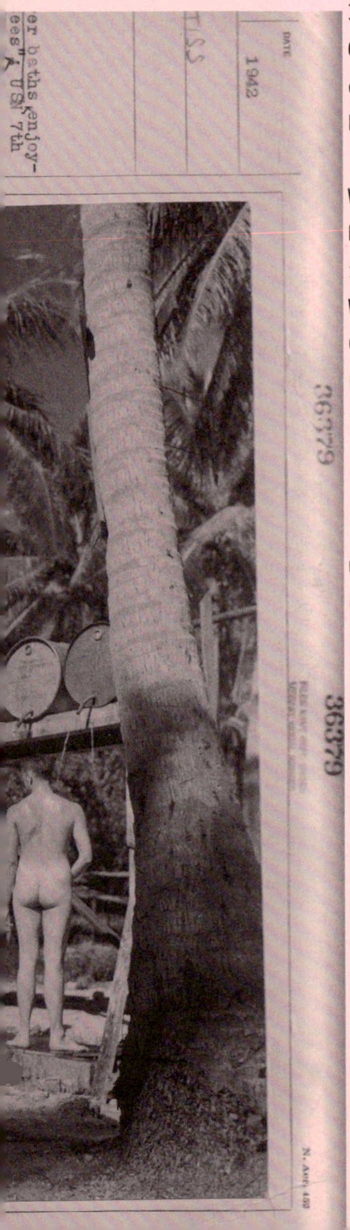

In his speech to Sulphur Bay, Cevin said that America's Second World War experience in Vanuatu represented for him the best of his country. Benevolent protectors of the Pacific – dashing, victorious, welcomed. Where in the world is America, or the West in general, still viewed that way? Where else do white faces still get a warm wave from the roadside? Perhaps Cevin's desire to realise the John Frum story was his own Ghost Dance, a kind of ancestor worship for an America that had run off the rails, been stultified by postmodernism and political correctness.

Or that may be too high-minded.

After the war, Americans were fascinated by being received as gods and kings in faraway lands. Take, for instance, an issue of the 1960s men's magazine ADVENTURE that has the coverline, 'The Yank who became an island god!' and features an illustration of a strapping sailor being fought over by amorous Polynesian girls. It was reprinted in a recent book by Sven Kirsten, a visual anthropologist and the world's foremost authority on

Tiki, America's mid-century craze for the South Pacific, which often had undertones of the deified castaway fantasy in its aesthetic.

"It's the epitome of being welcomed into a foreign culture," Kirsten told us by phone from California. "This was the Americans' experience during the Second World War."

Back then, America and the Western world still felt itself to be at the centre of the global narrative, the heroes in the story. After all, they'd fought off the Japanese in the Pacific and rescued the Old World from European tyranny. Simplistic self-belief, yes, but intoxicating all the same. This was before Vietnam, Nicaragua, before the Middle East invasions of the 2000s. "When you're liked you like other people back," Kirsten said. "But that has certainly changed."

Today, experience weighs heavy and power is shifting to new centres.

In Vanuatu alone, we watched over each successive visit as more and more Chinese money drifted into the archipelago, made manifest in new roads, rumours of a military base (denied by Beijing), and a very angular expo centre in the capital.

China sees Vanuatu as a strategic outpost in the Pacific. In return, it pledges prosperity and protection, particularly from those who wronged Vanuatu in the past.

Self-mythologising is a powerful force. It was at work when Europe's own empires were expanding too: Orientalism, as Edward Saïd viewed it, was about imagining the Other so as to conquer and control. But the way the West imagined *itself* proved to be just as potent. Exotic stories about 'civilising' explorers like Captain Cook being received as gods fired European imaginations at the very moment they were casting their eyes hungrily around the world. Owning the story could mean shaping reality. What is the message of Robinson Crusoe if not that Man Friday was willing and grateful of his own subjugation, and that Crusoe became a better man by ruling him?

As the world rebalances, the legacy of Europe's imperial iniquities is unpicked but old relationships linger on uncomfortably. However well-intentioned Cevin may be, his tale makes the notion of the so-called 'White saviour' queasily literal.

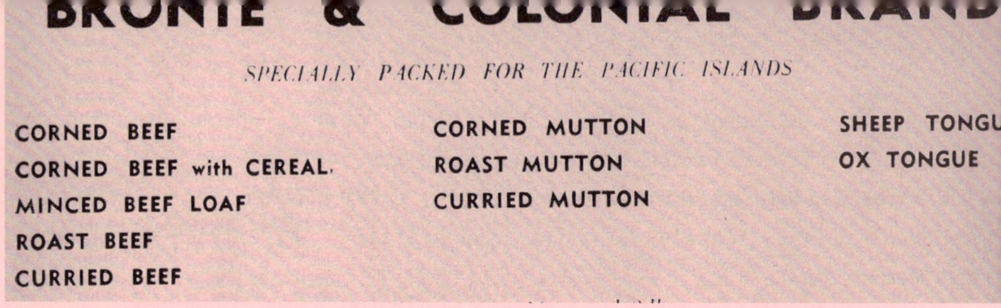

In the hours after our first encounter with Cevin at Sulphur Bay, Jon and I fulminated about the American in the baseball cap strutting around like God. We expected our shock to be shared by Ketty Napwatt, the Ni-Vanuatu woman from the night before in Hugh's hotel. But she just shrugged, disappointed that we hadn't had a profound cultural experience in Sulphur Bay. "We always have these crackpots showing up," she said, wearily, then turned to the same rosy-cheeked expats from the night before who had now reconvened for lunch on Tanna Lodge's veranda. "You see, the foreigners are not even watching our ceremonies anymore," Ketty said. "They're just watching each other."

Hugh, already shirtless, concurred there were crackpots: he told us about a New Zealander who had shown up a few years earlier and gone round the John Frum villages saying the prophet's arrival was imminent but that he was just waiting for a decent enough hotel to stay in. Oh, and it had to be one with a landing pad, because Frum was going to come from outer space. (The man's driver later confirmed this detail for us: 'Moon men', he said.)

A few chiefs were convinced to hand over cash and, incredibly, work actually began on a structure before the foreigner was deported on some misdemeanour. One of Hugh's staff took us out to all that remains: a septic tank and a ghostly sculpture of nailed-together plywood, teetering in a windswept coconut grove.

There were others. Ketty told us how in 1980, just months before independence, the British and the French armies sat around gripped by indecision as the islands were on the brink of war. A group of Las Vegas property developers wanted to create their own independent libertarian tax haven in Vanuatu, and had funnelled money to a charismatic community leader called Jimmy Stevens, sponsoring a cult-like secessionist uprising with echoes of John Frum. They went far enough to mint money and print passports

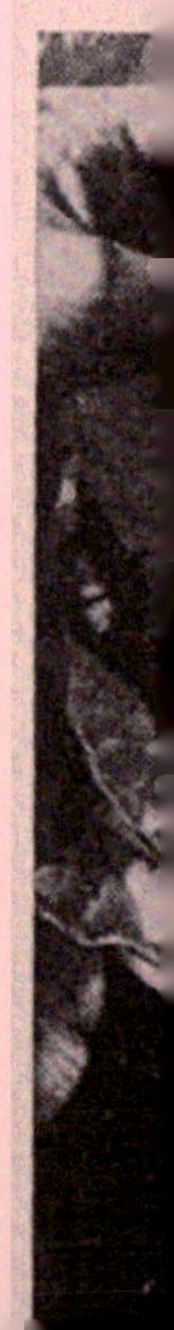

for their new nation before their scheme was routed: Jimmy spent the rest of his life in prison, while the libertarians sloped off into the sunset.

All this, unfortunately, gives an impression that Ni-Vanuatus are gullible people, too trusting for our corrupt world, exploited for kicks by foreign opportunists. But that is not the whole picture.

Many communities on Tanna believe to some degree in the John Frum movement. The legitimacy of their leaders rests on the promise that Frum will deliver prosperity. Internal island politics and inter-tribal feuds can be upended by the arrival of a man like Cevin offering to fulfil part of the prophecy for one group, especially if they come up with the goods. In a version of Cevin's documentary, there's a long scene in which the chief of Sulphur Bay, Isaac Wan, is examining the boxed-up foreign wares that Cevin has brought – pleased that the 'cult' is working, one could say, because the fabled cargo had started to arrive (It just happened to have been shipped there by a wealthy American filmmaker). One anthropologist who had done field work in Vanuatu explained to us that it can be expedient for tribal leaders to cultivate foreign contacts, even in some cases to indulge or humour their whimsies, if it gives them greater right to rule.

A couple of days after John Frum day, we returned to Sulphur Bay and found Chief Isaac Wan crouched in the palm leaf *nakamal*. Rather than his admiral's outfit, Isaac had on a shellsuit that clung to his frame. He was clearly fed up of dealing with the many foreign reporters who have come and gone over the years with their notebooks and dictaphones to hear him retell once more the tale of John Frum. "Pikanini i no go long skul," he railed at us, eyes blazing like two pieces of coal.

Isaac's son, clearly high on kava, joined us and stood at the door paraphrasing his father's diatribe about the perils of education. We shifted the conversation to Cevin Soling. "Yes, Cevin is a friend of Sulphur Bay.

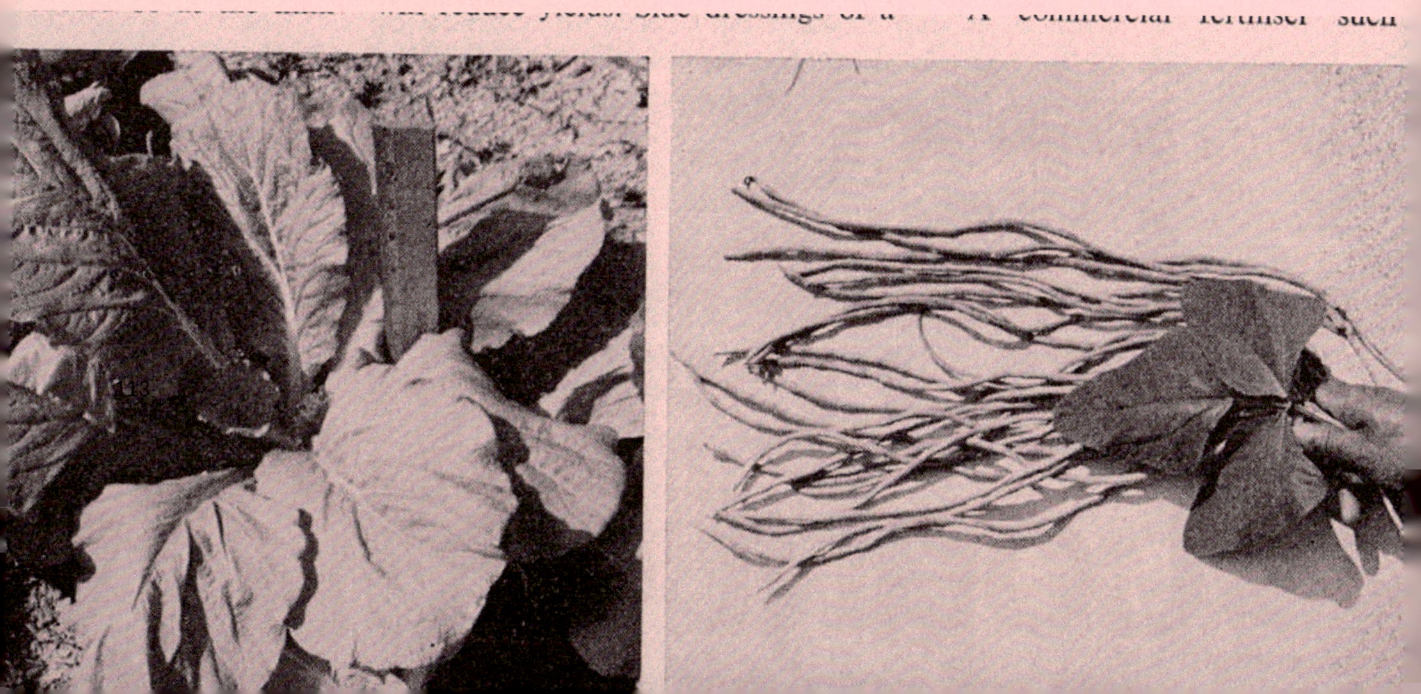

He is rebuilding a bond between Tanna and America." But, we asked, was Cevin John Frum? To this both were dismissive, despite the grandiloquence of the ceremony speeches, and would not give a straight answer.

Isaac got to his feet and with a wave of his hand, wandered down a dusty mud verge to a small clearing in the coconut palms. We followed him, and came to a circular platform of cracked stone upon which sat four kids, no more than six years old, their cheeks stuffed freakishly large with clumps of leaves, dribbling juices into coconut shells.

In ritualised form, the kava root is chewed first by pre-pubescent boys and spat out, creating a particularly potent pulp that imbues the drinker with a sense of wellbeing.

Shells of the stuff were passed round as more men from Sulphur Bay gathered. We were half-heartedly offered one but declined. The air was thick with the drinkers' need for silence. They wanted to be left to their slurping. Isaac occasionally cackled, and the others showed deference to him. There was a strange aggro in the air.

Watching this arcane scene, now the army uniforms were off and the journalists gone home, we were aware how cloistered this community of believers was. The notion of an outsider believing they could ever truly become part of it, and in doing so help these people in their mission, seems woefully picturesque.

On the drive back to our hotel, a torrent of rain blew over Tanna. Hugh's driver, we thought, must have had a nip of kava because he steered with a persistent grin, unfazed that the windscreen wipers were useless and none of us could see the road ahead.

Tanna is an eerie place after dark. When it rains the bush gurgles and the insects writhe and channels of muddy water work their way to the coast. Even in the dead of night you encounter men trudging the pitch black pathways, going to or from the kava shacks dotted around the island. These tiny bars light a coloured lantern at their gate when the brew is ready.

We got stuck in mud at the top of a hill. Fortunately there were a few passersby, looking for kava. We all gave the jeep a shove. The rain continued to pour down. Beyond our flickering headlights we could see the southern side of Tanna stretching to the ocean in a black, spiky expanse.

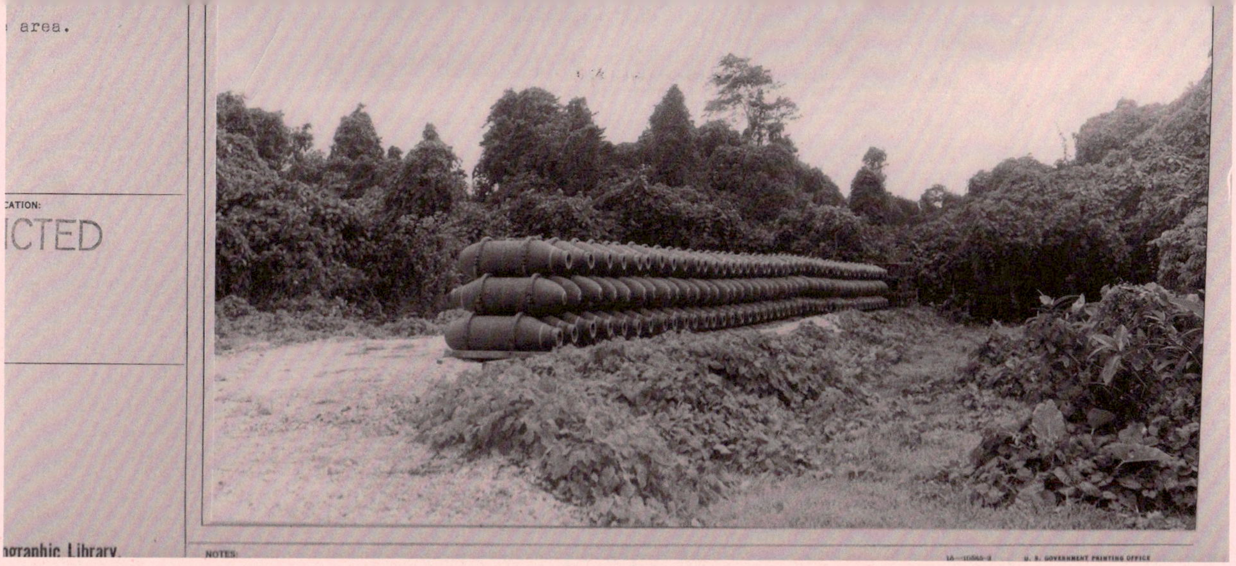

area.
ICTED
ographic Library.
NOTES:
U. S. GOVERNMENT PRINTING OFFICE

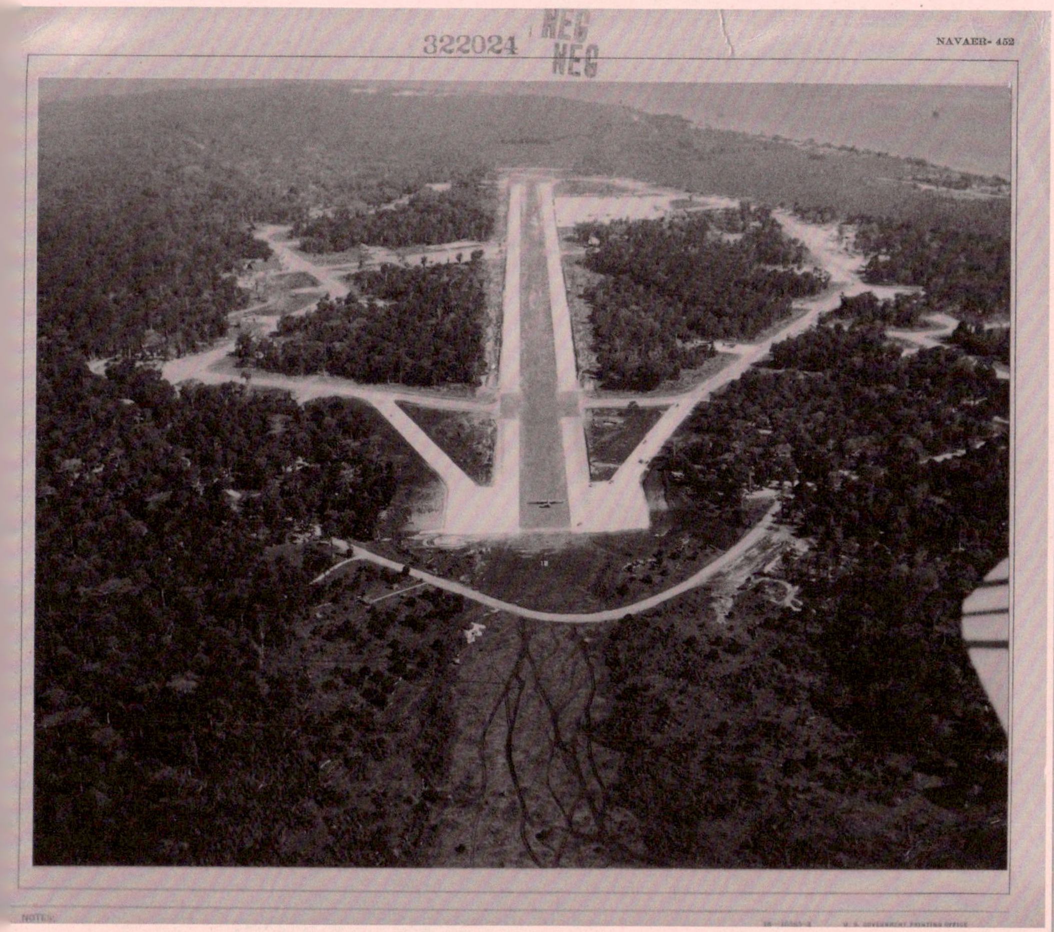

322024
NEG
NEG
NAVAER-452
NOTES:

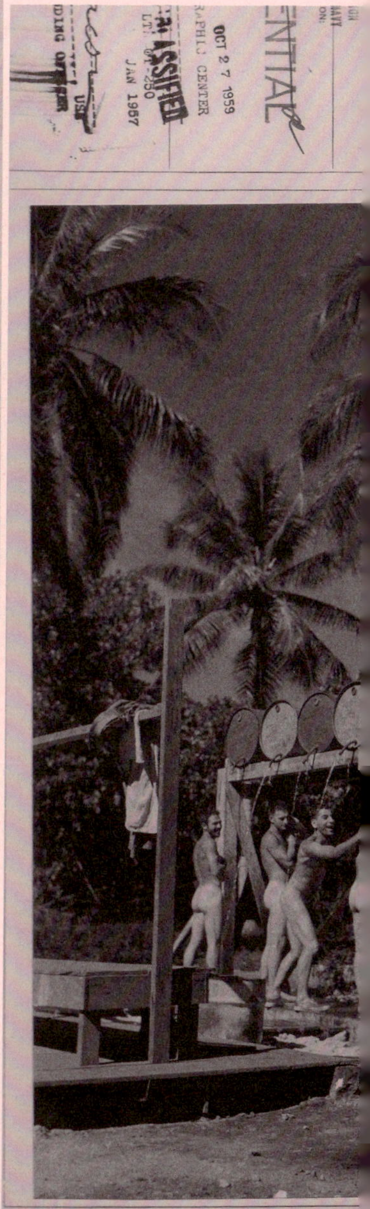

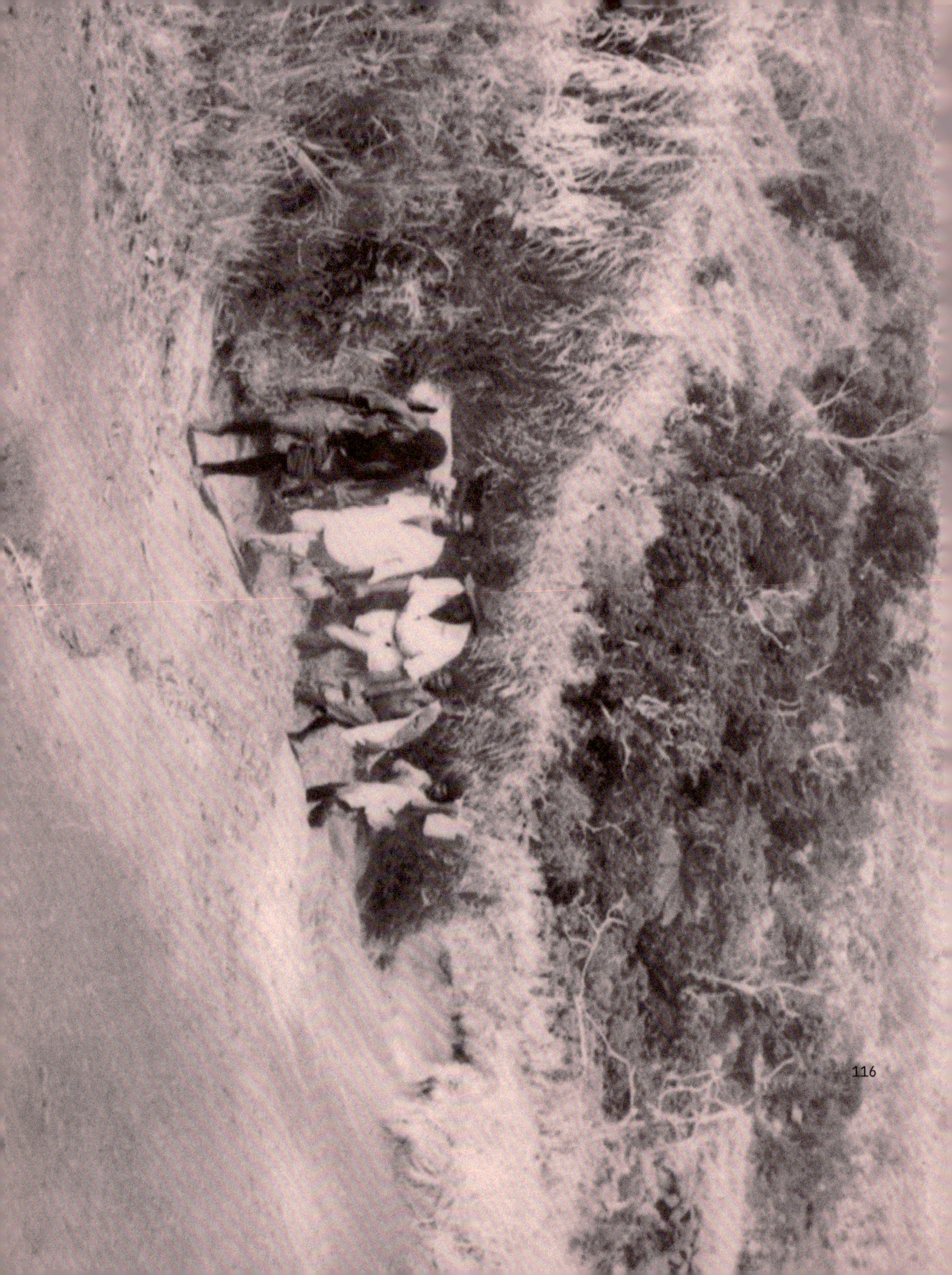

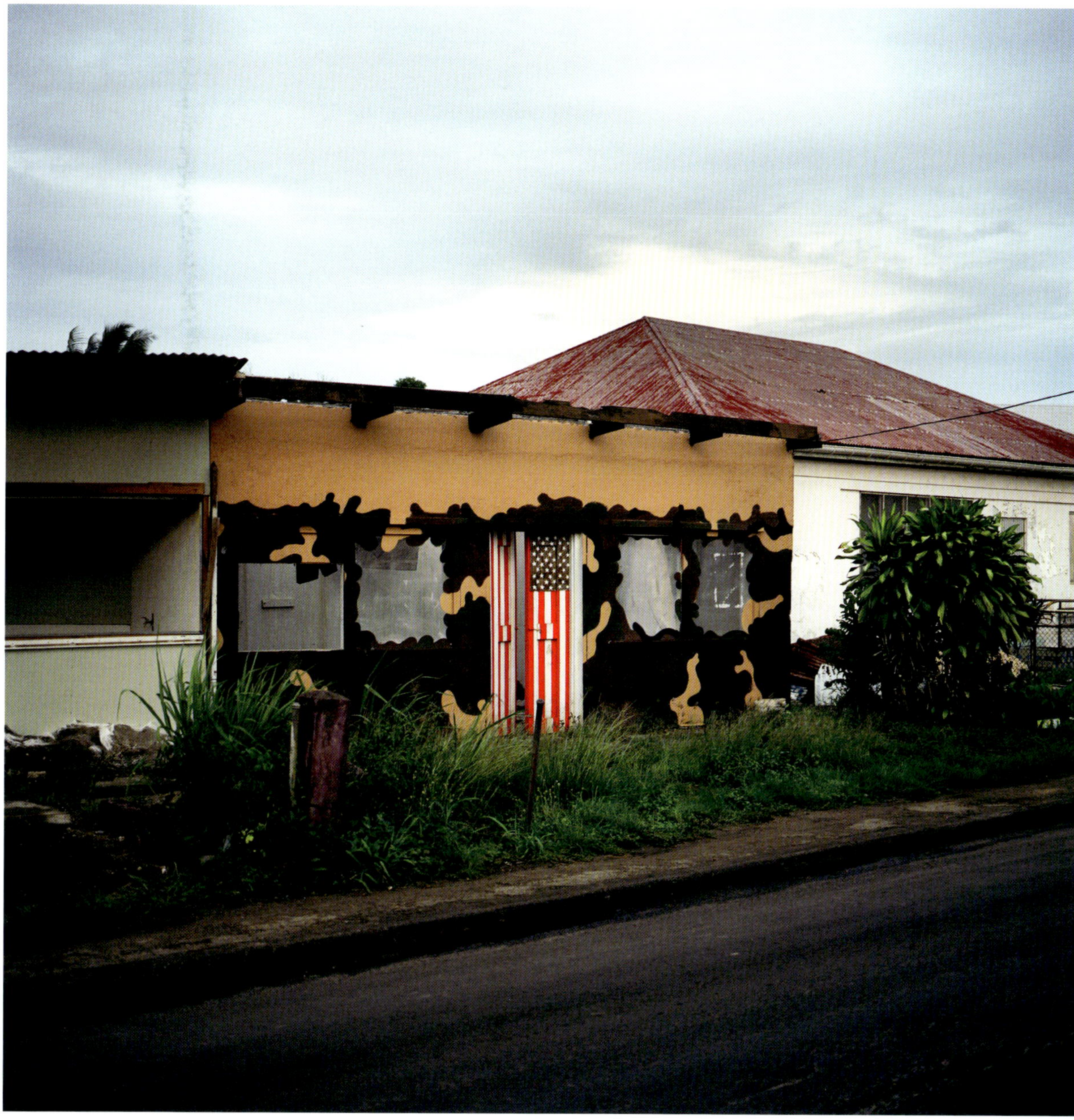

Jordy and Jérémie, Luganville, Espiritu Santo

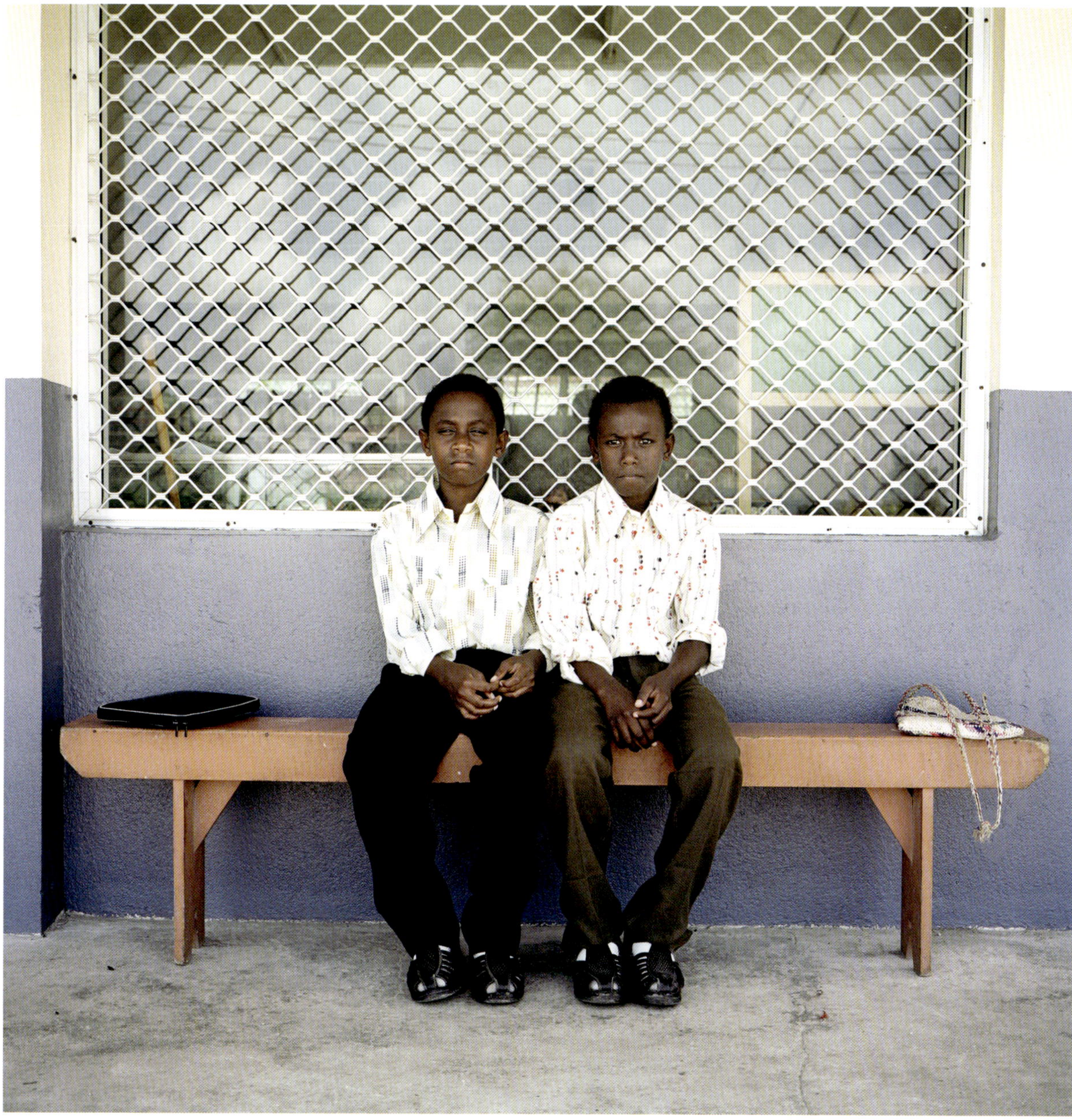

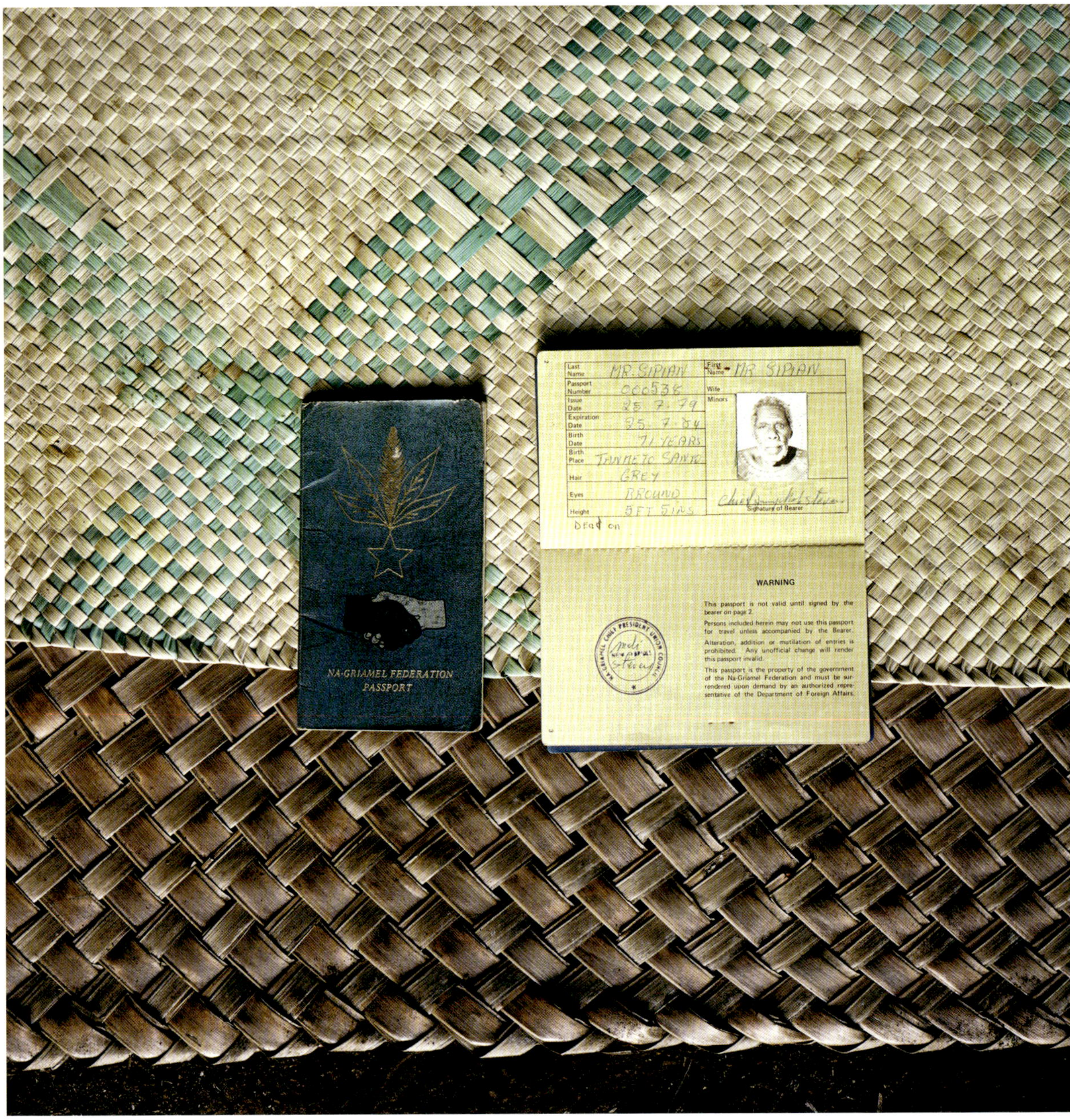
NA-GRIAMEL FEDERATION
PASSPORT
Last Name MR. SIPIAN
First Name MR SIPIAN
Passport Number 000538
Wife
Issue Date 25 7 79
Minors
Expiration Date 25 7 84
Birth Date 71 YEARS
Birth Place TANMETO SANTO
Hair GREY
Eyes BROUND
Height 5FT 5INS
Signature of Bearer
Dead on
WARNING
This passport is not valid until signed by the bearer on page 2.
Persons included herein may not use this passport for travel unless accompanied by the Bearer.
Alteration, addition or mutilation of entries is prohibited. Any unofficial change will render this passport invalid.
This passport is the property of the government of the Na-Griamel Federation and must be surrendered upon demand by an authorized representative of the Department of Foreign Affairs.
NA-GRIAMEL CHIEF PRESIDENT UNION COUNCIL

Passport produced for Nagriamel, a breakaway nation financed by Las Vegas property developers in 1980

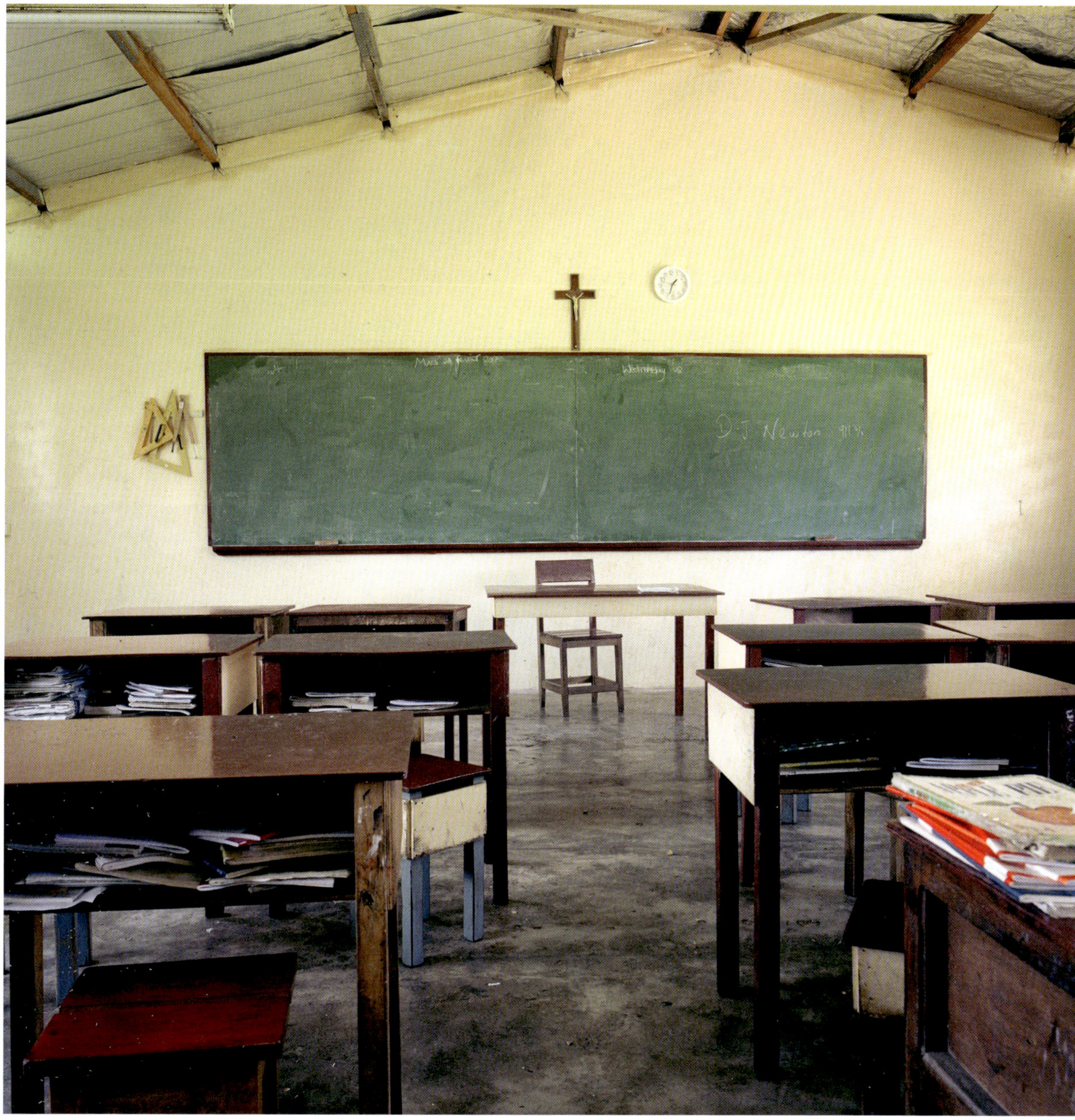
D J Newton

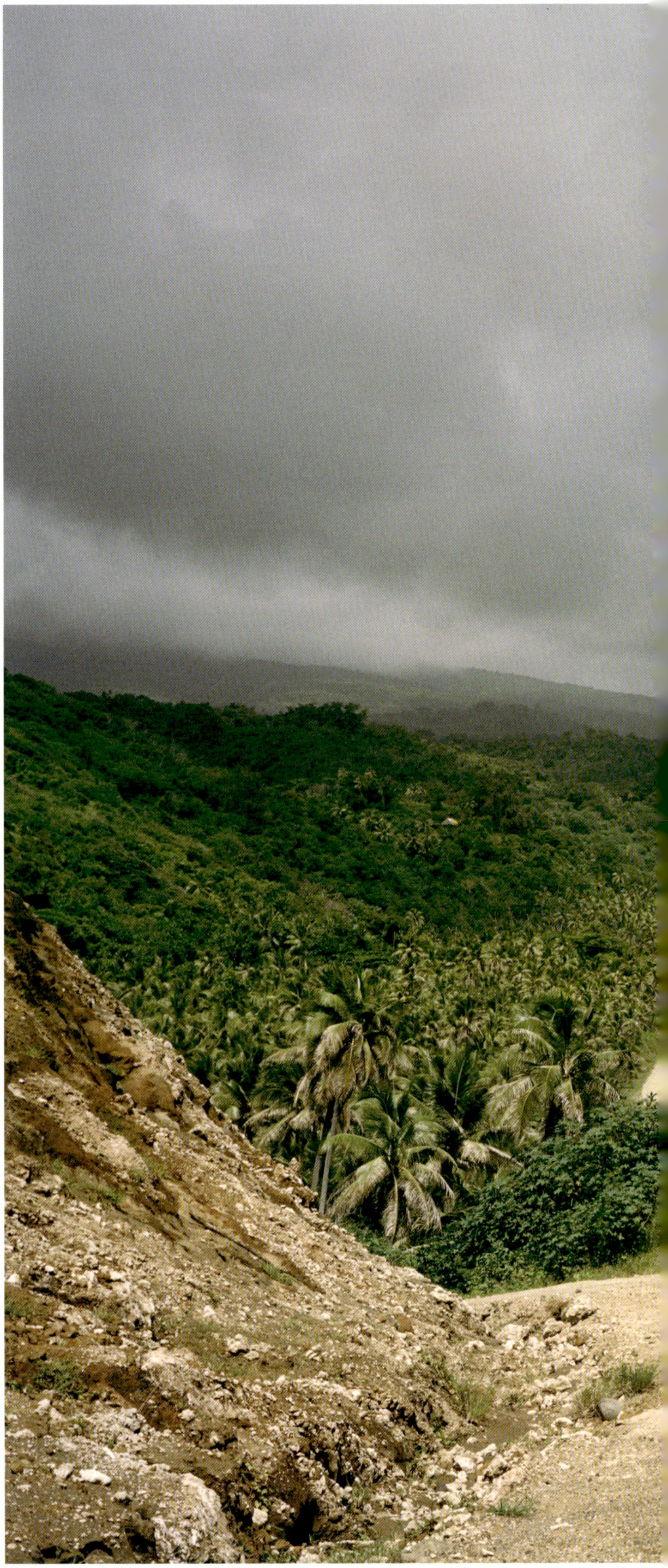

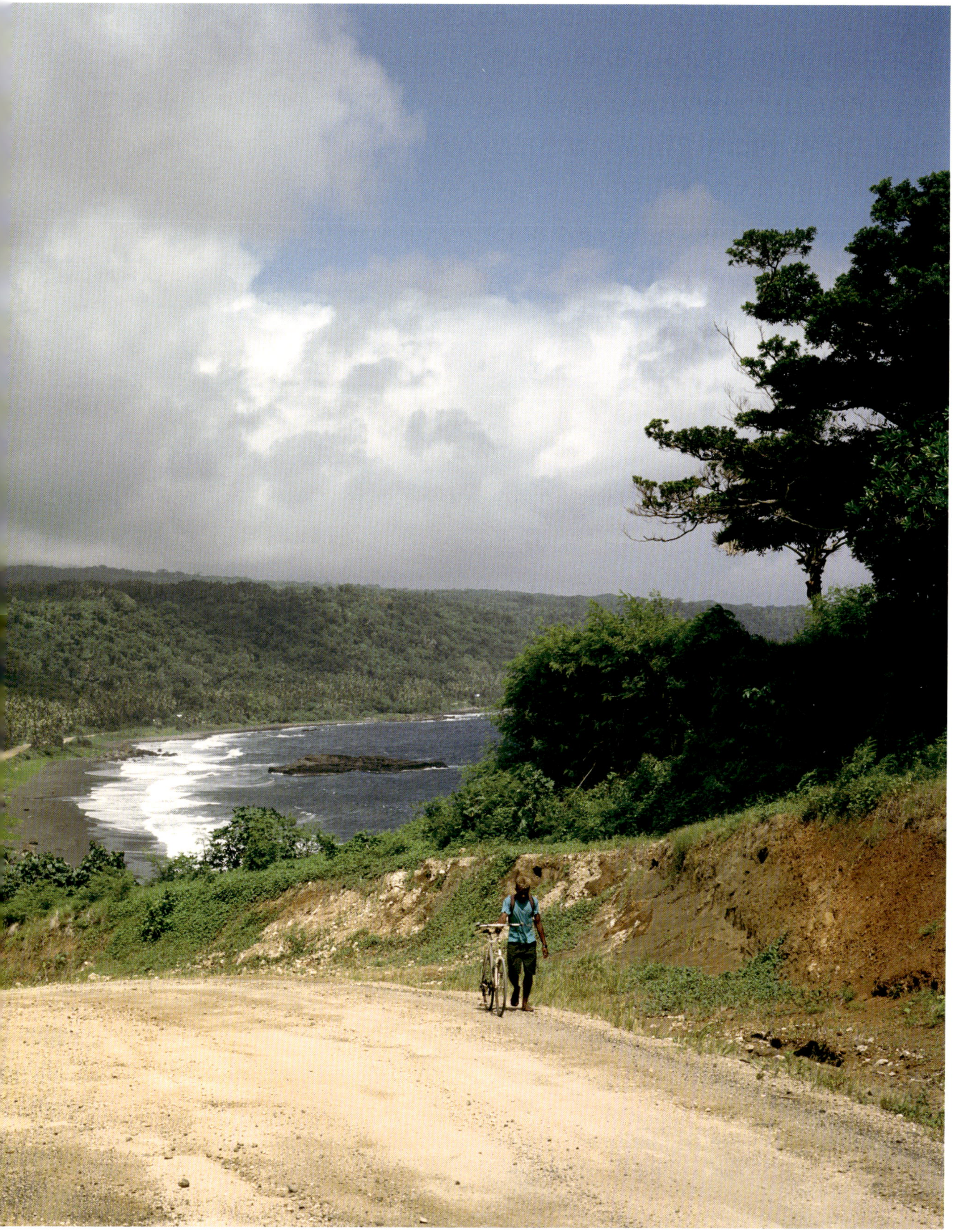

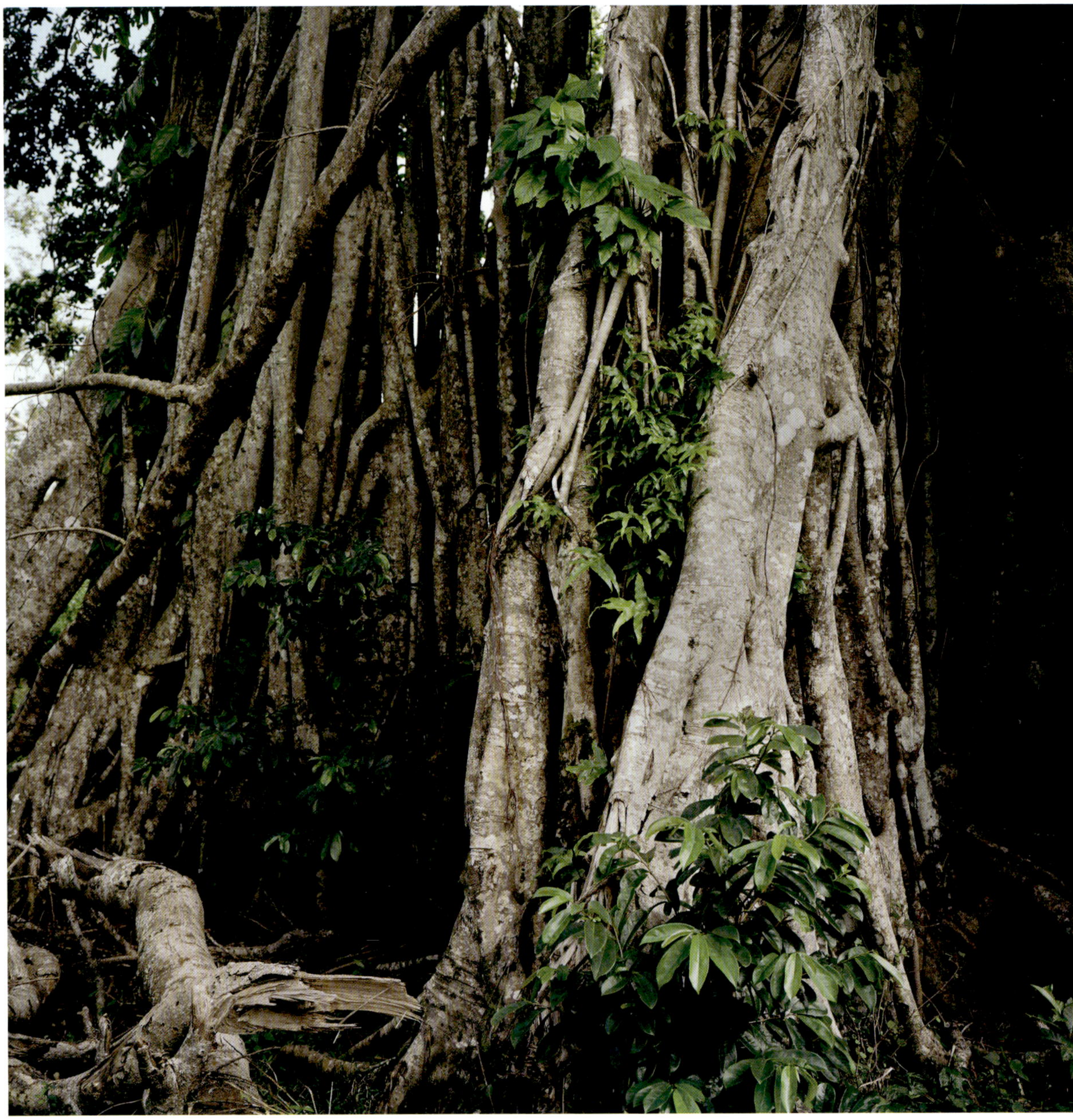

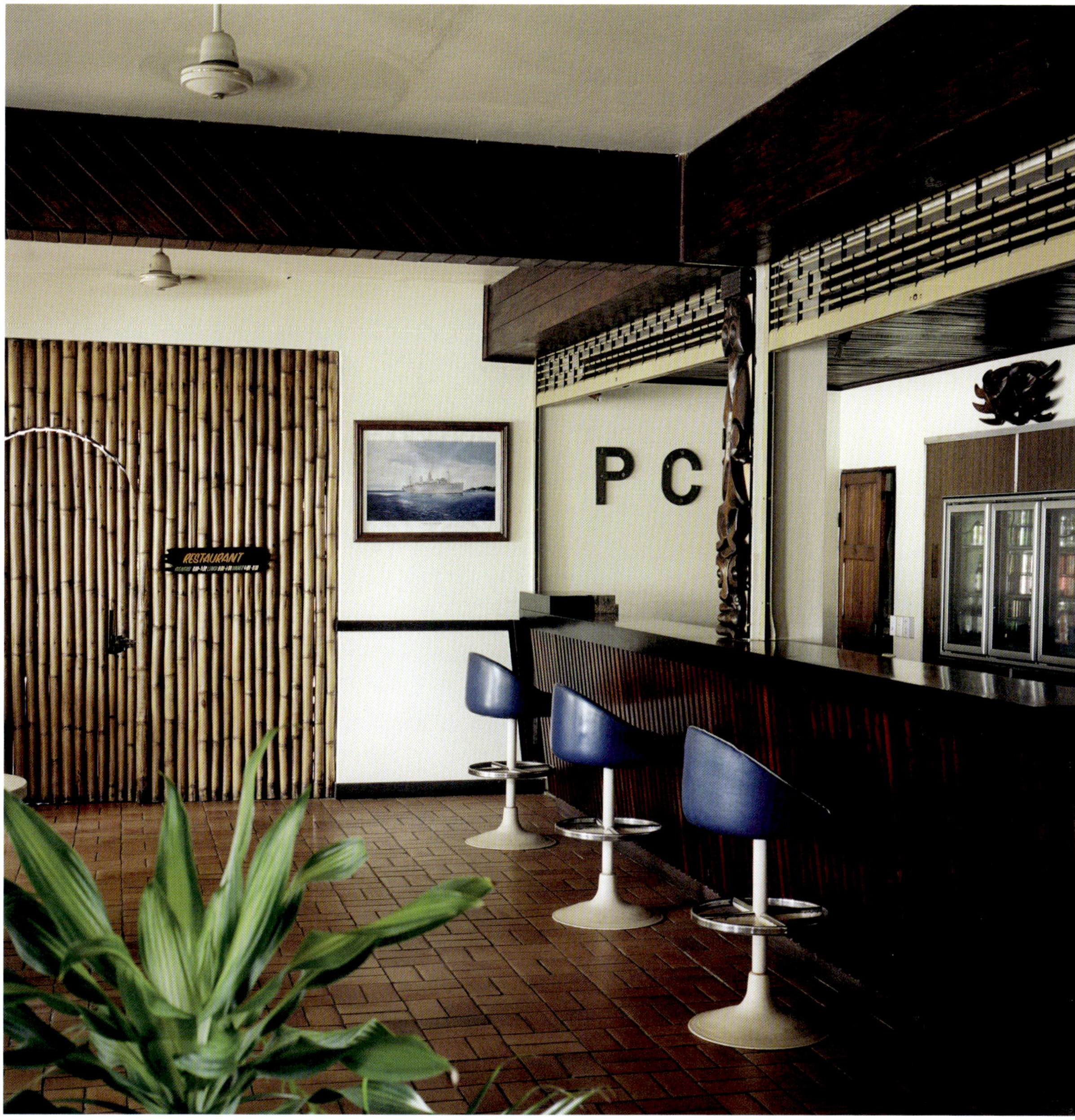
RESTAURANT
P C

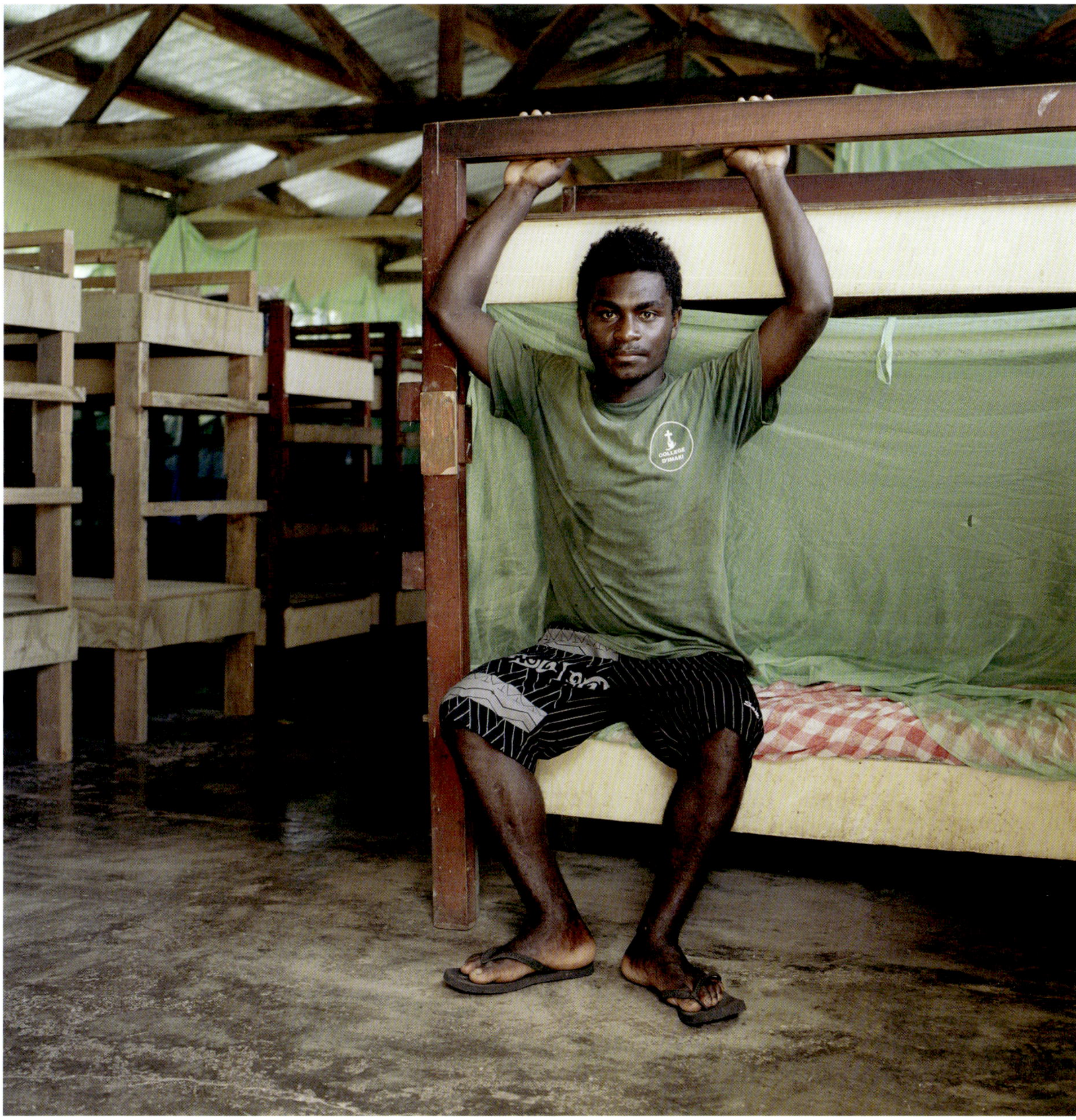
COLLEGE
D'IMAKI

Grave of Ni-Vanuatu nationalist leader
Jimmy Stevens, Espiritu Santo

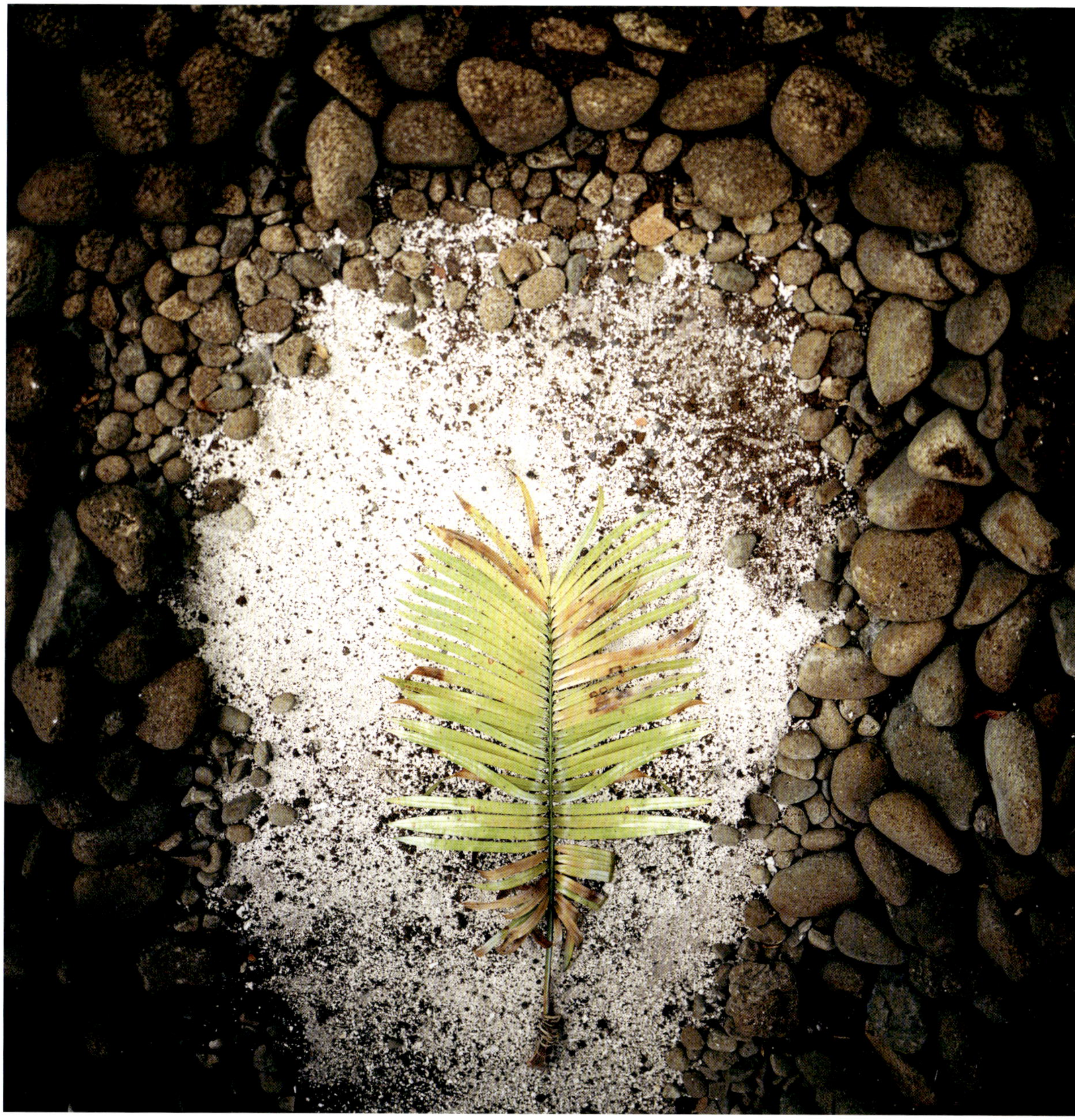

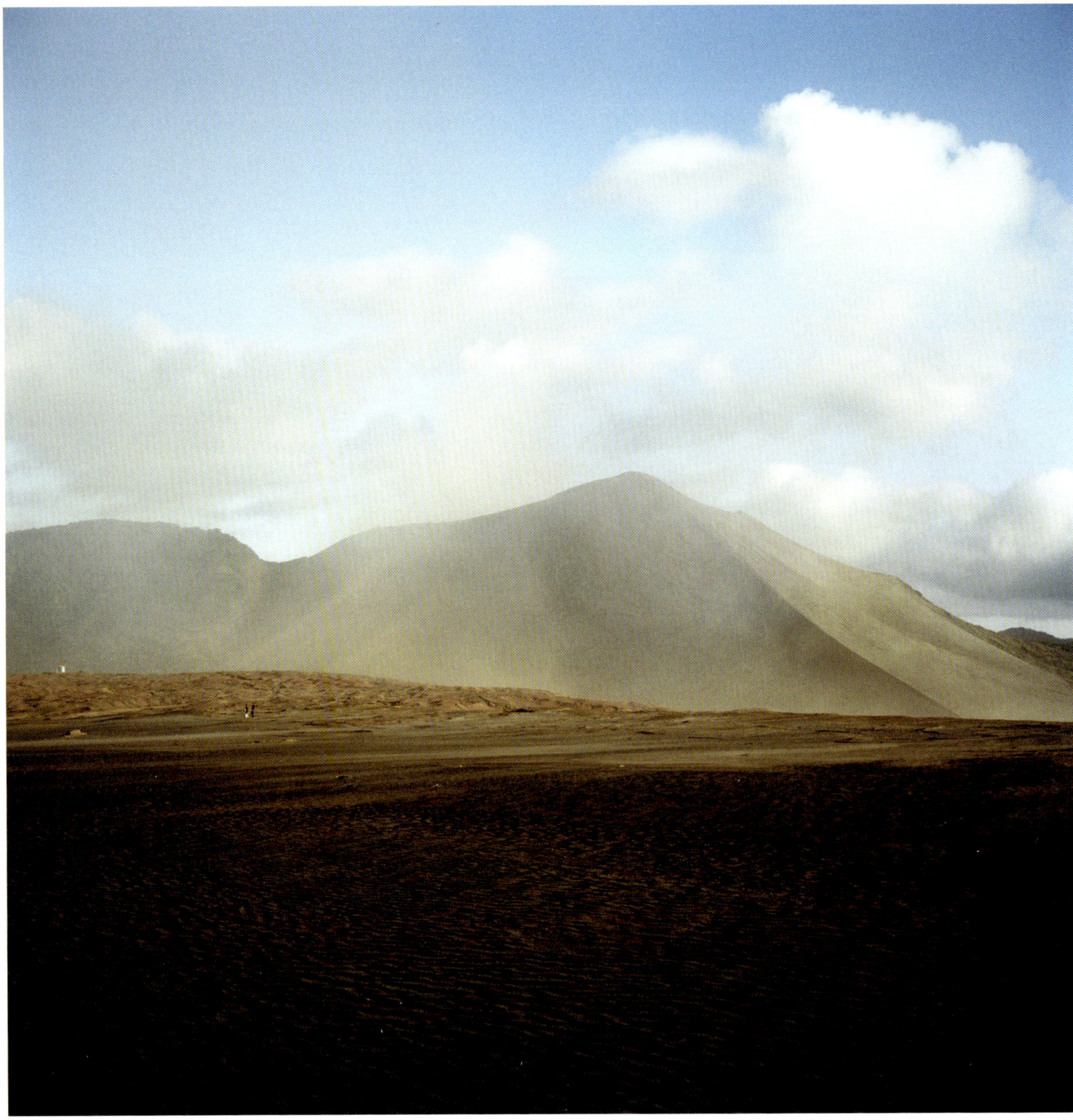

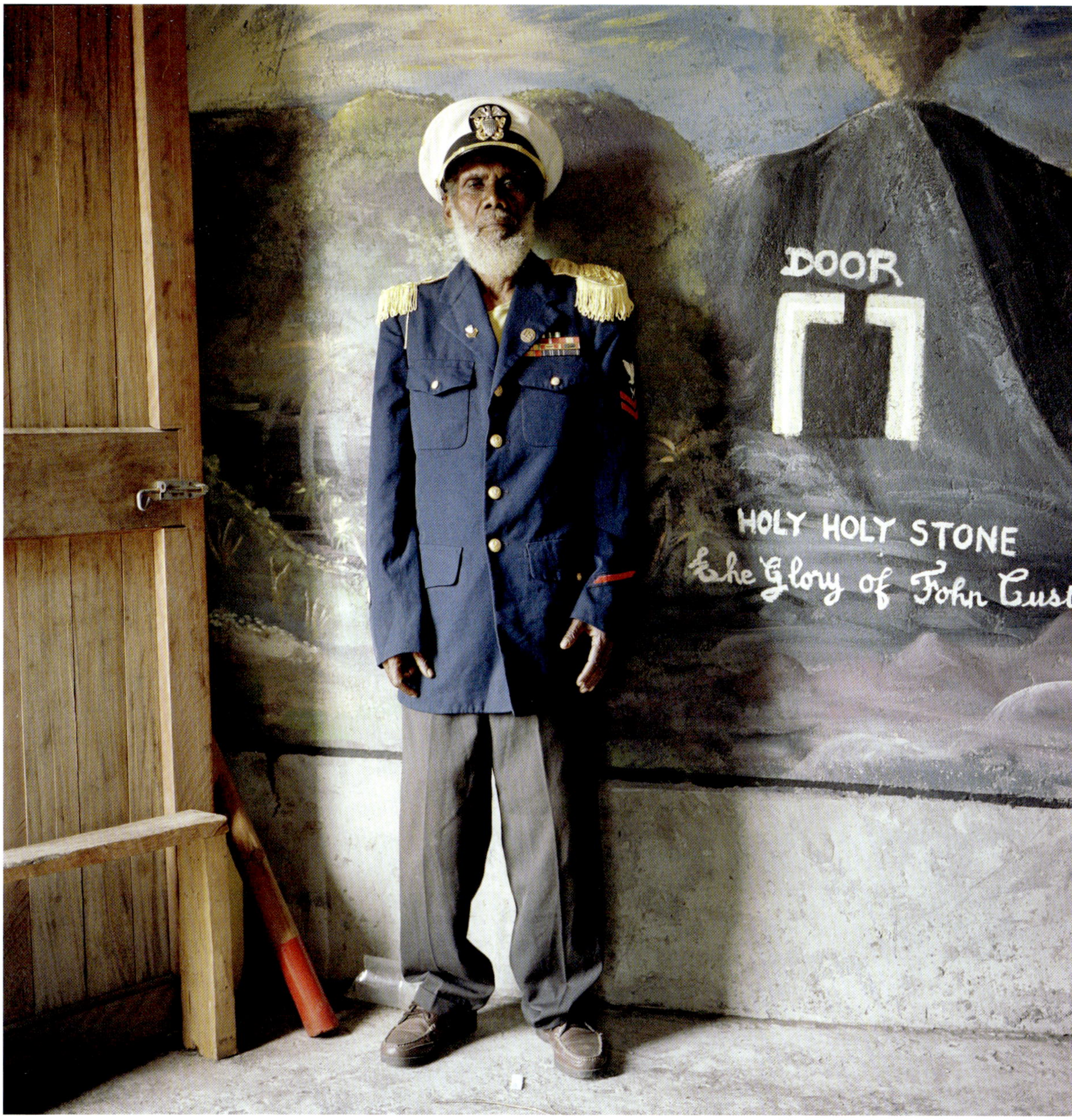

Chief Isaac Wan, Sulphur Bay, Tanna

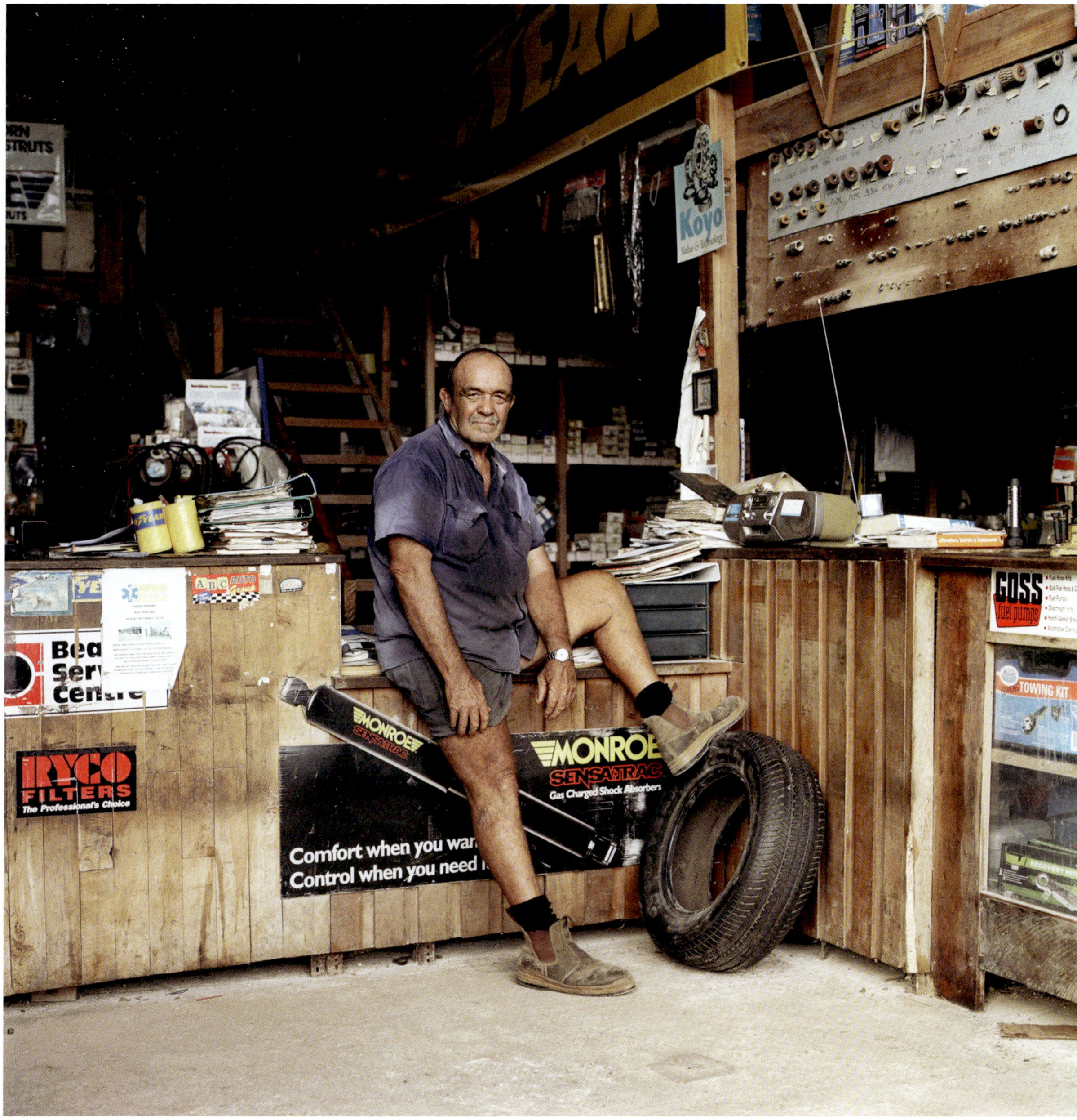
RYCO
FILTERS
The Professional's Choice
MONROE
SENSA-TRAC
Gas Charged Shock Absorbers
Koyo
GOSS
fuel pumps
TOWING KIT

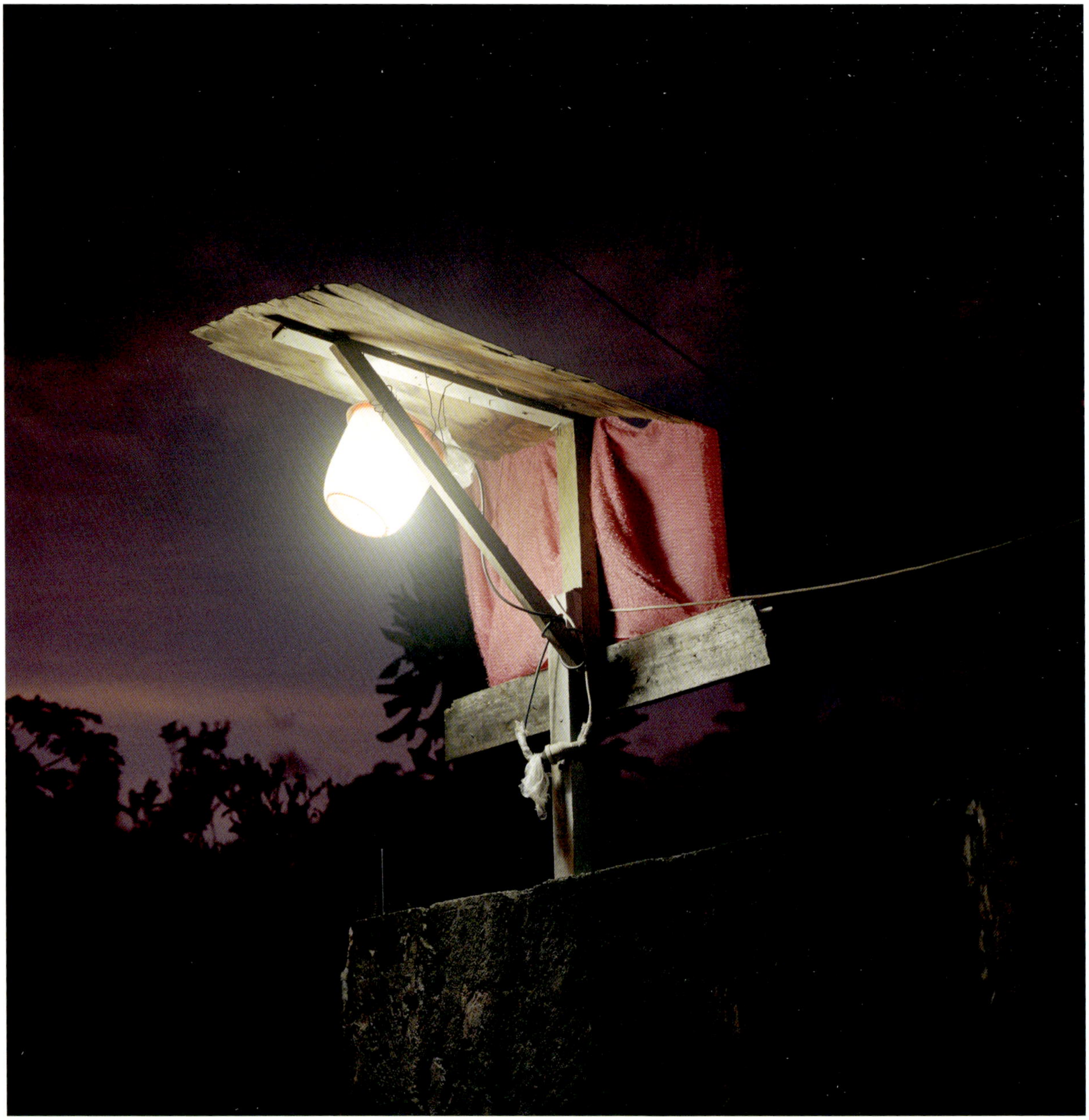

Elder West, Mormon Missionary from Idaho

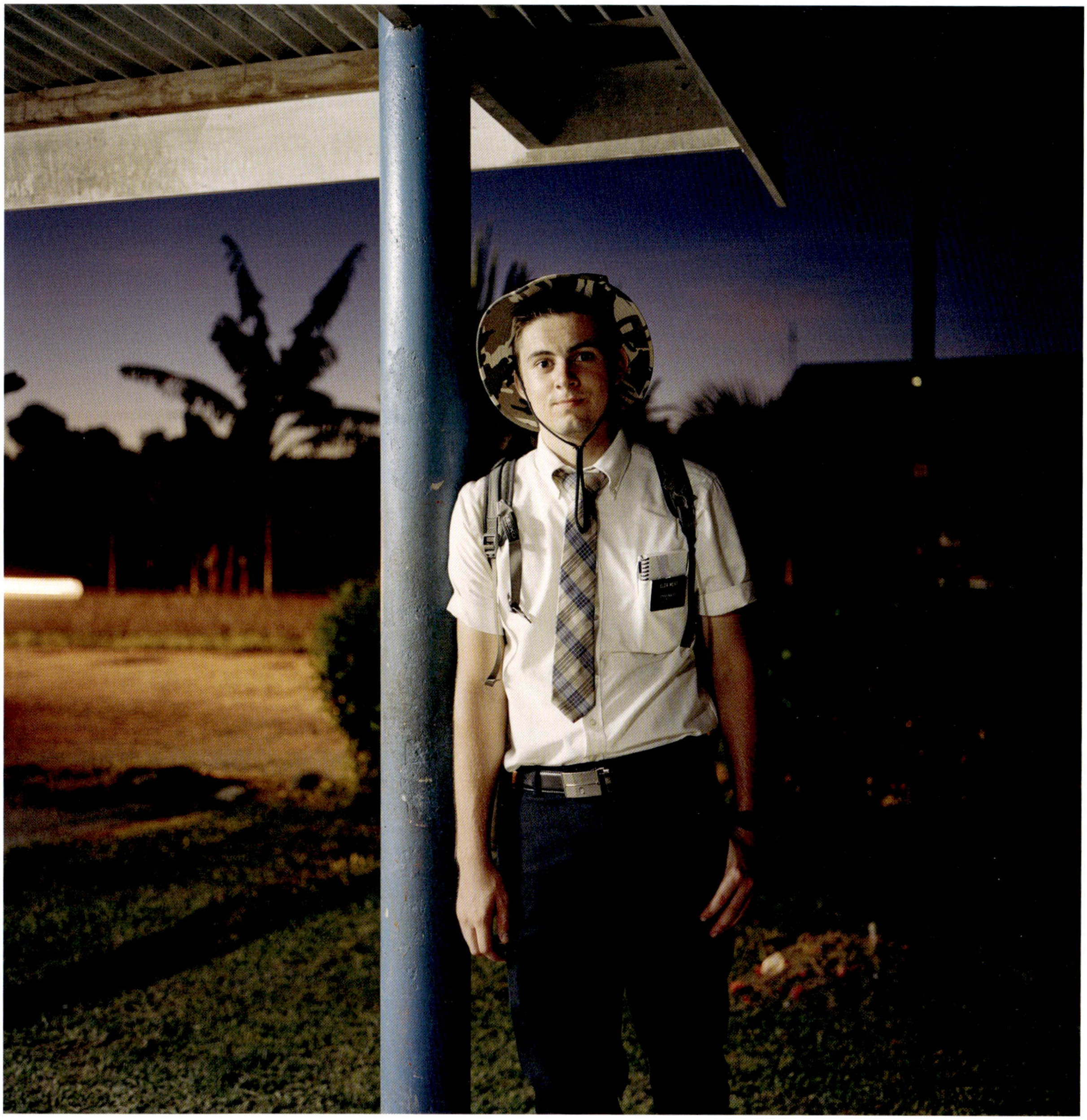

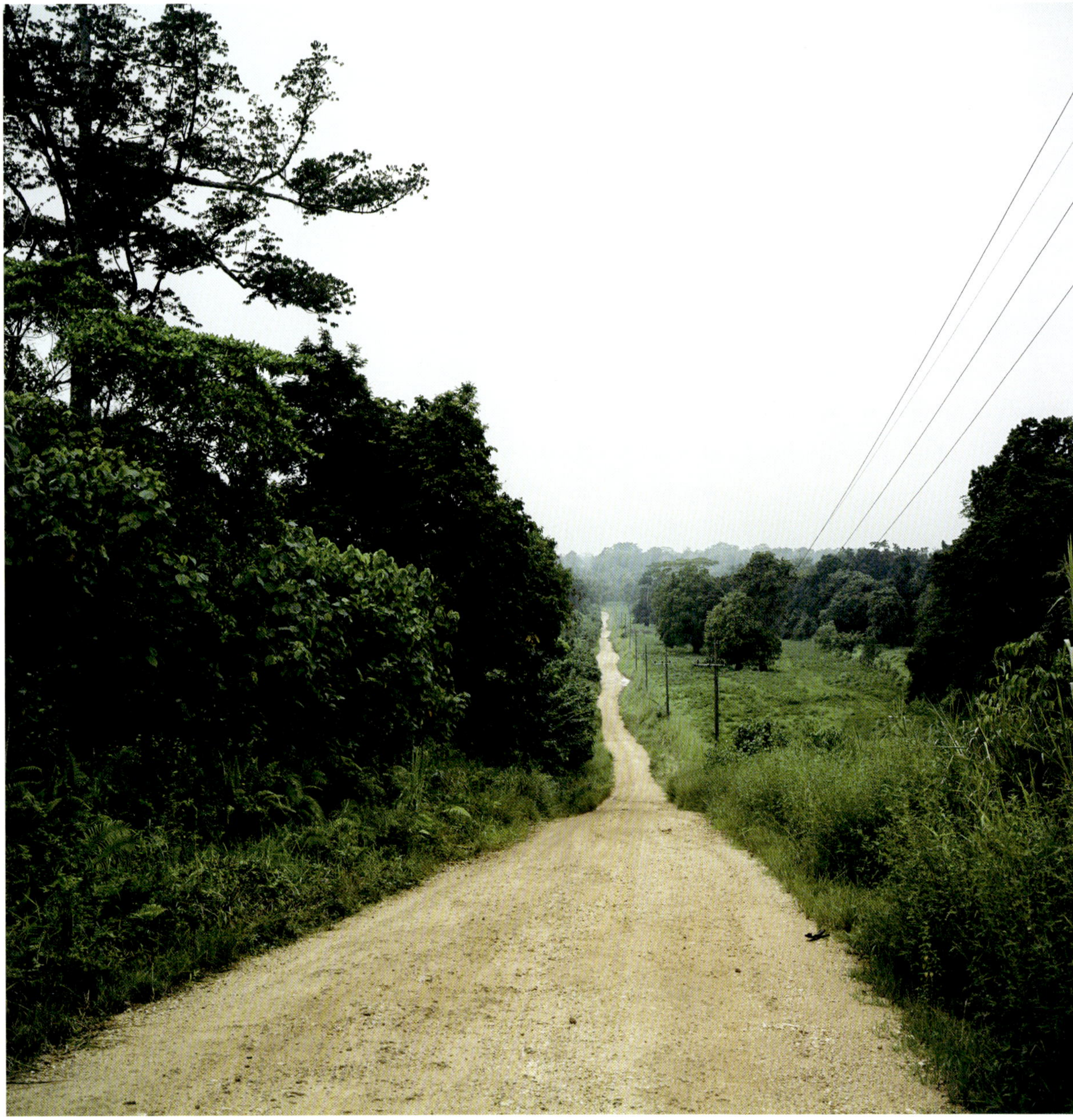

THE CORONATION

One of the earliest descriptions of John Frum in print was written, surprisingly, by a Catholic priest, Reverend Patrick O'Reilly, who heard that parishioners on Tanna were neglecting Jesus in favour of another magical foreigner. Writing in a 1950 issue of the Pacific Islands Monthly, O'Reilly described Frum as, "A mysterious little man with bleached hair, a high pitched voice, and clad in a coat with shining buttons." He promised riches and eternal youth.

Jon and I did eventually meet a mysterious little man loosely matching O'Reilly's description: Claude-Philippe Berger, 'King of the Royal House of Tanna', whose gala in Berlin I described earlier.

Claude's royal claim rides on the spirit of Frum – when he returns to run his kingdom, the prophecy will be complete – but unlike many of the Frum-fanciers who come to Vanuatu, this story has a historical origin.

At the foot of one of Tanna's many banyan trees is a stele wedged into the dirt and bracken. The name 'Antoine Fornelli' is etched into its surface. A local chief called Willy tended to the stele until he died, and he showed Jon and I several chunky medals and medallions that were given to him by Fornelli; they had worked together for independence of the island, the chief explained, during a short period in the 1970s when this man Antoine was installed as the first king of Tanna.

Antoine Fornelli was born in 1919 in Corsica. He became a gunmaker and served in the French army. As a child, he pleaded for his parents to buy him a gun and his life was a search for the kind of self-reliance that's often talked up by those who bear arms.

He fought in the French Resistance, refusing to hand over his weapons at the war's end, then he enlisted with the Foreign Legion in the last years of French Indochina. After the war, Fornelli lived with his wife and young children in Lyon but found civilian life tedious. One day, he came across an advert in a hunting magazine for a coconut plantation in the New Hebrides. Fornelli bought the plantation, legend has it with the cash he made from selling his collection of antique weaponry, and moved his family out to Port Vila in 1967.

At the time, the New Hebrides were jointly governed by Britain and France. It was, by most accounts, confused: each side had its own schools and administrations, its own respective police force (with both HM's bobbies and cap-wearing gendarmes) often at loggerheads with the other.

An independence movement was growing, spearheaded by islanders who'd gone through the local English education system. By the 1970s the UK government was keen to see a transition to indigenous rule within the following decade. For both French-speaking Ni-Vanuatus and the French plantation owners who cultivated great swathes of the New Hebrides, the fear was that post-independence their interests would be sidelined and their farms expropriated if the new Anglophone elites got their way.

Fornelli shared these concerns. But he had a sniffy attitude to the expats in Port Vila. "He was a bit of a rogue," recalled Anne Naupa, the long-standing, Welsh-born archivist at the National Library of Vanuatu, who said Fornelli could be found drinking on the boat he used for shark fishing.

When the Fornellis arrived, the farmhouse was in rack and ruin. Antoine used to say that it rained more inside than out. He also had no experience of farming coconuts. So he hired a group of French-speaking Ni-Vanuatus to help him on the plantation. These men were from Tanna island and had come to the capital looking for work, and the boss was reportedly generous with pay and cigarettes.

to trouble

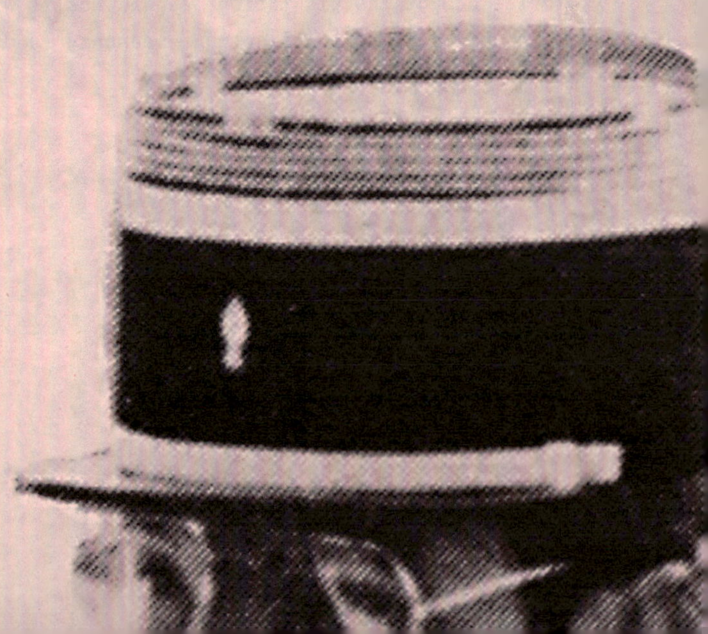

As the weeks went by Fornelli heard his crew discussing a prophecy about a messiah from a far away land. John Frum would bring them freedom and development; a champion of native rights. When he returned, the land would be equally shared. They could go back to Tanna to till their own gardens. Blacks and whites would be equal, planters and indigenous land-owners would coexist in harmony.

Hearing all this, Fornelli's thoughts took a significant turn. Over time, he too came to think that the island where his workers came from, Tanna, shouldn't be part of any independence project designed by the English. Instead, they should rule themselves according to pre-colonial, pre-missionary *kastom* ways. All they needed was a leader who could stand up for them on the world stage. Now, he may have been befuddled by booze or the long hot nights when the power conked out, but Fornelli came to believe that he was the kind of man the island was waiting for.

What followed was as wily as any fiction. In 1971, Fornelli went to Tanna for the first time, motoring into the north of the island on his fishing boat where he was received by a group of villagers who called him 'Tony'. They explained that independence, in which all 83 islands in the New Hebrides would form the new nation, was just another step in the church's long-held ambition to eradicate their traditions by subsuming tribal structures under the rule of a centralised elite in Port Vila.

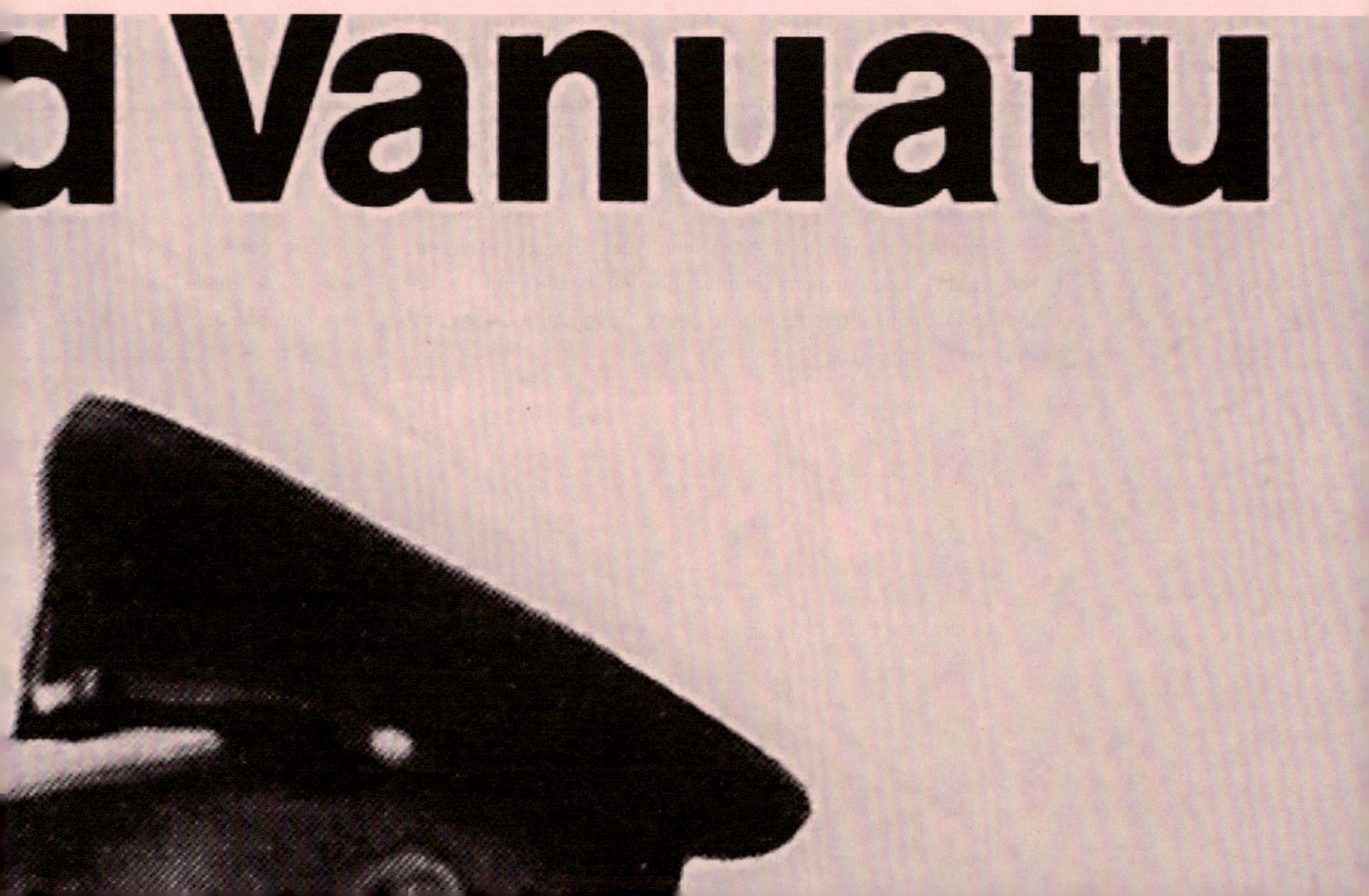

Over a couple of years of going back and forth to Tanna, Tony gained a sizeable following. It turned militaristic; the old gunmaker took to wearing a red paratrooper's beret and machined medals for the chiefs, giving them rank and file titles. They planned to make Tanna an independent nation in its own right, ruled by traditional *kastom* and the chiefs, with Fornelli's oversight over all four corners of the island. Hence the name given to their movement, Forcona, which was supposedly inspired by a brand of corned beef sold at the time.

On March 24 1974, a flag was hoisted that was Pacific blue with a yellow circle and a green star (the same flag we would see propped up in a Berlin business hotel some 40 years later). To mark the occasion, Fornelli gifted a restored World War Two Mauser rifle to one of the northern chiefs.

The colonial administration was worried about Fornelli. Rabble-rousing among the 'natives' was one thing; giving them guns quite another. Then word went round that the Forcona group were going to declare their independence on June 22. British and French police drove up to the north of the island and after a few scuffles confiscated the flag and the old Mauser. Fornelli, however, was nowhere to be found.

He was holed up on his plantation in Port Vila preparing to face his destiny. By this point, Fornelli had largely distanced himself from expatriate society, and his family. A young French photojournalist called François Giner was his confidant, and he asked him to come along to Tanna as press attaché.

Today, Giner lives in the shadow of a volcano in the Philippines. We met up in Paris during one of his rare trips home. Now in his 70s, Giner arrived wearing camo trousers with a baseball cap hooked onto a belt loop. Under one arm he had a folder of dusty negatives, which he laid out on the dining table, and animatedly described the extraordinary events to which he was witness.

"We got to the north of Tanna just before sunrise. And as we came up the hill, I could hear chanting: 'An-toine! An-toine!' There were about a thousand people gathered in the village and I realised then the scale of what was happening."

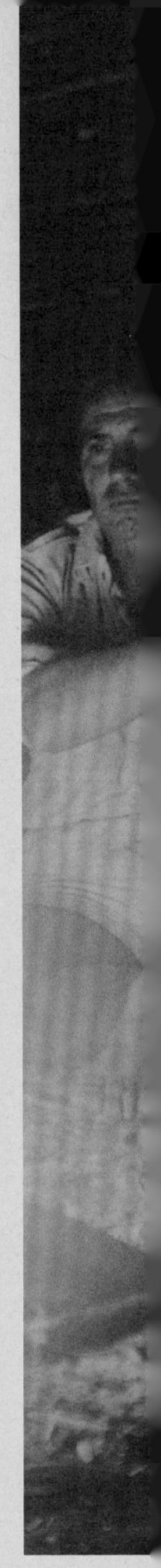

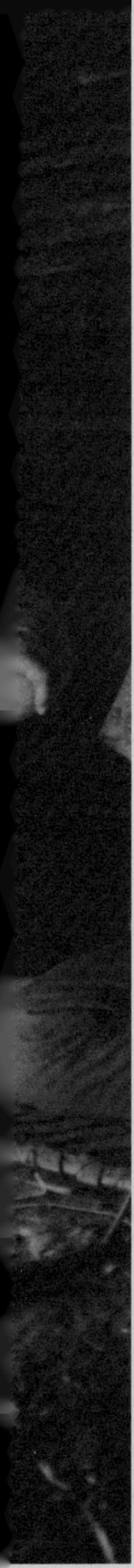

The photographer was shown to his own hut and, at dusk, found Fornelli brooding fireside. "He said to me, 'Tomorrow will be a big day, when I'll be crowned the king of Tanna.'" Giner paused. He held up a negative of Fornelli sitting on an earthen floor, a roaring campfire next to him. "I think somehow he lost himself then. In his mind he was thinking like John Frum; I think he was disturbed by the realisation of the power. And in a way he knew that he needed to go home."

The next day the 'coronation' happened. "I'll never forget this image in my life," Giner said. "My camera was six by six and I watched through the lens as Antoine came out of his hut." He stood up straight-backed, mimicking the militaristic rigmarole that by then was core to the Forcona movement. "Antoine pinned a medal on each of the chiefs, and held up the blue flag with the star on it. Then one of the chiefs said, 'Antoine Fornelli, king of Tanna.' And all the villagers shouted the same thing."

The new nation didn't last long. The French gendarmes broke up the party at dawn and in response, Fornelli wrote a letter addressed to the Queen of England and the President of France, demanding that the colonial district agents leave the young Nation or face 'armed hostilities'. Naturally, that didn't happen. Forty policemen stormed the Forcona village, to be met by men with pikes and bows and arrows who were arrested along with the local chiefs and, eventually, Fornelli in his bare feet.

The Forcona chiefs were chucked in jail while the foreigner was deported to New Caledonia, a French possession, and banned from returning to Tanna. From a prison cell in Tanna, where he was first detained, Tony sent a letter to the French commissioner: 'This nation will always find in its path, the weapons and despotism of powerful nations still encumbered with outdated colonialism,' he wrote. 'Born on 24 March 1974, the nation of Tanna was overthrown on 29 June 1974.'

Making sense of Fornelli's motivations is difficult. Most chroniclers of the period cast him as an agitator who initially set out to preserve French interests on the islands but got carried away by the mythos that swirls around Vanuatu.

We managed to track down one of Fornelli's sons, Frederic, who has one of the blue flags of independent Tanna hanging in his house in Lyon.

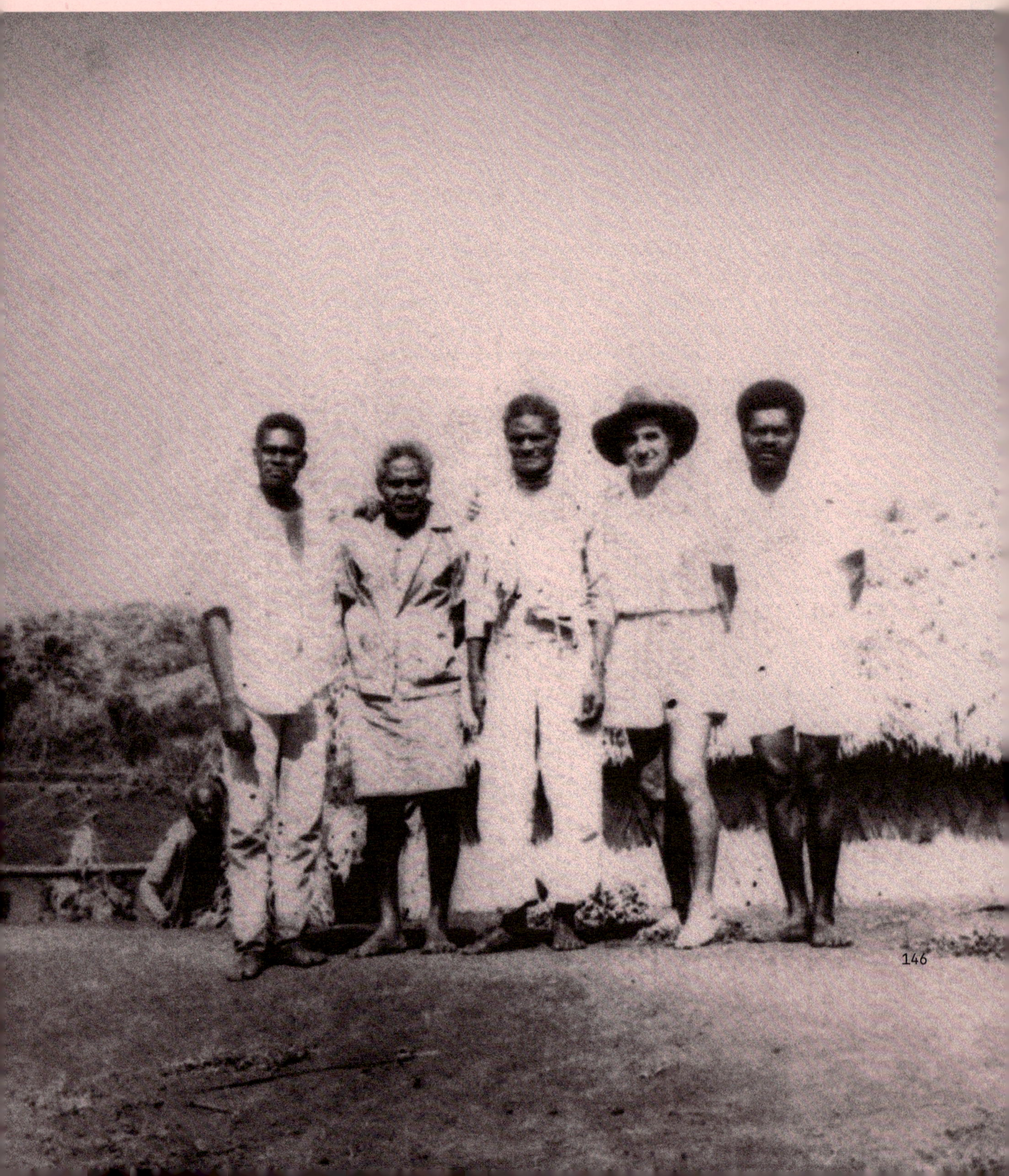

"My father was one of the last adventurers," Frederic told us. "He liked the people of Tanna and he fought for them. Certainly, in the beginning, he never wanted to be what he became. The environment pushed him to be like that. And then he continued until it became a sort of sport for him, and couldn't stop."

Frederic remembered Fornelli giving him a Winchester pistol for his 12th birthday. "What happened in Tanna was all part of his destiny, he was a fascinating character – I admire him but I don't always agree with him. He was not a good father."

Close study of Giner's photographs reveal a man with self-conscious eyes, a boyish desire to be cast as the ringleader – Butch Cassidy amongst the Sundance kids. Why else would he bring a photographer along to document his adventures?

Something else lurks in the images too: memories perhaps from his foreign legion days, helping beat back independence movements in France's name. Perhaps remote Vanuatu was somewhere he could fashion a new story for himself with his indigenous army.

In Joseph Conrad's novel Lord Jim, a young man grows up believing that he'll one day be a heroic sailor but disgraces himself on the job, then spends restless years drifting from port to port in search of retribution, fleeing east any time he overhears anyone talking about his past. Beyond the Makassar Straits he encounters a tribe being oppressed by bandits. Defending the tribe against these marauders, Jim is hailed as 'Lord Jim', their white rajah, and for a time finds peace believing he's become a hero, even if no one from home is around to see it.

We don't know how things stacked up for Fornelli. Claude-Philippe Berger could tell us surprisingly little about the character of the man. In Claude's telling of it, they met at a Masonic meeting in Paris in the '90s when Fornelli was seeking treatment for a terminal illness. He saw a kindred soul, someone who could continue his work – his kingdom in absentia – and in 1999, shortly before he died, abdicated in favour of his younger friend.

If Tony was a character out of Conrad then Claude-Philippe was more Walter Mitty. Where Fornelli donned military berets and safari shorts,

Claude indulged in pomp, from the tailored white jacket and medals to the year-round calendar of soirées and ribbon-cuttings around Europe.

In 2018, Jon and I visited Claude in Nice, where he lived. We met in the golden glow of the seafront (Claude said his house was undergoing repairs), and the king reeled off a litany of extraordinary claims about his aristocratic blood, and high-flying diplomatic career. He'd once returned a gift of a Bentley from the Saudi ambassador. At one point, he even claimed to have been inside the Ka'aba in Mecca. "I've lived seven lifetimes in one," he said, wistfully.

However hard we tried to get a sense of who Claude actually was, he would veer off into grandiose anecdotes about his dutiful role. He went on about how Tanna would be an important place geopolitically in the future and that he and the royal house were working to bring real change to the lives of the people there. The only time we glimpsed a person behind all this was when we mentioned the princess, who had left him after the Berlin gala – and he looked genuinely sad.

The royal story, which swelled exponentially throughout that afternoon in Nice, allowed Claude's love of theatricality to run riot. But it was unclear what else he got out of being the 'king of Tanna'. He insisted that the counts and countesses didn't fund his lifestyle, and that a family inheritance and the payouts from a motorcycle crash in Paris some years ago kept him afloat. All royal visits to Tanna had, so far, been borne on the air miles of a wealthy American count – "In business class!" said Claude, gleefully. There's no willing harem waiting for him there either because, he explained, touching him was taboo.

For the counts and countesses who attend the galas, their motivations are outwardly philanthropic, inwardly provincial. Mostly, it's the thrill of being swept up in an elaborate cosplay where tropical kings and princesses cavort around in laundered finery, knighting each other in conference suites. They get to clink glasses with – as one count put it to us – "a cast of characters like something off the Cluedo board" and in doing so, slough off their lives in Europe and America as landlords or bosses or retirees. For a night, they become a fixture in the group's collective imagination.

Claude-Philippe readily dismissed any suggestion that he was not a real king. It was only "jealous whites" who said that. He claimed to have had some recognition from other European monarchs, including the Queen of England. Apparently, the chiefs told Claude they'd prophesied a man from the French Riviera would one day arrive, and he maintained that Tanna should one day be an independent country with him in situ as a 'traditional king'.

On the islands themselves, this view became hazy: Passing round photographs of the king in his courtly gear tended to elicit a bemused response from most islanders. Very few, we found, knew who he was.

He did have a right-hand man on Tanna called Tom Kuai, a stern Ni-Vanuatu whose father Willy, mentioned earlier, was one of the original Forcona chiefs working with Antoine Fornelli in the 1970s. Tom happened across the Maison Royale de Tanna's website while researching the life of the much-fabled Antoine, and reached out. This led to the king's first visit to Tanna in 2011, and the almost miraculous reception he received when large numbers of old Forcona members and their descendants greeted him off the plane.

Claude made all sorts of pledges on that first visit. Tom Kuai told us that the islanders were still waiting for the full promise of John Frum to come true: "Fornelli did one part already," he said. "But now we are waiting for Maison Royale to bring more development to Tanna." So is Claude-Phillipe recognised as king on the island? To this he was oblique, but did remark, "We know we have a traditional king in exile."

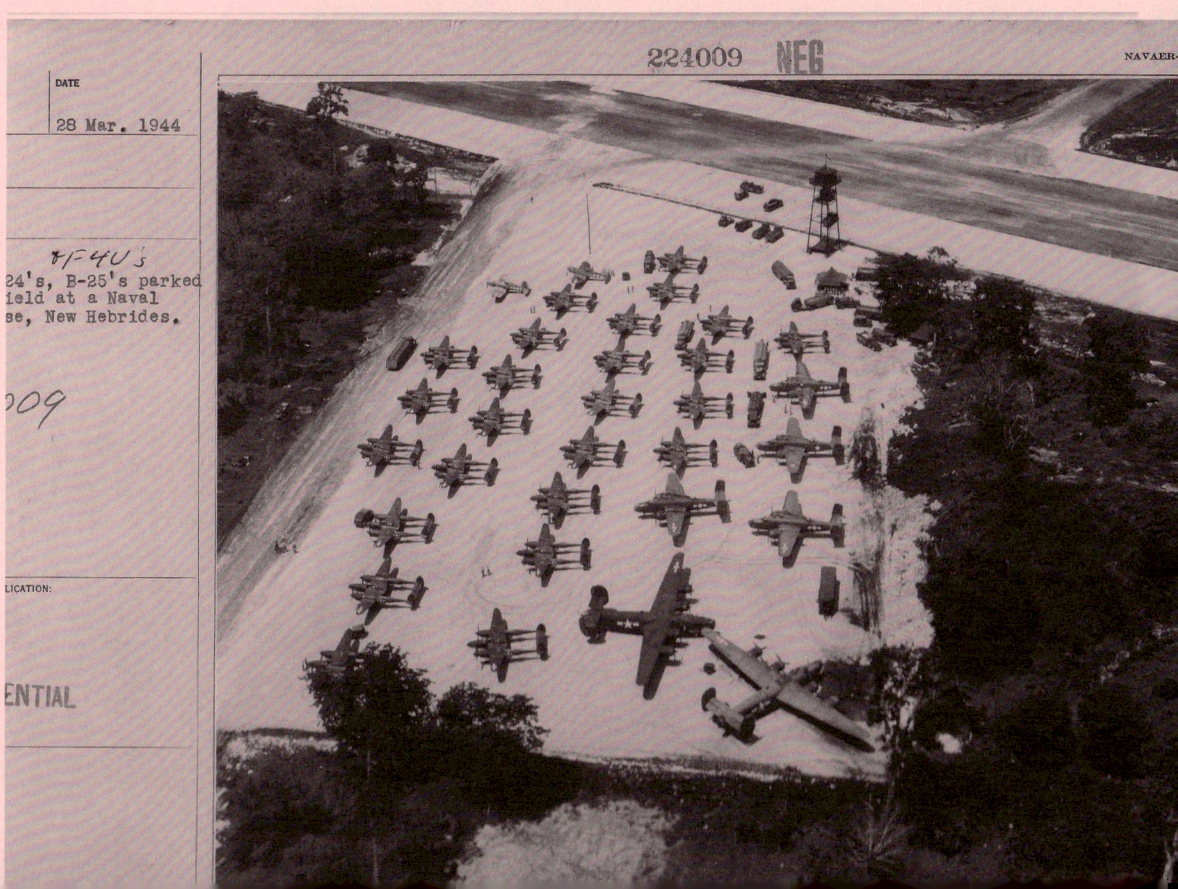

Tom Kuai administered the donations sent from the royal house to Tanna, including shipments of solar lights and water tanks. It was explained to us that, in the bright future to come, the independent nation of Tanna would have Tom for its chief.

There were ambitious counts among the ranks too. They whispered about the prospect of diplomatic passports, and dreamt of developing tourism and logistical businesses on the islands. King Claude could be a way in, perhaps, as a man with influence: the Maison Royale has over the years flown a few regional politicians from Vanuatu to their annual shindig in San Remo to curry official favour. Yet, for all this, the 'traditional king' still got the cold shoulder from central government.

Frederic Fornelli was unambiguous about the royal house: "It's a joke. I've never met this man," meaning Claude-Philippe, who he described as a 'usurper.' One of the Fornelli family went to Tanna several years ago and denounced the Maison Royale to the chiefs there. "This story belongs to my father, and was between him and the people of these islands."

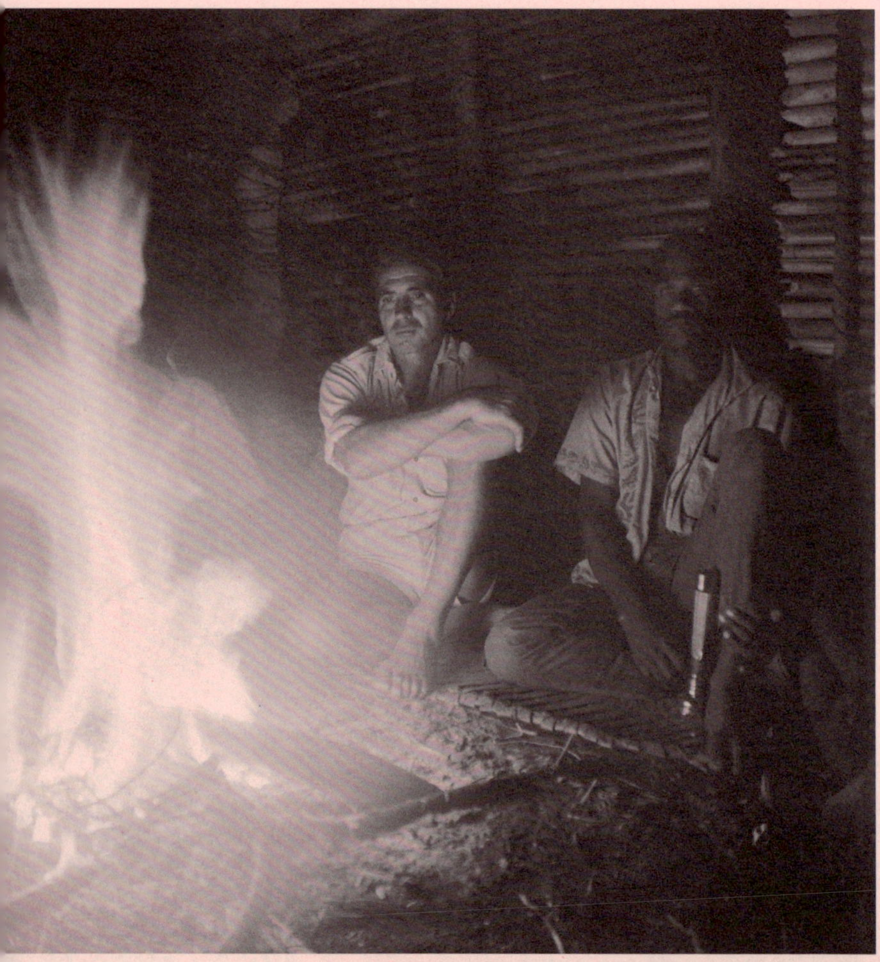

In March 2016, Claude was dispatched to Vanuatu (again on airmiles) for the annual Forcona day celebrations. It marked the day Fornelli first declared independent Tanna, and Claude was expected to attend. Jon and I met him in a polite crepe café in Port Vila, where he showed up wearing a garish yellow Hawaiian shirt and a nauseous pallor to match.

"I'm so very sick," Claude told us, and loudly imitated vomiting. He seemed fed up, tired, eager to get back to the Riviera.

Tom Kuai was also in tow, silent and suspicious of us, along with two other Ni-Vanuatus who were there as chaperones. One of them, a mean-looking man in blue overalls, snapped a few times that we should be more deferential to the king. But this felt more like a test of what we made of Claude's royal credentials rather than a real telling-off.

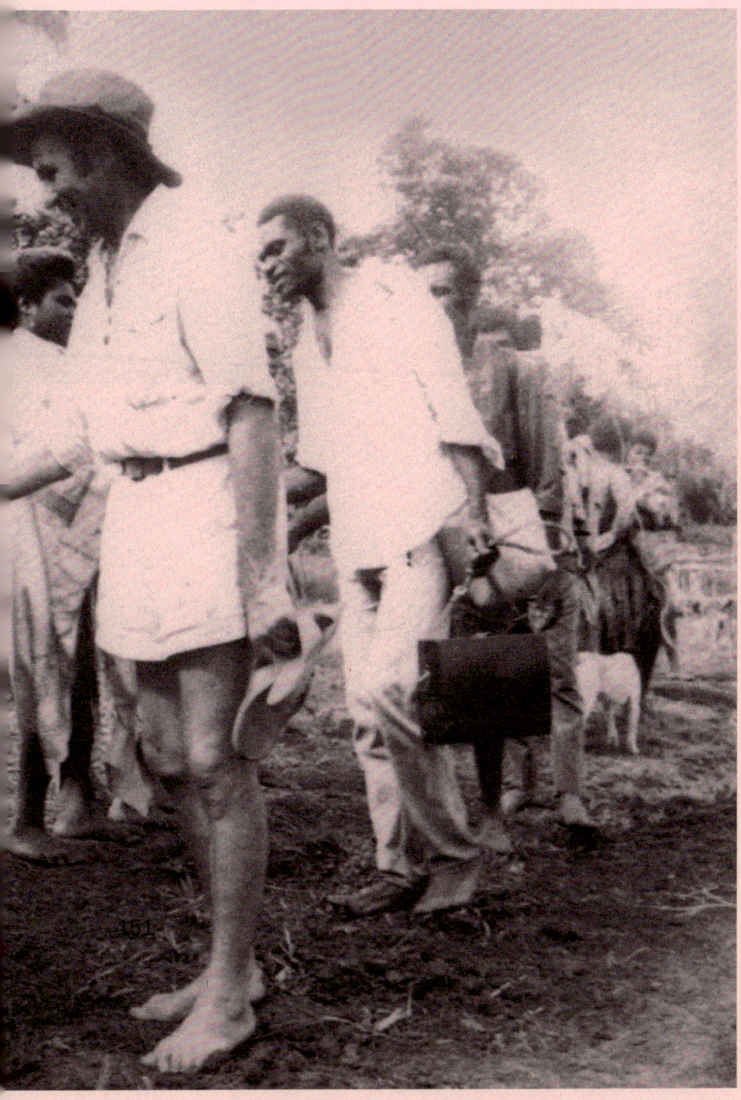

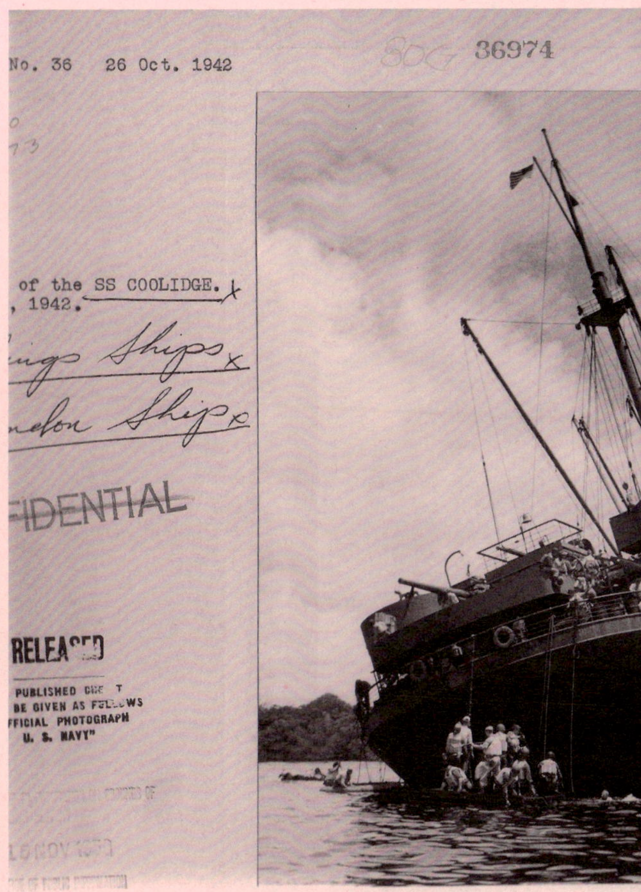

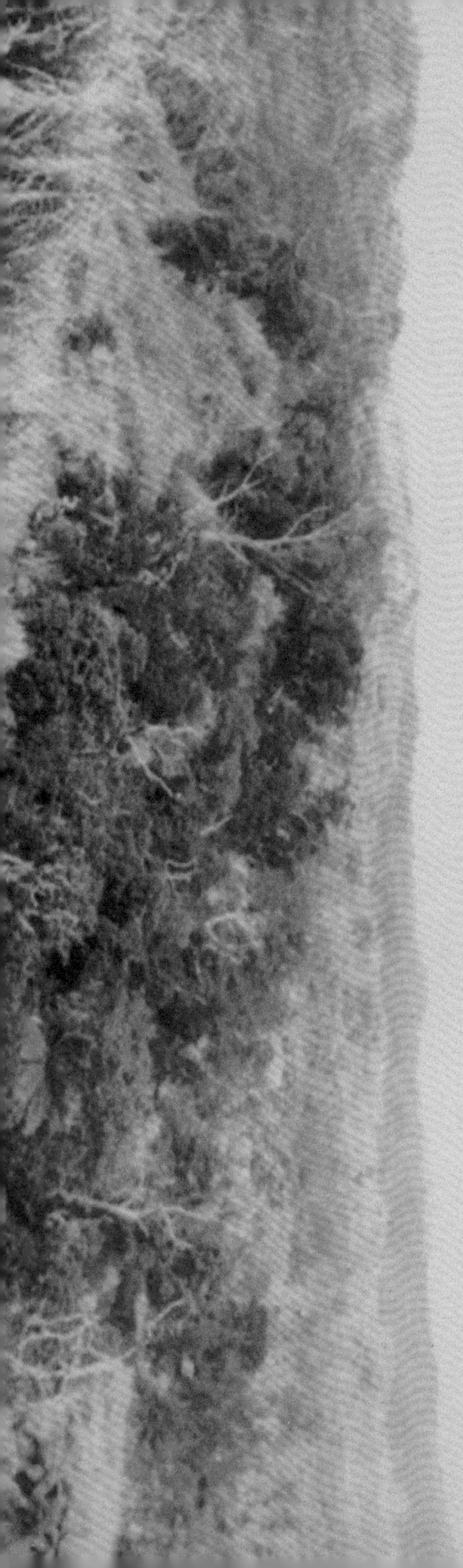

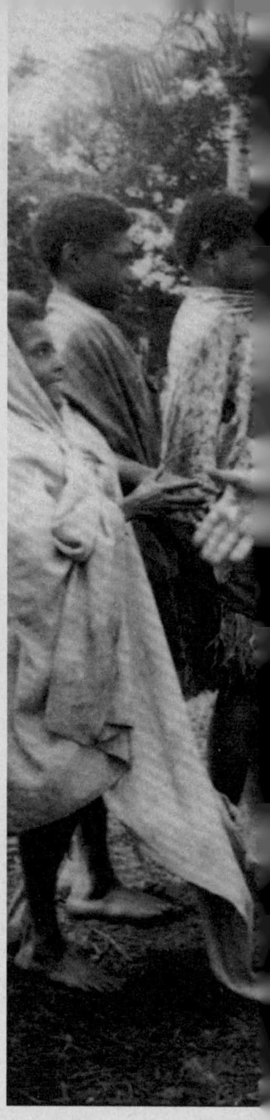

Claude wasn't well enough to travel on to Tanna for the proper Forcona party, we were informed. A small gathering would be held at his hotel in Port Vila instead.

It had rained all week. Water gushed out of the gutters and cascaded off the corrugated iron roofs, forcing Claude's small group of followers (mostly Tom Kuai's extended family) in from the garden to a cramped sitting room. His kids hung garlands around our necks and sang jaunty songs about Tanna, while Claude made a great show of laying out and talking us through all his various flags - the Berger coat of arms, that of the Maison Royale itself, and the Orthodox Church of the Pacific, for which he was a bishop. There were several costume changes - at one point he had a pontiff-like gown and cap on, anointing us all with a raised hand. The Ni-Vanuatu owner of the hotel occasionally popped his head around the corner and surveyed this scene with a cocked eyebrow.

It was clear to Jon and I that we were at the heart of the absurdity. Even Claude's usually hardy stomach for the dissonance between his royal affectations and the reality seemed to be wavering. Nevertheless, when the rain briefly subsided, we were told we couldn't leave without attending the traditional Forcona kava-drinking session at a nearby village.

To get there, we all piled into Tom Kuai's minivan, and turned off the highway onto a muddy track dotted with potholes.

The village was mostly migrant workers from Tanna. They had come to the capital looking for work, just like the original Ni-Vanuatus who had first inspired Fornelli. Under a great banyan tree, the men of the village were swilling kava mix in a plastic bucket.

A strange unease descended when we arrived. Claude had had the good sense to put his Hawaiian shirt back on, and stayed close to us. Still, he didn't let up: "All these people are here for me," he said with a magnanimous sweep of the hand.

By the time the kava was ready, people were steadily emerging from their homes and gathering under the banyan tree. The king was handed a coconut shell full of the earthen-smelling drink and together with Tom Kuai and a few other hangers on, they raised a toast to Fornelli and the bright future of independent Tanna. Claude, we noticed, had the merest sip then tried to palm the drink off on us, before giving the customary blow-out through the nose that is a libation offered to the old gods.

"Happy Forcona day!" shouted Tom Kuai. Was there a note of cynicism in his voice? The rest of the village watched on in silence with folded arms.

Night falls quickly in Vanuatu. As it did, more shells of kava were handed out. The tall grass around the village darkened. Torches and lanterns were lit and the hanging creepers of the banyan tree cast a chaos of shadows on the earth.

Amid the rising drunken clamour, it seemed the right time to say goodbye to Claude. We wished him well, even embraced him in the oddly charged feeling that we were leaving behind a sickly man who didn't really know why he was there, far from home, and – despite his pomposity – he wasn't so sure these rowdy people cared for him at all.

When we shook hands, Claude tried to explain something in English but instead just said, "Thank you, merci, thank you." Claude-Philippe Berger, traditional king of Tanna, scion of the Holy Roman Empire, gave us an imploring look, a high-pitched chuckle, and then we left him amid the creepers.

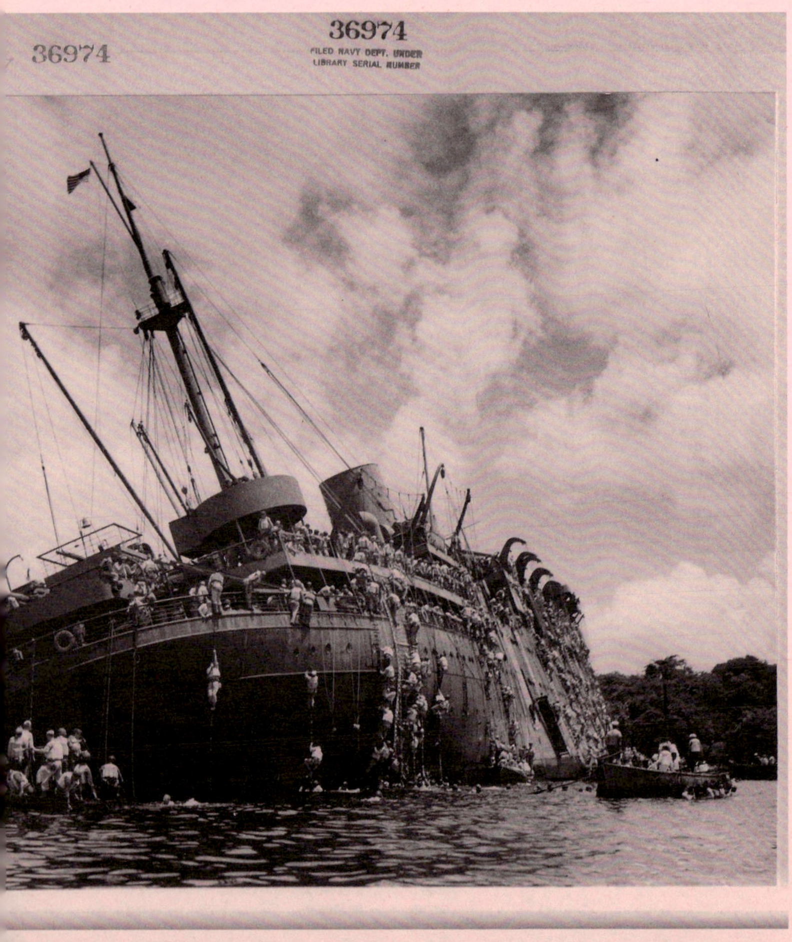

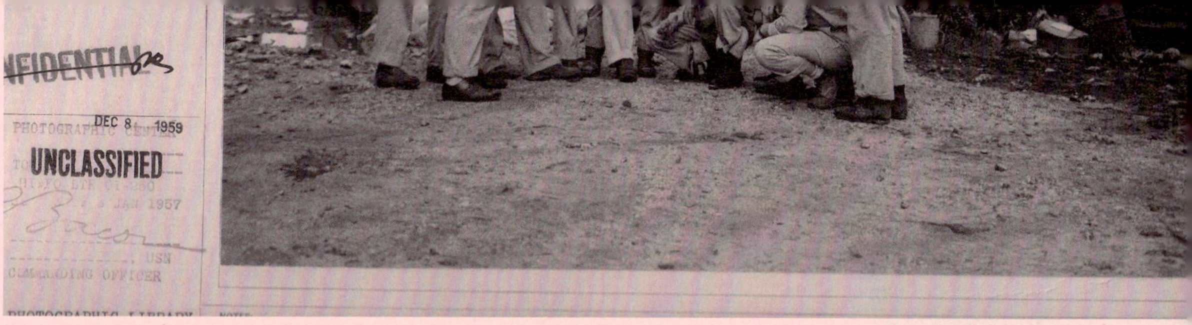
NFIDENTIAL
DEC 8 1959
UNCLASSIFIED
USN

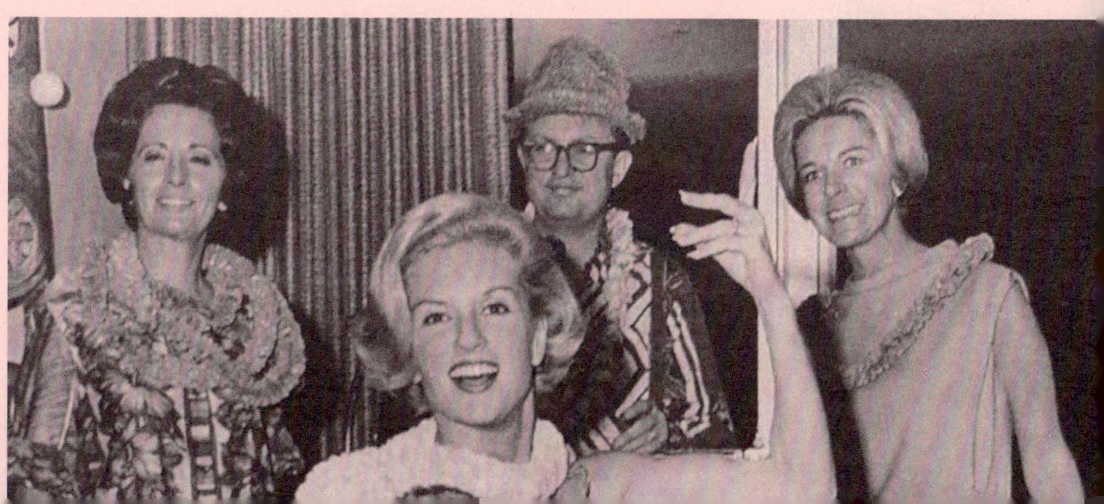

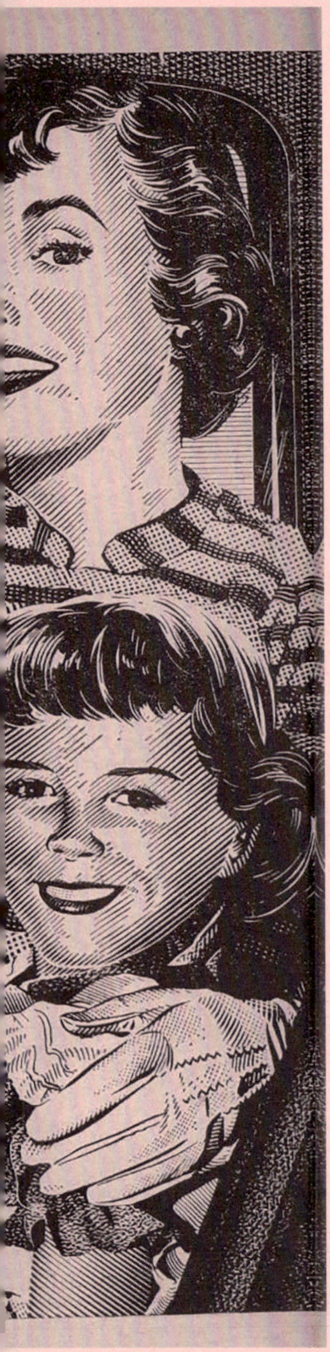

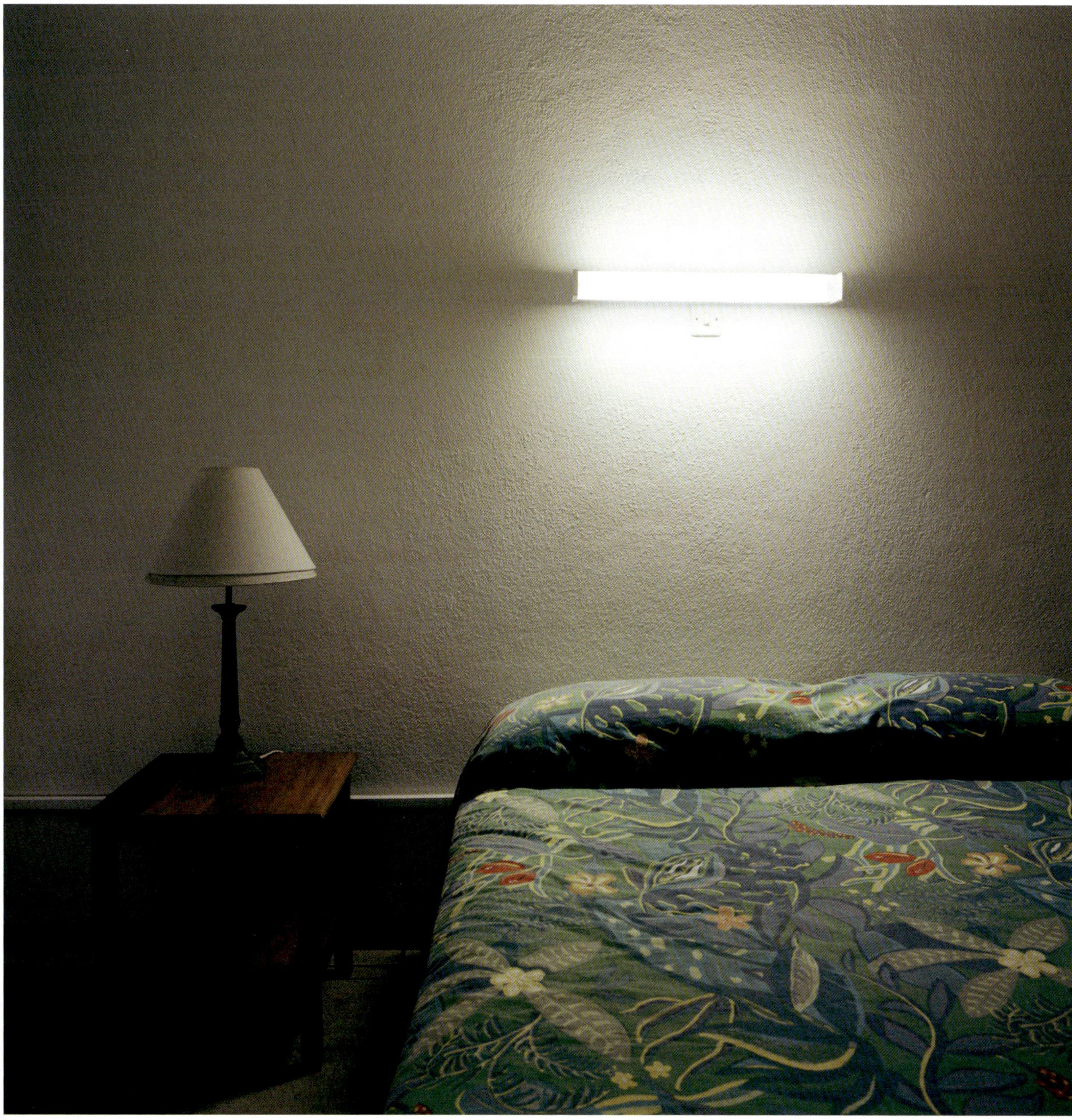

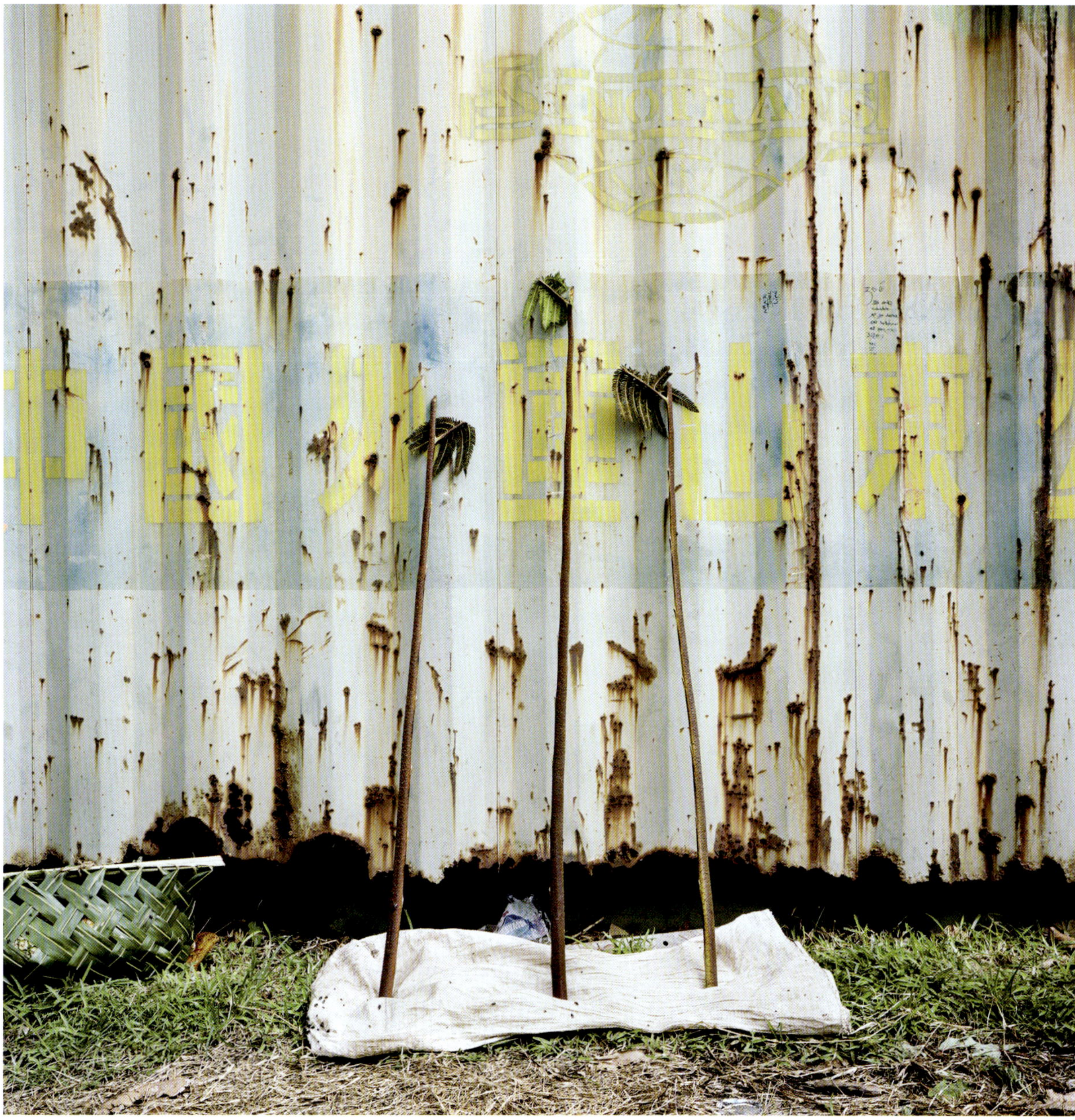

Ernest Kalkoa, WW2 Museum founder, Efate

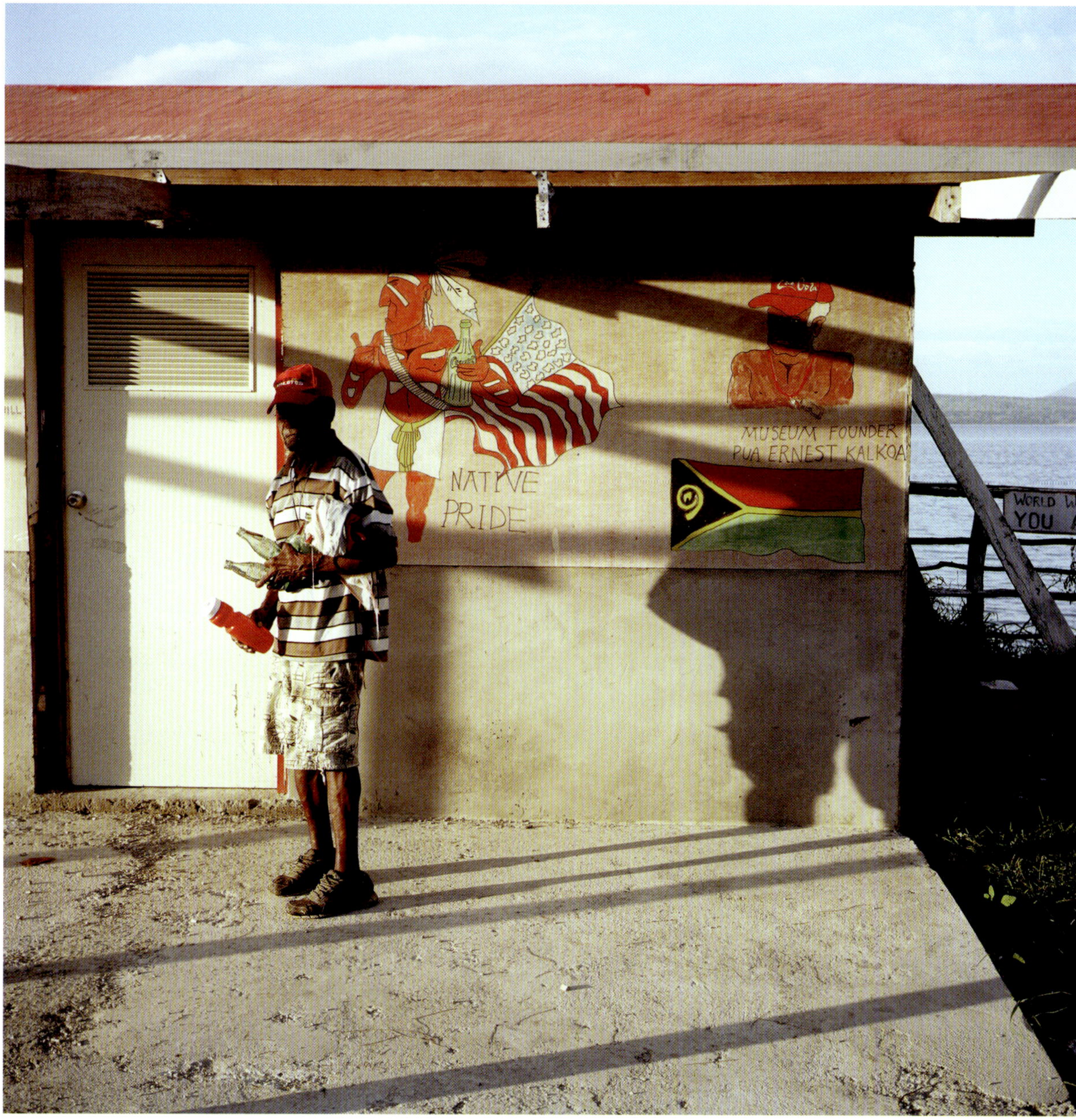
NATIVE
PRIDE
MUSEUM FOUNDER
PUA ERNEST KALKOA

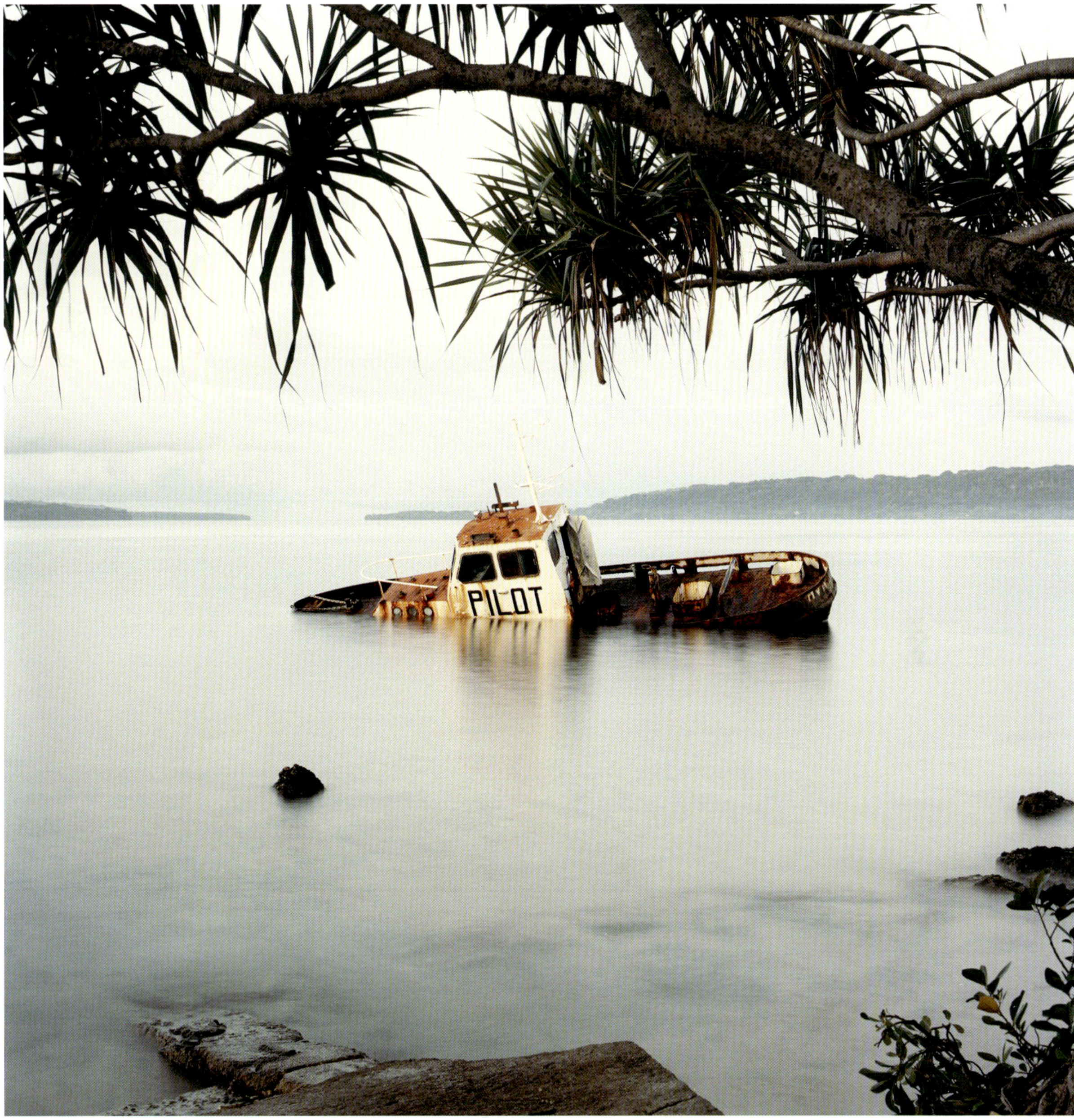
PILOT

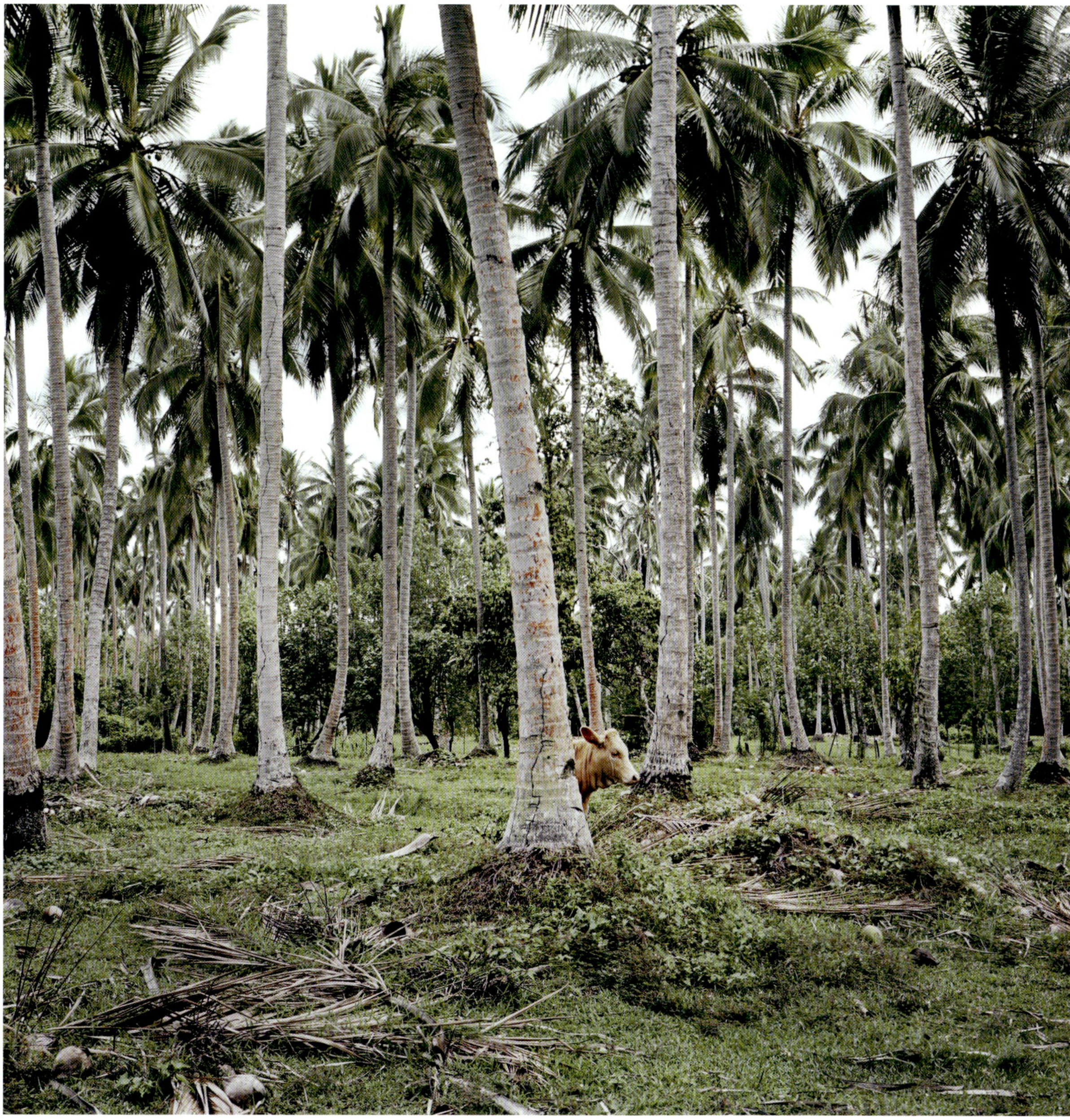

JT - What brought you here?

FB - I wanted a different life from Norway.

JT - How did you come across the tribe?

FB - Computer, internet. A lot of researching and then I found Yakel.

JT - How did you first make contact, did you come to Tanna?

FB - I came to Whitegrass airport, then I took a car to here. This was in the evening. I met a guy here and we talked some, and then I had a sleep here. It was nice, simple and nice.

JT - How long do you hope to stay for?

FB - I plan to stay here permanently.

Frank Alexander Berg (right) at Yakel Village with Jimmy Joseph Nako, Tanna

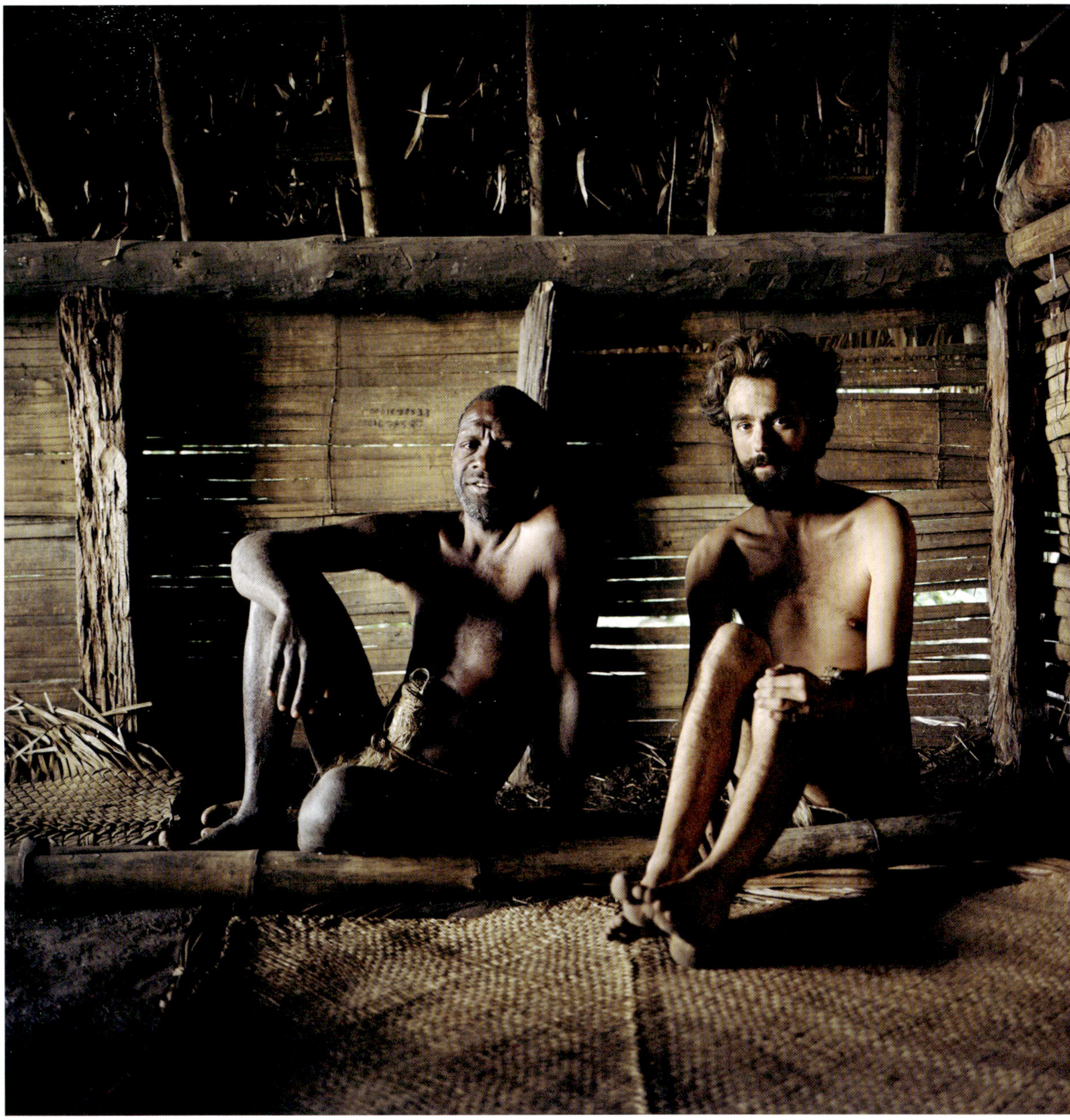

Gao Ying and Rosina Rapuen,
Brother Restaurant, Port Vila

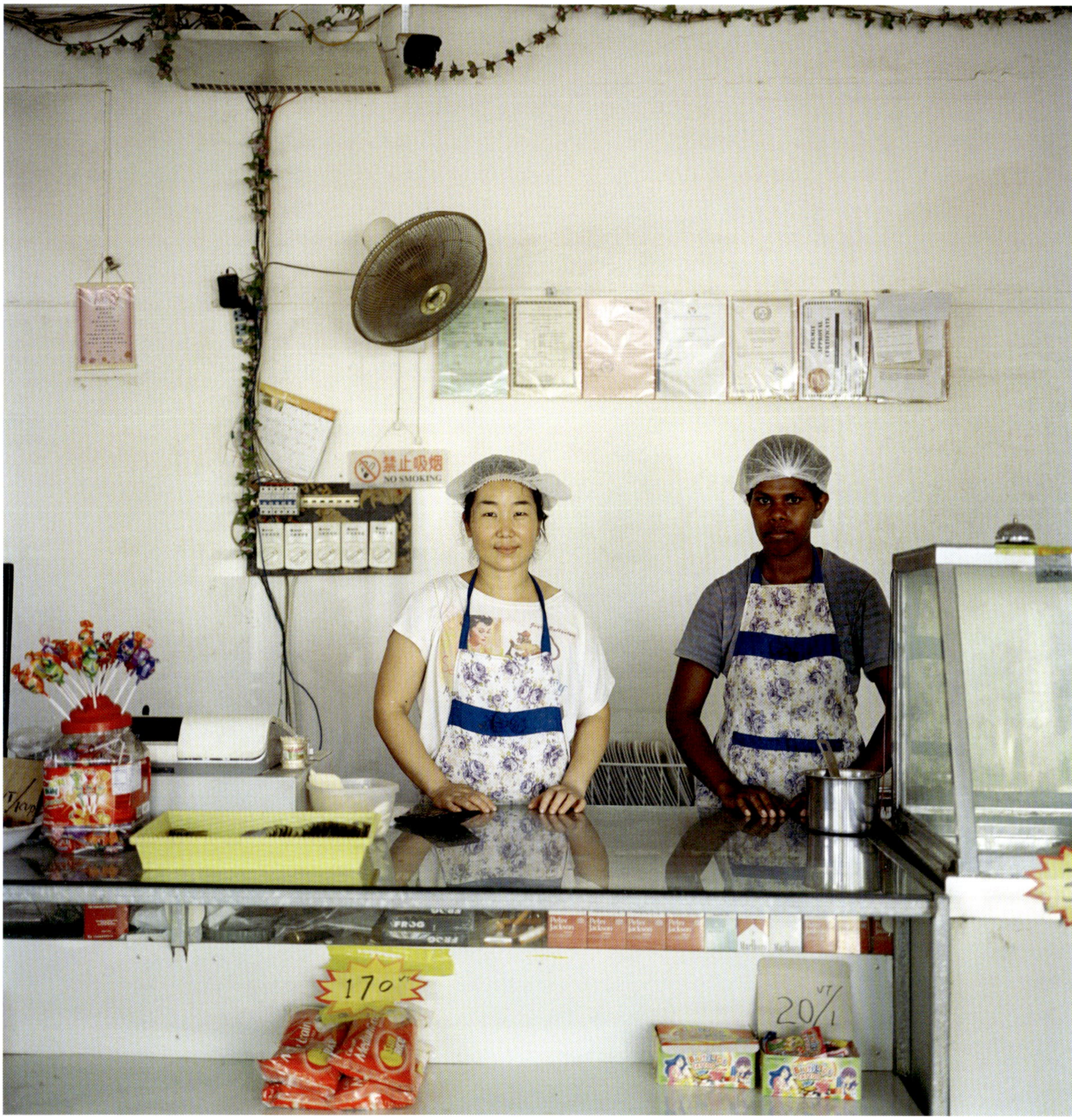
禁止吸烟
NO SMOKING

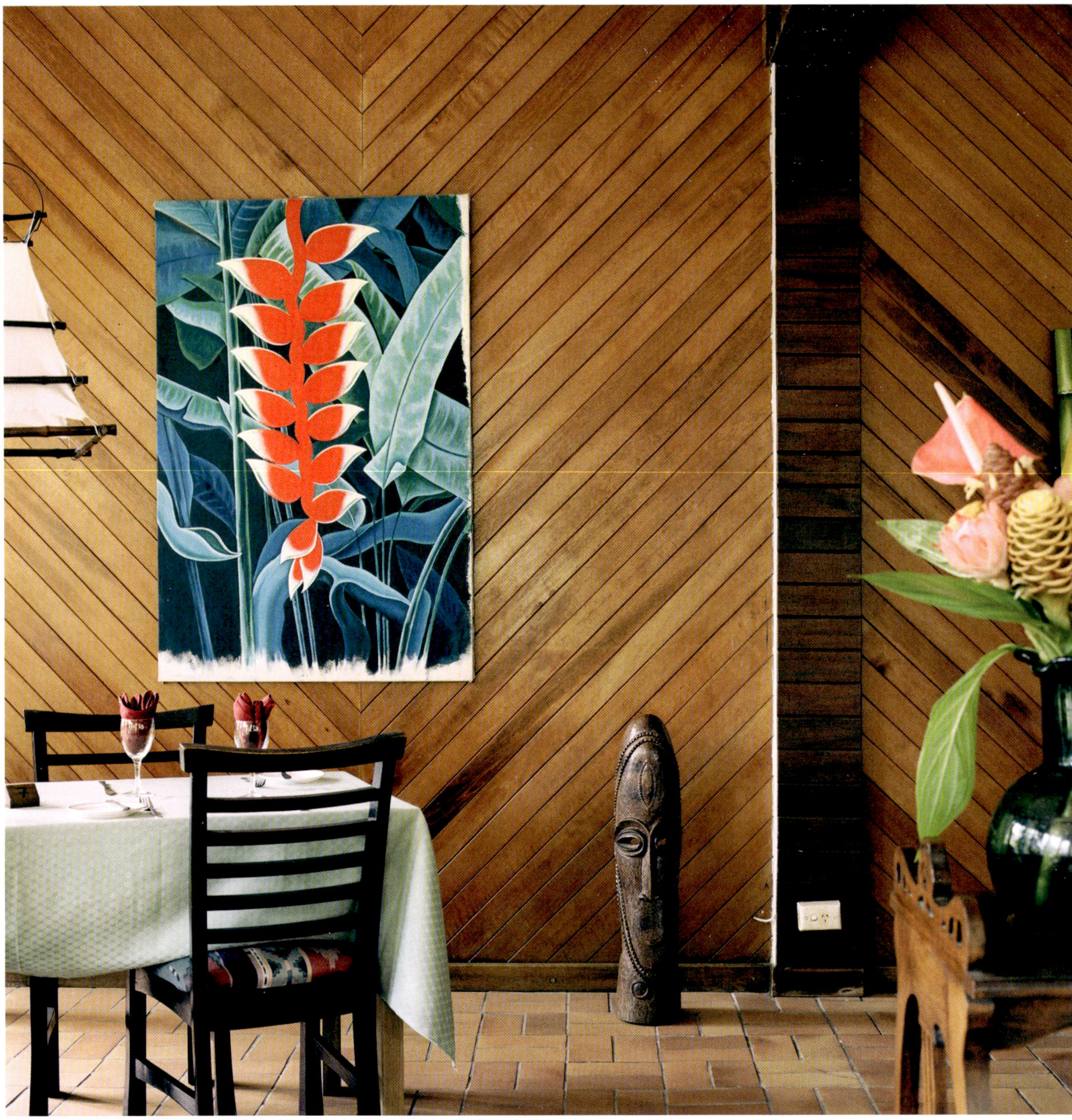

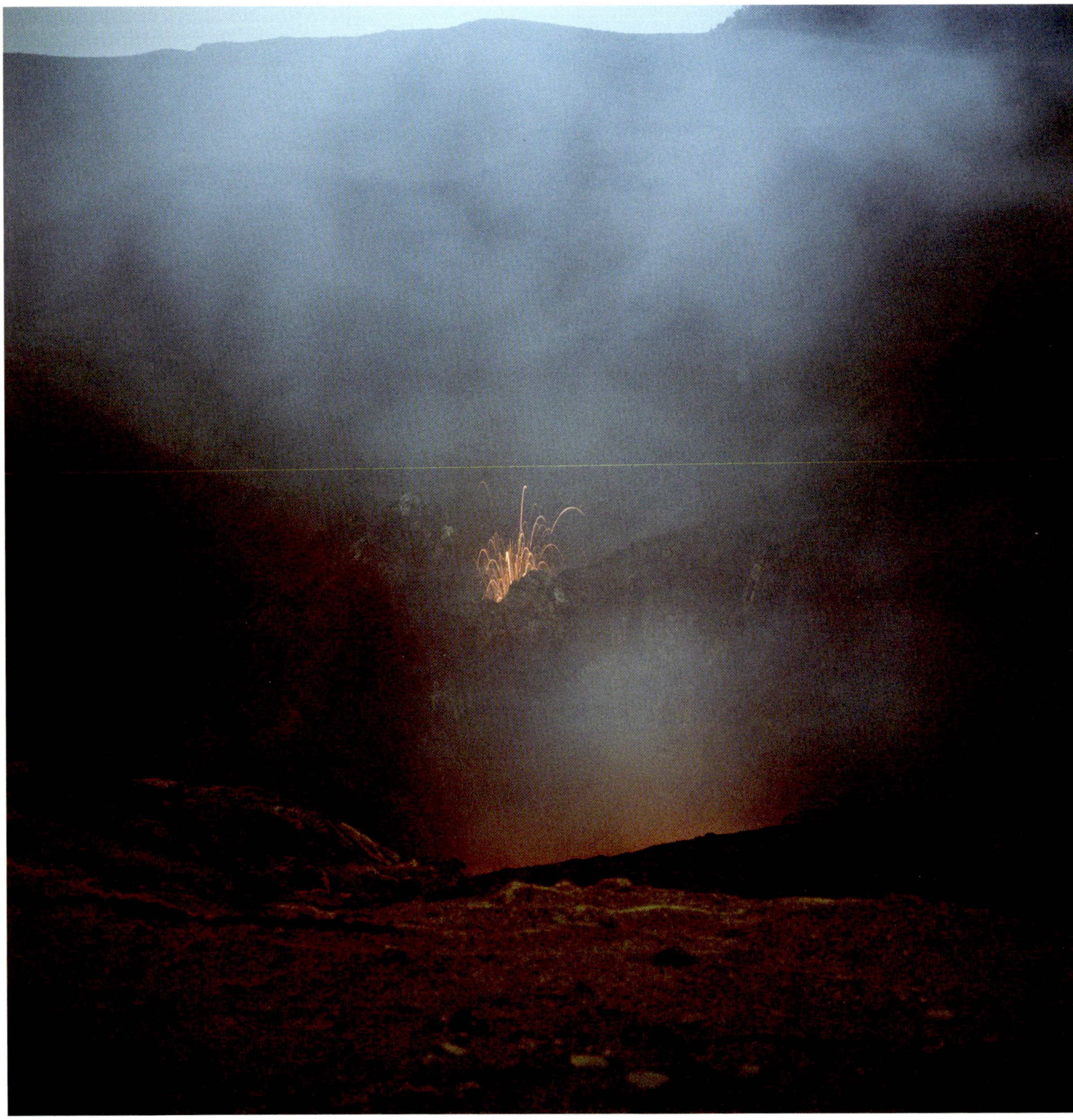

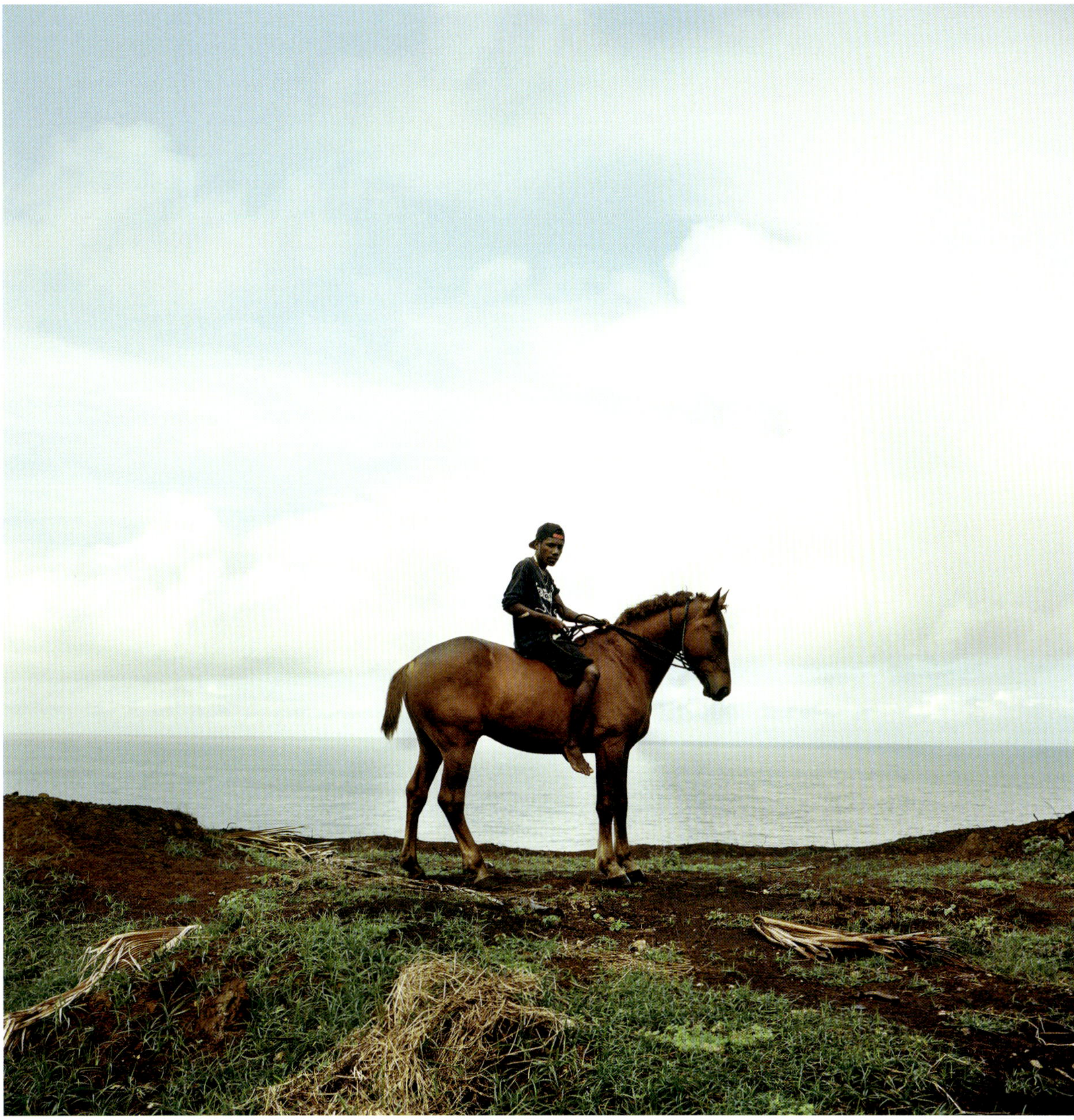

Charlie Phillip and Jackie, Tanna

Our elders sustained and maintained the traditional rituals and kastom ceremonies of this island, and so our history was maintained. But there was a time when Christianity first came to the island and a law called Tanna Law started threatening these traditions, forbidding us from drinking kava and performing certain dances and our native, traditional rituals. Life was hard at that time.

Then came the spirit of the son of our ancestral god in the name of John Frum.

John Frum was on our side - strengthening our kastom, opposing Christianity and other influences from the West that threaten our culture. John Frum said that it was difficult to get rid of these hardships from here in Tanna, from the front, in the face of it. So he advised us, "Stick to your kastom and culture, and fight against Christianity, while I destroy the source of the fighting that threatens our culture."

So he went to England and there he is, Prince Philip. So the spirit in Prince Philip is the spirit of John Frum from Tanna: The spirit of kastom.

Chief Charlie of the Yakel, told via Jimmy Joseph Nako

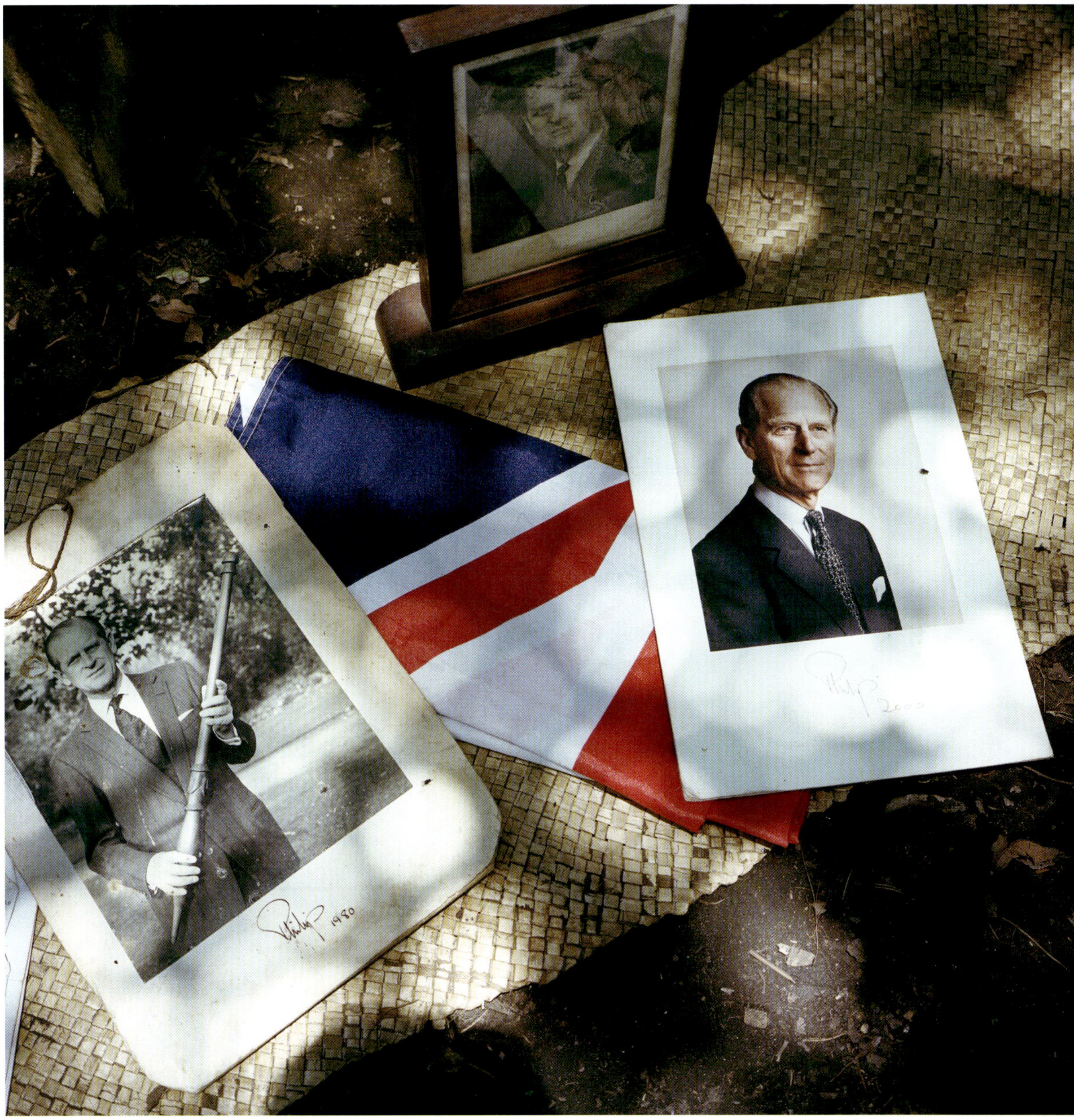

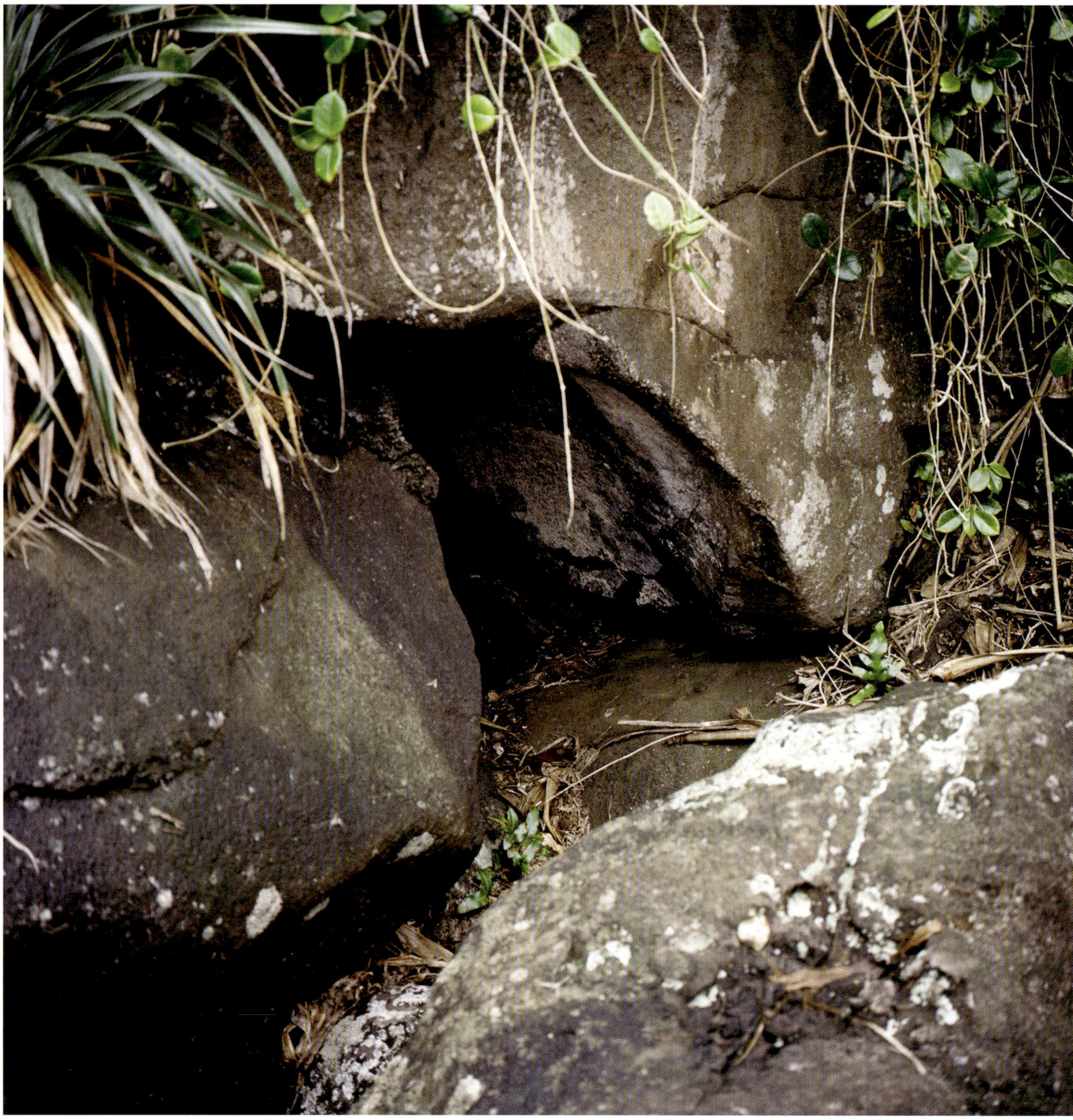

The cave where John Frum was last seen, Green Point, Tanna

Cevin Soling, Tiki Island Restaurant, Boston

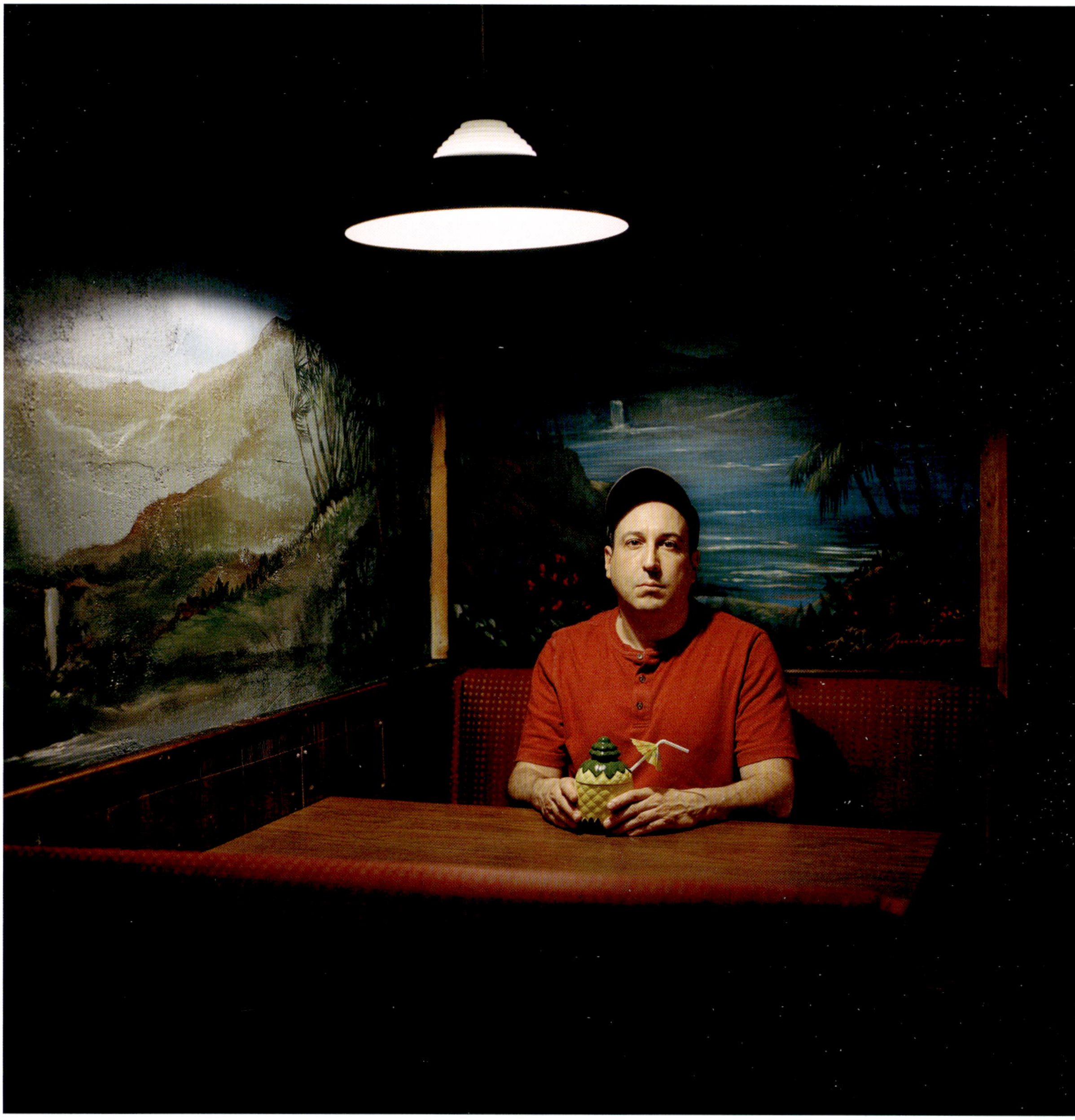

The way that the banyan tree sprawls and grows is like the pathways of tales that criss-cross Vanuatu. On the surface are the hanging ancient tendrils that are both confusing and marvellous as they interlace. Yet beneath our feet, a plant is always growing, spreading its roots unseen, ever more complex and circuitous. Like the John Frum stories, its origins are hard to follow, to make sense of, and maddeningly so.

Over the years of going back and forth to Vanuatu, Jon and I were taken to several caves that Frum entered but from which he never emerged. We witnessed long debates about which sacred rocks he once sat on, which chicken bones he picked clean between his teeth. Was his staff a torch too? And what about the Ni-Vanuatu guy, Prophet Fred, who went to Africa and came back with a spinning dance that would make everybody immortal, and took his people up to a town called New Jerusalem on the side of the volcano, only to die riddled with cancer a few years later? There's even a faction who call

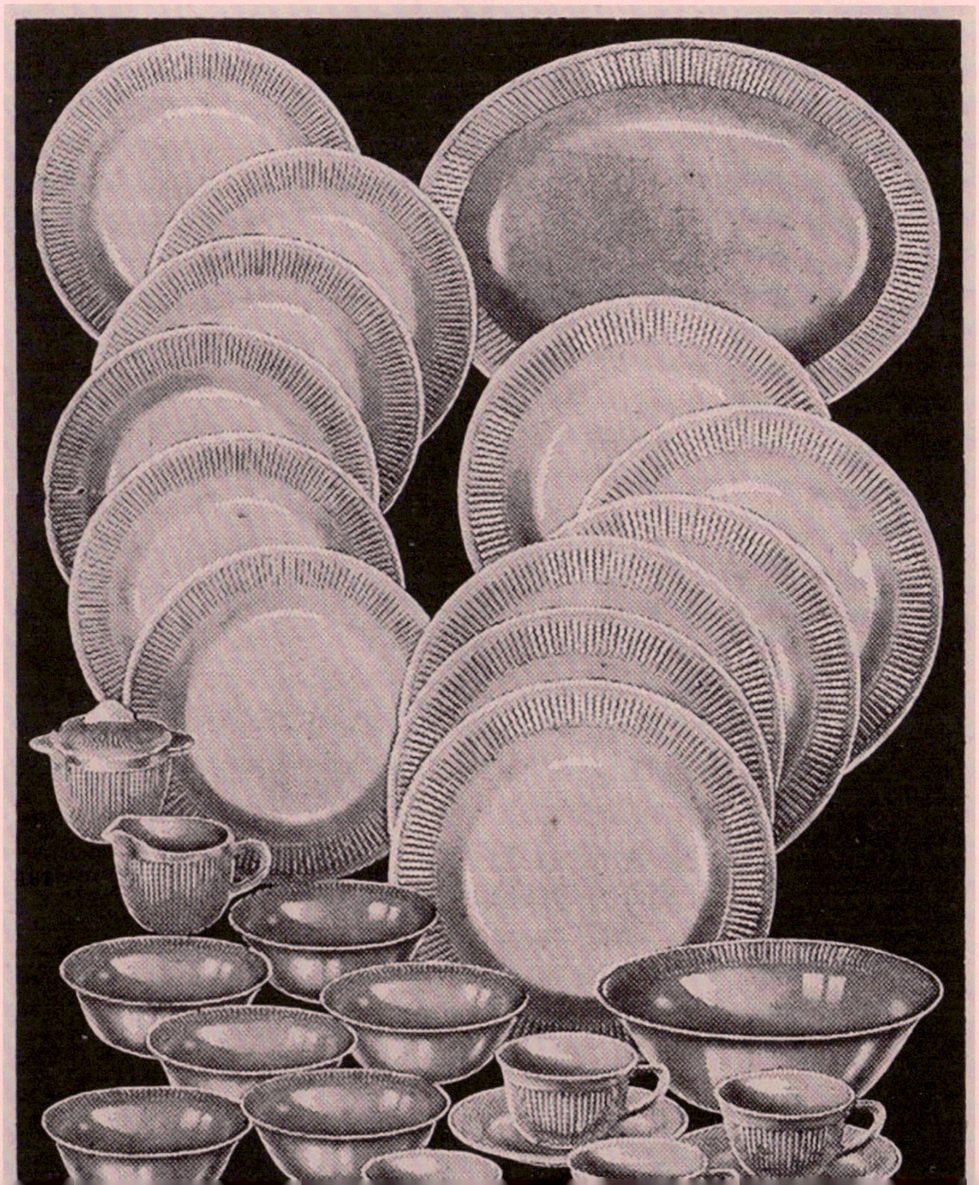

themselves The Real John Frum Village; they tried to take other groups to court to assert their claim - and won.

Those who go into the world of John Frum looking for linear logic will be disappointed. Stories can, to outsider ears, sound as if they're being made up on the spot. In Bislama, the verb *storian* captures the way details creep and entwine and enmesh as tales are told - as contradictions become cogent, as kava visions and hearsay encounters transform into truth - usually in night-time whispers. But ask enough people, drill down, and you'll find commonalities between stories; the roots of the banyan tree do eventually link up somewhere.

John Frum stories, so far, are mostly unwritten and uncodified. They hang on kava-fattened tongues. And, in that way, never really end. There is always more *storian* to do. Such is their allure and frustration for the outsider: These beliefs are alive, always ripening and responding to change. Quite a few times we'd discover that the arrival of Jon - Tonks, that is, camera and all - had been interpreted as a foretold step in the fulfilment of the greater Frum prophecy. The possibility to be made part of the mystery is as true for anybody. Situate that in a fantasyland of too-white sands, star-filled skies and the gentle susurration of sunlit palms; how could this not be seductive?

No wonder so much lurid stuff has been written about John Frum over the years. Probably the most over-exposed - and misrepresented - of the beliefs on Tanna is the cult of Prince Philip.

The *storian* itself is worth recounting. According to one version, the spirit of John Frum hopped aboard an American warship at the end of the war foreseeing that the repressive colonial policies were about to resume on Tanna. He landed in Europe just as the Queen of England was looking for a consort. She invited him and the world's most powerful chiefs to her grand *nakamal* in London, and swooned over the lava-like blood coursing through Frum's veins.

Henceforth, he disguised himself as the gaffe-prone Greek, secret avatar of Mount Tukosmera, a great dun rock that looms over the south of Tanna.

Close to the mountain is a village called Yakel where Frum-as-Philip is venerated. Wrapped in a pristine palm leaf are photographs of the prince.

In one, he is holding a traditional Tannese club – a photograph sent by Buckingham Palace in the 1970s. It's thought the British administration of Tanna at the time was keen to encourage this surprising but welcome sympathy. Amid the public grief at the death of the Duke of Edinburgh in 2021, there was also a scramble by the Western press trying to get word from this tiny village on what would happen next. It was speculated that Prince Charles might take up the mantle. At the time of writing, the future is unclear. A mystery of the faith.

The Yakel are more orthodox in their adherence to tradition; men are usually naked except for the pandanus leaf penis sheath called a 'namba' and the women wear grass skirts. Like other Frum factions, they grow kava and keep pigs, they believe Prince Philip will return to usher in an end of days scenario, and like their fellow Frummers they get one or two prophetic arrivals in the meantime.

For instance, a skinny 30-year old from Norway called Frank showed up one day. When Jon met him, Frank was sat by a dying fire wearing only the 'namba'. "I like Norway but this is better," the young man said, shuffling in his nudity. "I always wanted to live in nature ever since I was a child."

He had read about the Yakel's beliefs and way of life online and convinced himself that this village was where he should be. He planned to

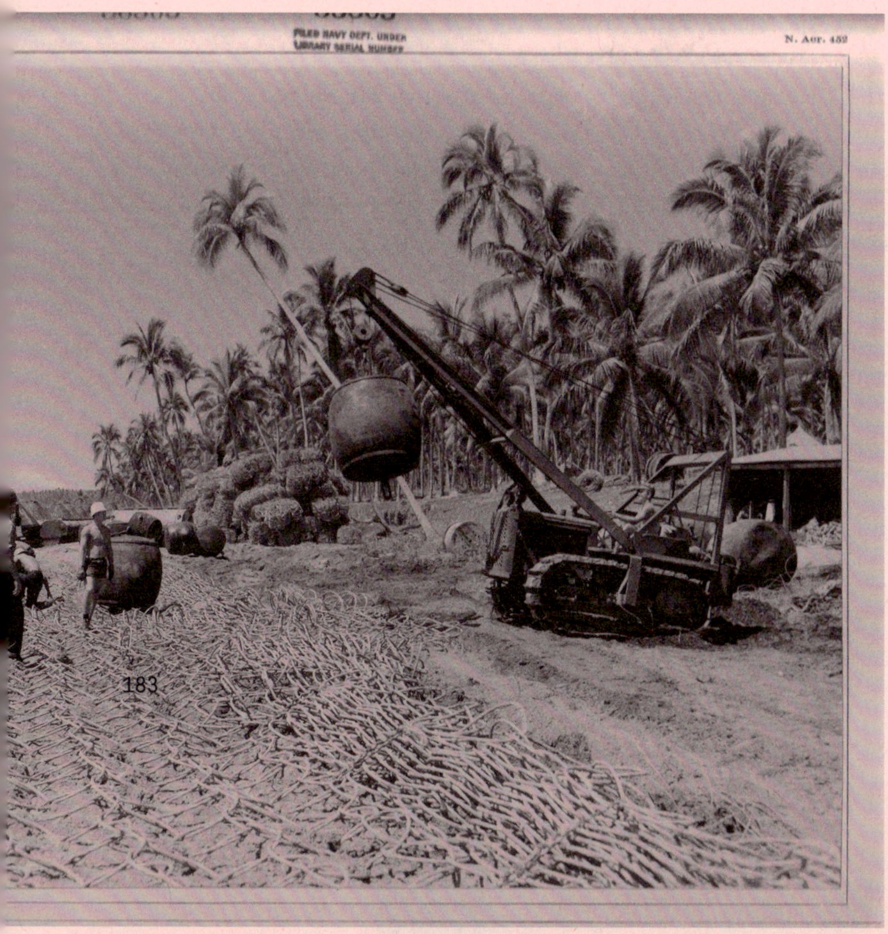

remain with the Yakel tribe indefinitely and burned his travel documents soon after arrival.

However out of place Frank was, the Yakel welcomed him. "Having Frank here is the fulfilment of a prophecy," said Jimmy Joseph 'JJ' Nako, a sort of spokesperson for the tribe, who is savvy to the ways of the outside world after a stint in college in Port Vila. "We believe that when the spirits of our ancestors and of our food crops return to this world to live with us they will come in the form of white people. These spirits are coming here because we are turning away from them, so Frank is here to get us back."

Frank appeared content with all this. He hugged his knees close to his chin and stared ahead, wood smoke dancing in front of his eyes. "Him staying here permanently is something we accept because it's a means of sustaining, maintaining and refining our culture and traditional way of life," said JJ.

Predictably, things didn't quite work out: a few months later Frank was spotted walking despondently around Port Vila wearing Western clothes. Some mysterious rupture had occurred between him and the tribe and he'd been effectively cast out, back into the world to wait for a new passport.

Regardless of what exactly went on between Frank and the people of Yakel (we heard rumours that it escalated from a row about tidiness), one thing is certain: neither found what they were hoping for. The young Norwegian didn't find prelapsarian bliss. He wasn't delivered back to nature. And the villagers didn't get their prophecy. Although, perhaps they did: we were told by JJ that the whole sorry experience had brought the Yakel closer together.

Frank is not the only one going to Vanuatu searching for utopia, an enclave out of time. At the time of writing, a very old man who used to own a low-cost airline is living naked with his wife in the jungle of Vanuatu's largest northern island. He calls his bamboo settlement Edenhope because it'll be the last bastion in the Earth's imminent ecological disaster –

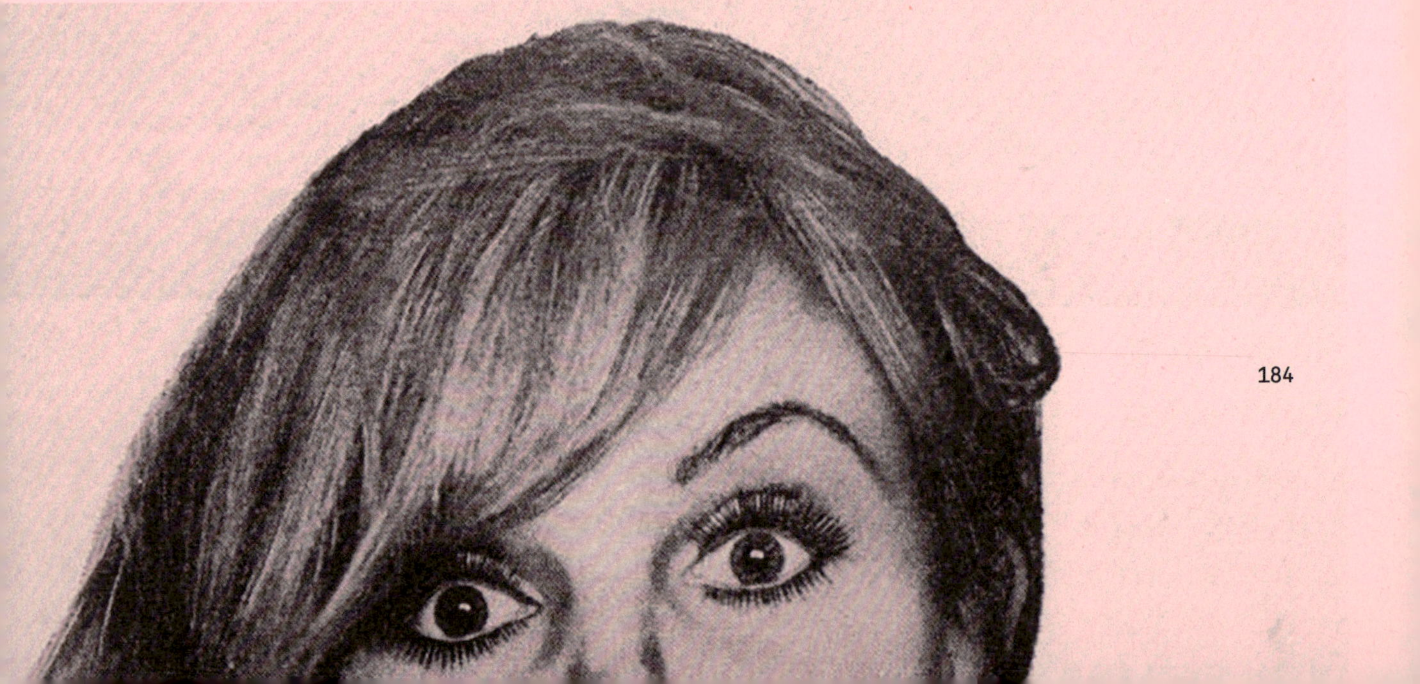

a disaster no doubt his planes contributed to – and about which he's very bitter. We met him while he was trying to find a hospital to treat his wife's persistent malaria.

Vanuatu attracts such people, those searching for the miraculous. They believe they've found a place where they can create their own story, reinvent themselves, where the boundaries of what's possible are slackened by geographical obscurity, inequalities, and a living oral tradition. The age of imperialism was full of similar stories; the colonies were a place where the occupiers could be whoever they wanted to be. That's what Kipling's *The Man Who Would Be King* is about: his royal pretenders don't go to Kafiristan looking for riches but to set themselves up *as kings*, to fashion their own story – even if only one of them lives to tell their tale to a tabloid newspaperman.

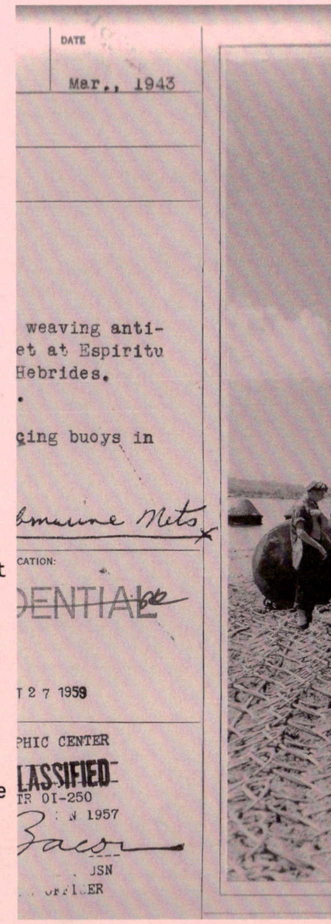

That said, whose heart doesn't flutter at the story of John Frum? Every inch of our planet is mapped, every obscure practice soon unravelled or exposed to the glaring light of day, yet here is a happening barely trodden by tourism, oblivious or defiant to so-called common sense. To world-weary eyes, John Frum's marching militia do seem like a miracle.

Among the older expats in Vanuatu, it's said these islands slowly do something to outsiders; that at the ends of the Earth one is liable to drift into a sort of dreamworld. It's partly to do with the South Pacific. That vast blue ocean, as deep and splendid as the night sky, peppered with what look like fragments of heaven, is lodged deep in our imaginations.

Joseph Banks, a botanist and illustrator who accompanied Captain Cook on his early voyages, wrote this in his log: "The scene we saw was the truest picture of an arcadia – of which we were going to be kings – that the imagination can form."

Only later was paradise lost, through sickness, environmental degradation, the loss of old ways. The disputed story goes that Cook was eventually killed on a Hawaiian beach at the hands of the exact people who had venerated him as a fertility God.

When Gauguin first got to Tahiti, he could see only what it lacked. He kept looking ever further afield in pursuit of primitive purity, eventually to the remote Marquesas Islands, where he spent his last few isolated years.

A REVEALING ARTICLE FOR MEN THE TRUTH ABOUT OVERSEXED GIRLS

ADVENTURE

THE MAN'S MAGAZINE OF EXCITING FICTION AND FACT

STILL ONLY 25¢ DECEMBER

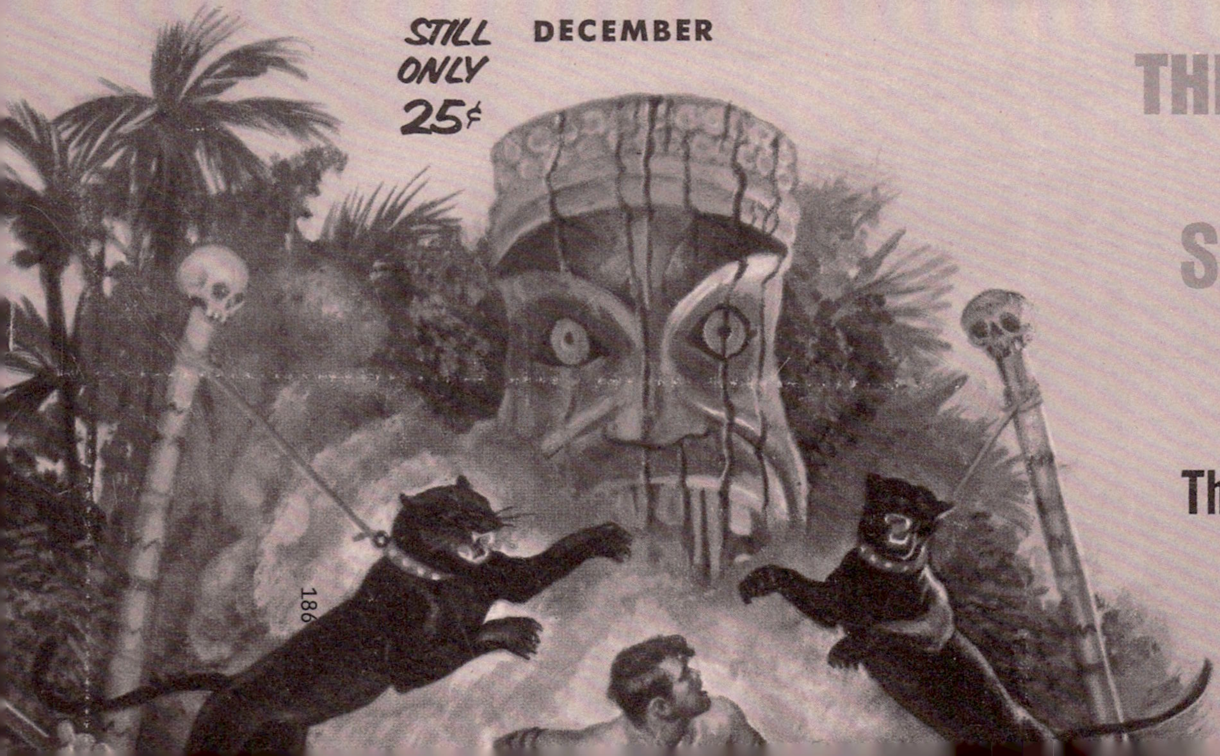

THE YANK WHO BECAME AN ISLAND GOD

Sailor Morrell and His Hundred Brides

AN EXCLUSIVE

The Murders You Never Hear About

RUB-OUT

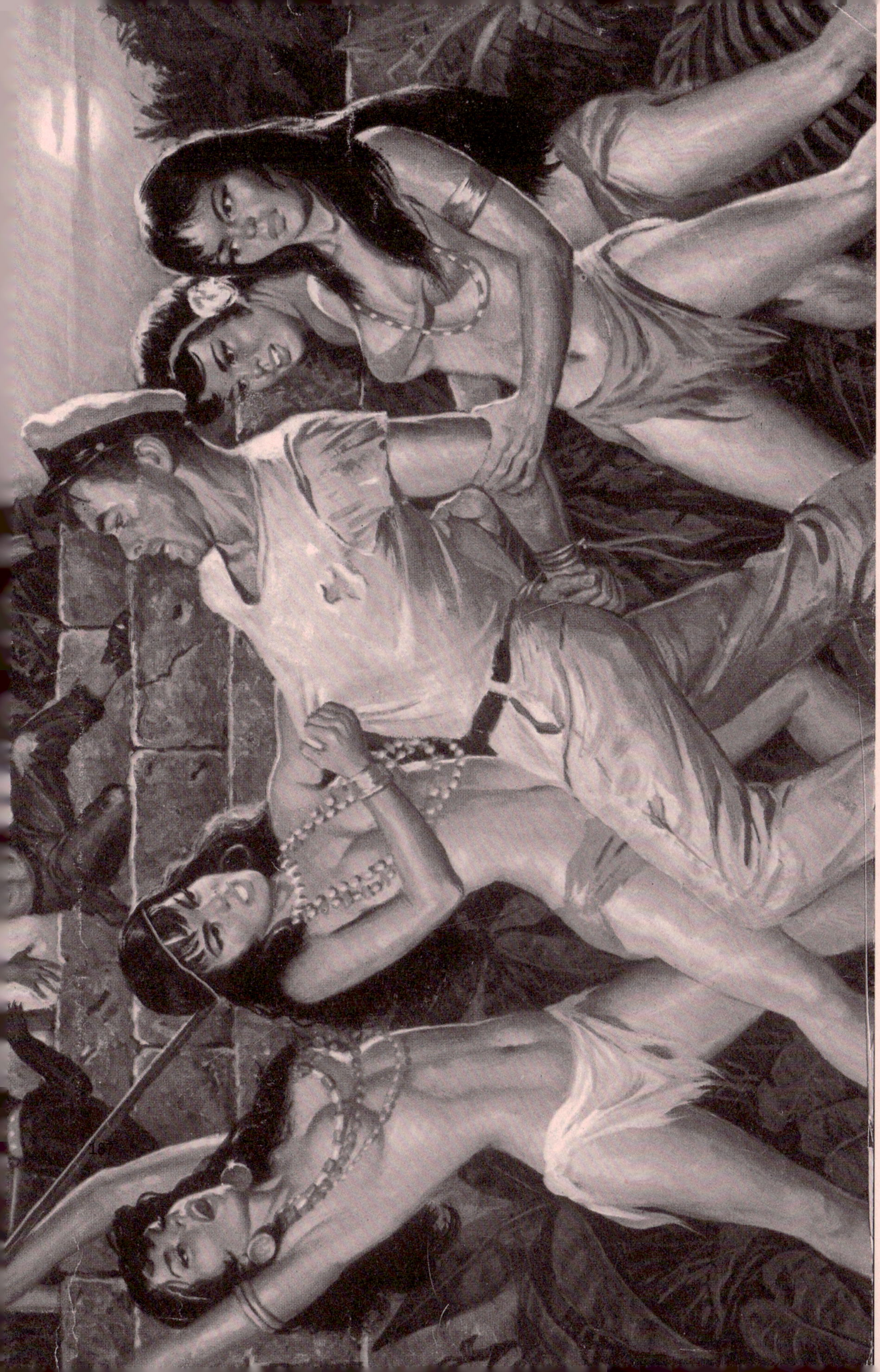

The title of Gauguin's great clairvoyant canvas of the period sounds like a startled cry, like someone who has been awoken abruptly from their dreams: *Where do we come from? What are we? Where are we going?*

Jon and I are just as culpable. Travelling to Vanuatu in search of our own elusive dream - a great, untold story - we too got tangled up in John Frum. Years after that first journey, our notebooks have filled with dates and miscellany about the prophecy and those who ingratiate themselves in it.

We started out wanting to know if there were people on the other side of the world still waiting for their American messiah. Our question has become in the end: who are the 'cargo cultists' here - the men of Sulphur Bay reenacting American army drills, or the ageing counts of the Maison Royale de Tanna, who host their galas and raise their glasses in the hope, the belief, that Claude-Philippe could be a real monarch?

People often ask us what motivates the men who would be king. Their reasons, as we've shown, are disparate: Can they cut it as an island god, be recognised as an illustrious monarch, be a hero among oppressed peoples, be delivered back to Eden. What unites them, though, is an attachment to a certain kind of adventure that runs deep in the Western imagination. It was writ on the sails of Europe's first voyagers to worlds unknown, drifting across oceans and continents to new frontiers, the blank spaces on the map. Amidst such possibility, the imagination ran amok - not only in the form of undersea krakens and the fountain of youth but also about the very act of striding out into the unknown, which became mythologised. The myth was alive in the woodcut print found in the early pressings of Robinson Crusoe, showing a stranded barefoot buccaneer taking his first fateful steps on an uncharted island. It endures in the tropes of Hollywood exotic: the hero prising open a sealed tomb, the intrepid searching for lost cities in the jungle, the solitary explorer making first contact with a hostile tribe. However innocent these seem, such tales are echoes of a brutal past - fictionalised re-enactments of lands claimed, peoples conquered, pillaging done in the name of 'civilisation'.

Adventure of this kind runs like rivulets through the films and books many of us are inculcated in from childhood. It permeates Western culture, however enlightened we think we are. Yet it has also led to a crisis of confidence - the loss of moral footing on the actions of those who came before us. As we unravel layer after layer of the onion of history, the marriage of heroism and adventure in how we imagine ourselves and how we once walked the earth becomes ever-more suspect. The result is an identity crisis. Stories that sustained the West for so long have become the very circumstance of its stasis and division.

Among the men who would be king, their common quest is essentially nostalgic: Not for a time when black men were subjugated by white men - despite how this tale first appears - but for a more 'innocent' time, before this crisis of identity, when white men could comfortably play the hero, the rajah, the adventurer in distant lands, without all the baggage. When they felt they were the protagonist in the story.

People also ask us whether we came to like these men in the end. The answer is simple: there's a bit of them about us - photographer and writer on a 'wonder voyage'. We travelled back and forth to the South Pacific, wandered into distant lives and beliefs looking for miraculous or undiscovered things, where blank spaces could still be found. We tried our best to leave John Frum as we found it - never daring to fix the stories down - but know our endeavour is inherently flawed. There will be those who object to the very premise of two white men going to the other side of the world to frame this story, however much bearing it has on our own. This we must accept.

We think John Frum itself emerged from a desire for self-representation. For centuries, these islands were at the mercy of whatever came over the horizon, shaped by missionaries, foreign armies, scores of anthropologists, and before them all Captain Cook with his incongruous Hebridean name for the archipelago. John Frum took back control. It remains a creative rebellion, a refusal of passivity; it delivers the narrative back into local hands.

At its most basic reading, we could say Frum commandeered the loosest shape of the Christ story. But the spirit of the prophecy has endured not in the romantic idea of Pacific Islanders earnestly scanning the horizon for returning Americans - waiting for their cargo ship to come in - but as a living corpus of stories in which these islands, their people and traditions are the centre of the world.

In our post-colonial age, the old imbalance hasn't gone away. Vanuatu's tides are rising as climate change threatens to swallow the islands completely. There's a growing gyre of plastic bags swirling out in the Pacific. Both are environmental disasters that the Ni-Vanuatu people had no hand in creating but which will shape their future. In 2015, Cyclone Pam ripped through Vanuatu and laid waste to villages and infrastructure. For a spell, the march of international aid came over the horizon. Just as abruptly it was gone again. How isolated it must be out there in the middle of the ocean, unsure what might come over the horizon next. Who wouldn't be intrigued at the promise of an emissary, a useful foreigner – John Frum, Cevin Soling, even Claude-Philippe Berger – who can tell your story to the world as you see it? Because these men are really just the supporting cast in the stories that sustain these islands. As one of Antoine Fornelli's Ni-Vanuatu confidants told an anthropologist: "We are believed to be Tony's partisans but that is not true – he is *our* partisan*".

Jon and I did go back to the village where we'd left Claude-Philippe; partly to check he'd made it out of the rowdy kava party but also to hear what the locals made of the royal visit.

Amid the pools of muddy water and discarded kava buckets, there was a morning-after feel about the place. In the *nakamal* meeting hut, a group of hungover men gathered and carefully considered our questions. "We don't know exactly who he is," said a man with a dense curly beard. "But we were told he's the representative of Forcona in Europe, not much more." Their families back home on Tanna were part of the movement associated with Antoine Fornelli. "We heard that, last time he came to Tanna, Claude-Philippe promised a lot of things – development, roads, electricity. So far, he hasn't brought those things to the island." Frustration is growing, the man explained, to a murmur of assent.

We had a photograph of Claude in his regalia in Berlin, knighting a Flemish count. The Ni-Vanuatu with the thick beard took the portrait in his hands and stared hard at it. Then he turned to us and asked, with a deep frown, "Does it make this man rich to say he's the king?"

---

* *The Tree and the Canoe: History and Ethnogeography of Tanna*, Joël Bonnemaison, translated by Josée Pénot-Demetry, University of Hawaii Press, 1994

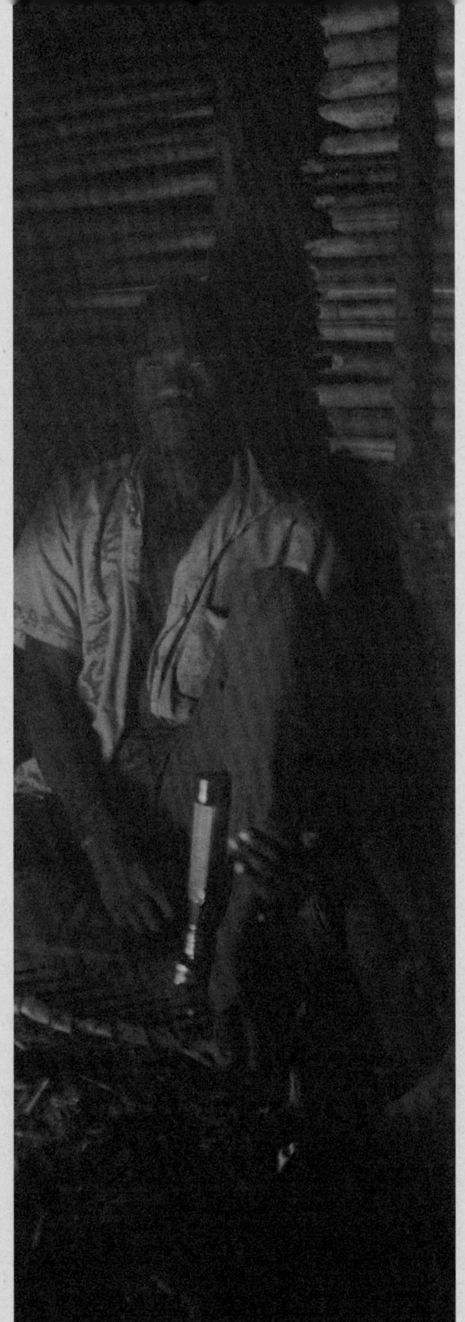

We would very much like to thank the following people for their help and support with this book:

Dewi Lewis, Ania Nałęcka-Milach, Francois Giner, Lamont Lindstrom, Dr Haidy Geismar, Sven Kirsten, Jimmy Joseph Nako, Ketty Napwatt, Ruth Naiu, Anne Naupa, Mary-Jane & Lisa Dinh, Mia Dalglish, John Kaurua, Frankie Stevens, Ian G. Kerr, Frederic Fornelli and all the people in Vanuatu who showed such kindness.

Christopher Lord would like to thank particularly the following people for believing in this story from the beginning, for their ears and eyes, and for their encouragement: Andrew Bulley, NJ Stallard, Gabriela Maj, and James Alexander.

Jon Tonks would also like to thank the following people for their kind support, advice and patience over the years with this work:
Sir Brian Pomeroy, Joan Morgenstern, Martin Parr, Louis Little, Tom Groves, Steph Bentham-Green, Roman Franc, Dr. James Hyman, Christiane Monarchi, Stephen Vaughan, Sarah Allen, Mark Power, Glauke Bogaert, Ella Cousins, Colin Pantall, Carol and Roger Tonks, Simon Tonks, Jon Robson, Andrew Jones and to everyone else who has helped along the way, you know who you are.

In fond memory of Pete James.

In writing this essay, Christopher Lord is indebted to the following publications.

The Endeavour Journal of Sir Joseph Banks (1743-1820), Project Gutenberg of Australia
The Santo Rebellion: An Imperial Reckoning, John Beasant, University of Hawaii Press, 1984
Joël Bonnemaison, The Tree and the Canoe: History and Ethnogeography of Tanna, University of Hawaii Press, 1994. We are particularly indebted to the author for the section on Antoine Fornelli and the quote of Fornelli's letter to the French administration in Tanna appears here courtesy of his work.
Lord Jim, Joseph Conrad, 1900
The God Delusion, Richard Dawkins, Houghton Mifflin, 2006
The John Frum Movement in Tanna, Jean Guiart, published in Oceania: *A Journal Devoted to the Native Peoples of Australia*, New Guinea, and the Islands of the Pacific, March 1952
The Sediment of Voyages: Re-membering Quirós, Bougainville and Cook in Vanuatu, Margaret Jolly, part of Oceanic Encounters, published by ANU Press, 2009
The Man Who Would Be King, Rudyard Kipling, Brentano's at 31 Union Sq, New York, 1888
Tiki Pop: America imagines its own Polynesian Paradise, Sven Kirsten, Taschen, 2014
Cargo Cult: Strange Stories of Desire from Melanesia and Beyond, Lamont Lindstrom, University of Hawaii Press, 1993. The quote from Sir David Attenborough on page 69 is courtesy of this book.
Kill a Bird with Two Stones: A Short History of Vanuata, Jeremy MacClancy, Vanuatu Cultural Centre, 1981
Tales of the South Pacific, James A. Michener, 1947
The Last Heathen: Encounters with Ghosts and Ancestors in Melanesia, Charles Montgomery, Douglas & McIntyre Ltd., 2004
The Coconut War: The Crisis on Espiritu Santo, Richard Shears, Cassell Australia, 1980

In the South Seas, Robert Louis Stevenson, 1896
Antoine Fornelli and the Forcona Movement on Tanna: The Story of One Man's Quest for Utopia in the New Hebrides, Zorian Strech
Dreams of Unity, Traditions of Division: John Frum, "kastom" and Inter-Manipulation Strategies as Cultural Heritage on Tanna, Marc Tabani, published in Paideuma, 2019
The Trumpet Shall Sound: A Study of 'Cargo' Cults in Melanesia, Peter Worsley, Paladin, 1970 edition
Melanesian Politics: Stael Blong Vanuatu, ed. By Howard Van Trease, University of Cambridge and University of the South Pacific, 1995
Translations of Chief Isaac Wan's speech on page 104 are courtesy of Cevin Soling and the crew of *John Frum He Will Come*.

POSTSCRIPT

In July 2021, shortly before this book went to print, we received word that Claude-Philippe Berger, 'Traditional King of the Royal House of Tanna', had died. According to one insider, there was no service held for the 'King' in France but on Tanna 300 people walked "in very heavy rain" to pay their respects. At the time of publication, Claude-Philippe's successor was yet to be determined.

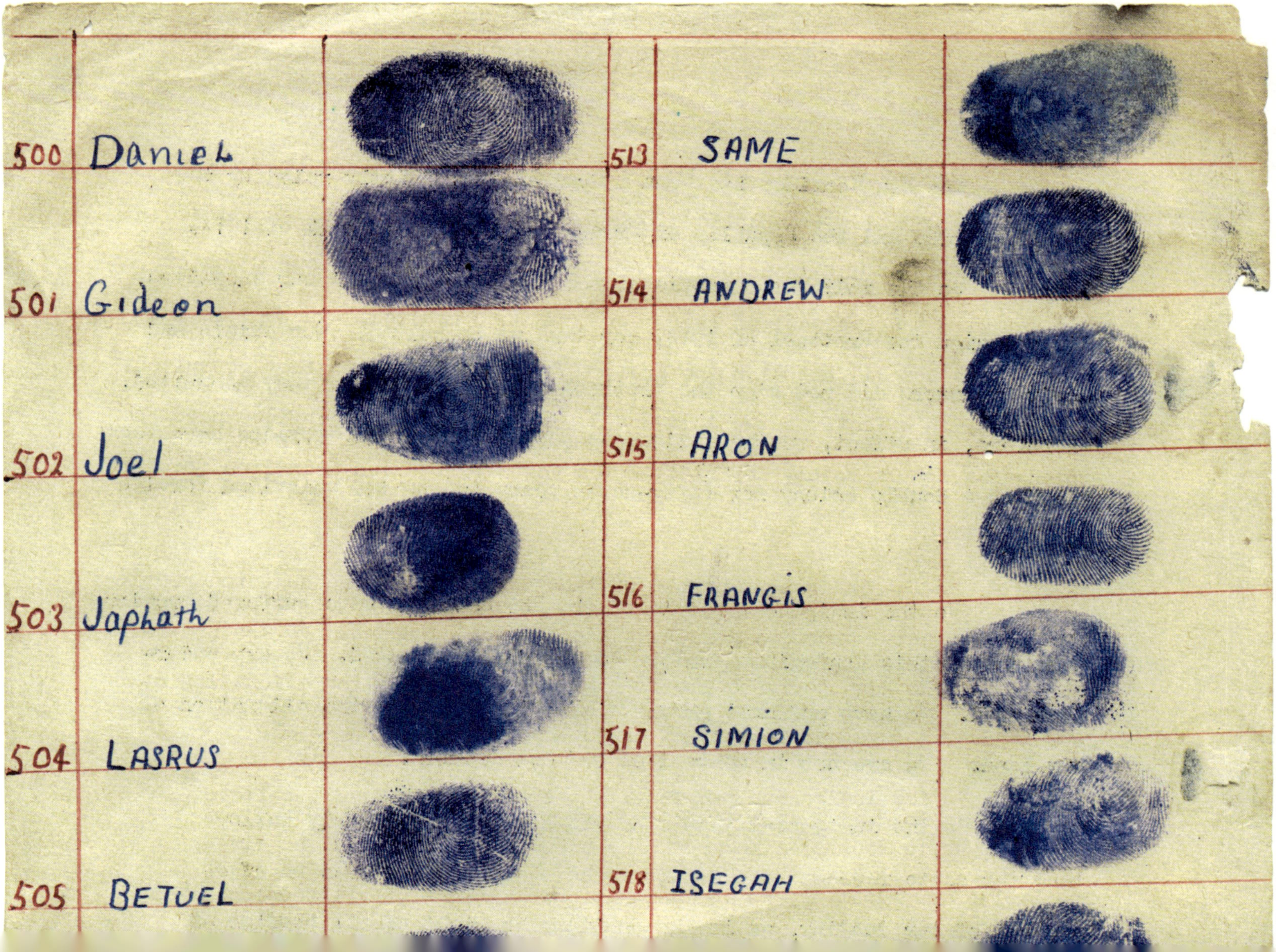
500 Daniel
501 Gideon
502 Joel
503 Japhath
504 LASRUS
505 BETUEL
513 SAME
514 ANDREW
515 ARON
516 FRANGIS
517 SIMION
518 ISEGAH

The New Hebrides has been a Condominium, jointly ruled by the United Kingdom and the Republic of France, since the Protocol of 1914.

We the indigenous people of the New Hebrides, and our ancestors, did not sign the Protocol of 1914, nor were we consulted. Our chiefs and their ancestors did not sign the Protocol of 1914, nor were they consulted. Therefore, in effect, we the indigenous people of the New Hebrides have been ruled as a double colony for fifty-seven years by the two uninvited foreign powers.

We the indigenous people of the New Hebrides have suffered grevious harm under this Condominium rule. We are under-educated. We are under-developed. We have suffered grevious harm in regard to the alienation of our land. We are not in control of our own destiny.

We the indigenous people of the New Hebrides firmly believe that for us to redress the wrongs we have suffered we must be given control of our destiny, as is the unalienable right of all peoples as

We the indigenous people of the New Hebrides therefore draw attention of the United Nations to our plight and urgently request that action be taken by the United Nations to direct two of its member nations, the United Kingdom and the Republic of France, to guarantee a definite time for Independence for the New Hebrides and to quickly prepare us, the indigenous people of the New Hebrides, to exercise our right of self-determination and join the comity of nations as a mature and responsible member.

We the indigenous people of the New Hebrides hereby request that the Government of the Dominion of Fiji, as our closest Pacific neighbour with membership in the United Nations, to direct this petition to the urgent attention of that body.

Signed, Jimmy T.P.S Moses

NA-GRIAMEL CHIEF PRESIDENT UNION COUNCIL NEW HEBRIDES

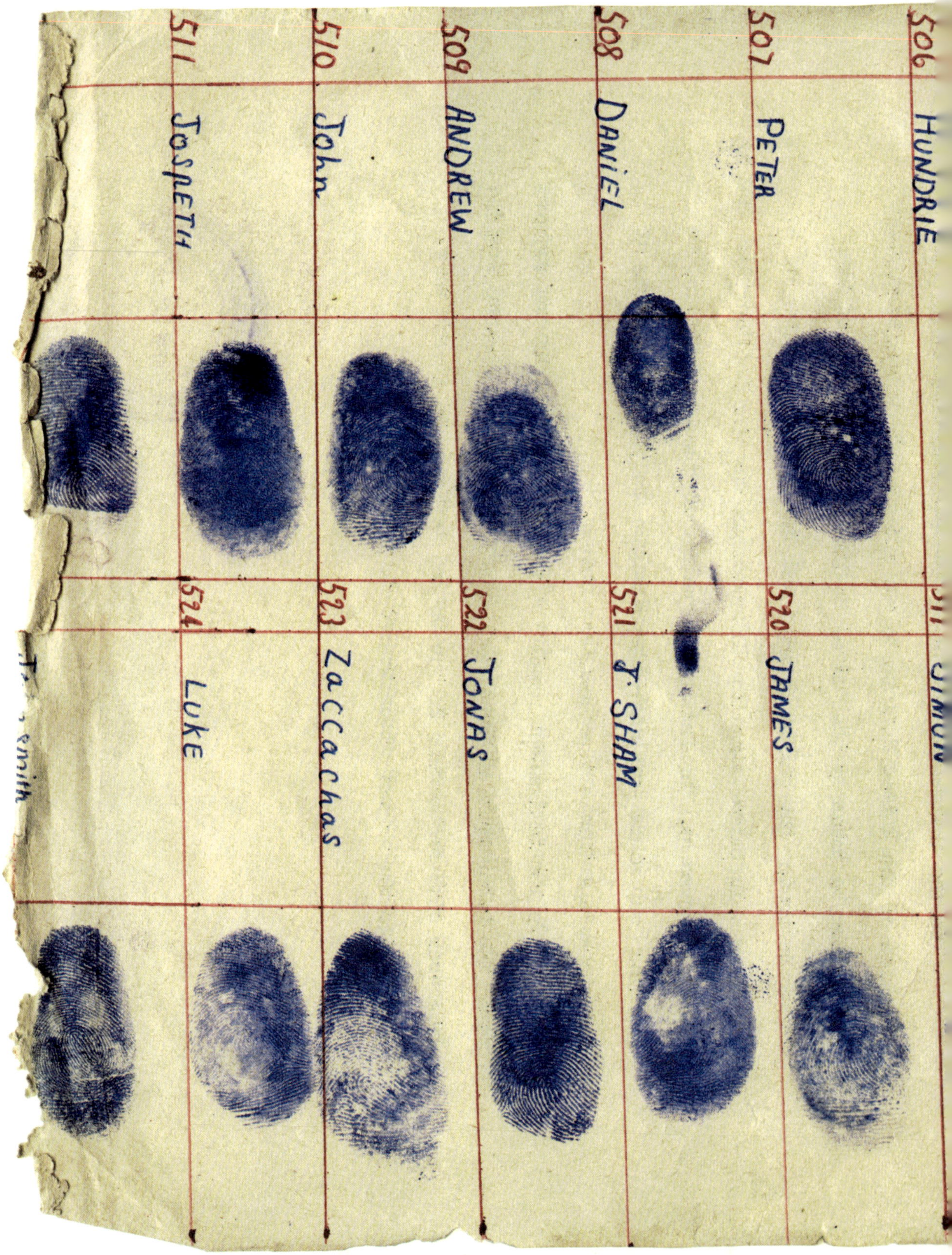
506 HUNDRIE
507 PETER
508 DANIEL
509 ANDREW
510 John
511 JOSPETH
520 JAMES
521 J. SHAM
522 JONAS
523 Zaccachas
524 LUKE

THE MEN WHO WOULD BE KING

First published in the UK in 2021 by
Dewi Lewis Publishing
8 Broomfield Road
Heaton Moor
Stockport SK4 4ND
England
www.dewilewis.com

All rights reserved

Copyright © 2021
For the photographs: Jon Tonks
For the text: Christopher Lord
For the book design: Ania Nałęcka-Milach
For this edition: Dewi Lewis Publishing

ISBN: 978-1-911306-43-6

Type set with Gravitica Mono & Sonny Gothic
Printed on papers: Garda Premium Natural & Burano Pink
Print & bound: EBS Verona

www.jontonks.com
www.christopherlord.co.uk

Archival imagery courtesy of:

Pacific Island Monthly Magazine - courtesy of the Fiji Times & National Library of Australia
Bradley Wood & the South Pacific World War II Museum
Antoine Fornelli photographs courtesy of Francois Giner
The Sven Kirsten Collection
Letter to the United Nations (attached) courtesy of Frankie Stevens

comes t

Y

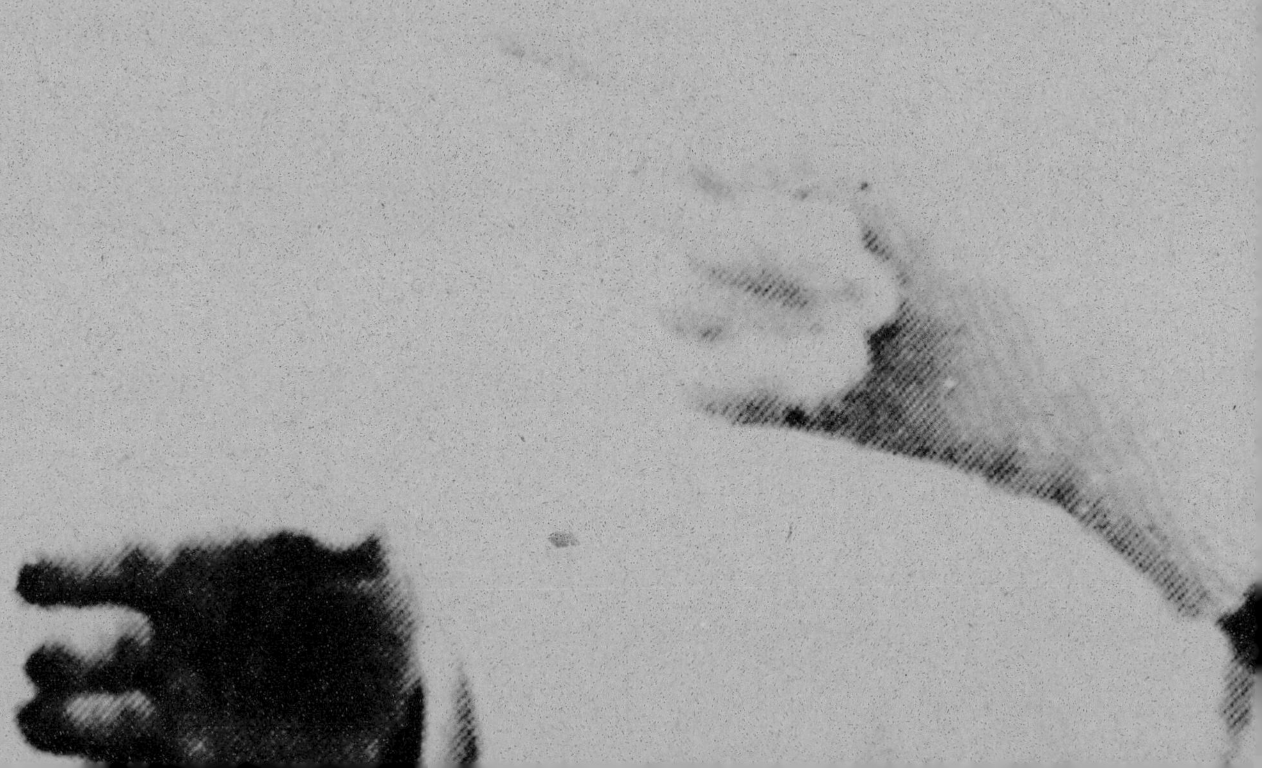

NO, NO, SIR
GOES THAT W

THIS WAY, M'
IT GOES THIS